WITHDRAWN

Politics Without Process

Politics Without Process
Administering Development in the Arab World

Jamil E. Jreisat

LYNNE
RIENNER
PUBLISHERS

BOULDER
LONDON

Published in the United States of America in 1997 by
Lynne Rienner Publishers, Inc.
1800 30th Street, Boulder, Colorado 80301

and in the United Kingdom by
Lynne Rienner Publishers, Inc.
3 Henrietta Street, Covent Garden, London WC2E 8LU

© 1997 by Lynne Rienner Publishers, Inc. All rights reserved

Library of Congress Cataloging-in-Publication Data
Jreisat, Jamil E.
    Politics without process : administering development in the Arab
world / by Jamil Jreisat.
        p.   cm.
    Includes bibliographical references and index.
    ISBN 1-55587-333-2 (alk. paper)
    1. Arab countries—Politics and government—1945–   2. Arab
countries—Economic policy. I. Title.
JQ1850.A58J74   1997
338.9'00917'4927—dc21   96-39894
                                                         CIP

British Cataloguing in Publication Data
A Cataloguing in Publication record for this book
is available from the British Library.

Printed and bound in the United States of America

        The paper used in this publication meets the requirements
   ∞   of the American National Standard for Permanence of
        Paper for Printed Library Materials Z39.48-1984.

        5 4 3 2 1

Contents

List of Tables   vii
Acknowledgments   ix

PART I   INTRODUCTION

1   Perspectives on National Development   3
    Change and Domination: A Thesis, *5*
    Reconsidering Basic Premises of Development, *11*
    The Arab World and Converging Obstacles, *18*

2   Ideological Setting of the Arab State   23
    Modern Arab Nationalism: The Embryonic Phase, *24*
    Political Movements After World War II, *29*
    Evaluating the Nationalist Legacy, *35*
    Conclusions, *40*

PART II   ADMINISTERING DEVELOPMENT

3   Managing Development in the Troubled Arab State   45
    Development Policies and Their Consequences, *46*
    Mismanagement of Capital, *48*
    Waste of Human Resources, *50*
    Bureaucracy and Reform, *56*
    Perpetual Problems of Administration, *58*
    Other Adverse Effects on Development, *62*
    Conclusions, *67*

4   Building Administrative Capacity   71
    Egypt, *72*
    Jordan, *76*
    Iraq, *77*
    Syria, *78*
    Saudi Arabia, *80*
    Tunisia, *81*
    Sudan, *83*
    Bahrain, *84*
    Qatar, *84*
    United Arab Emirates, *84*
    Yemen, *85*

Comparative Analysis, *86*
Conclusions, *88*

5   Egypt: An Exhausted System   93
    Structural Dimensions, *93*
    Public Policy Formulation and Its Context, *96*
    Bureaucracy and Reform, *106*

6   Jordan: Surviving Economic Scarcity   113
    Structural Dimensions, *113*
    Development Policy and Economic Reality, *119*
    Public Administration, *123*

7   A Comparative Analysis of Common Problems   135
    Jordan: The Problem of Implementation, *136*
    Egypt: Centralization Is Not Control, *147*
    Conclusions, *150*

        PART III   ASSETS, OBSTACLES, AND CHOICES

8   Political Islam and Matters of Governing   155
    Islamists and the Crisis of the Arab State, *156*
    Opposing Is Not Governing, *161*
    Islamism Between Persecutors and Advocates, *166*
    Demand for Independent Appraisal, *168*
    A Distinct Islamic Economic Order? *172*
    Which Islamic Management? *176*
    Conclusions, *177*

9   A Strategic Resource: Oil   181
    The Past Shapes the Present, *186*
    Oil Revenues and Arab Development, *188*
    Focus on Saudi Arabia, *192*

10 Alternative Development Strategies   203
    Economic Liberalization: Privatization, *206*
    Future Strategies: Some Choices, *212*

11 Politics Without Process,
    Administration Without Discretion   223
    The Political Domain, *226*
    Administrative and Institutional Capacity, *234*
    Foreign Connections, *240*
    Conclusions, *242*

    Bibliography   245
    Index   255
    About the Book   261

Tables

3.1	United Nations Human Development Rankings	51
3.2	Females per 100 Males in Secondary Schools in Selected Arab Countries	52
3.3	Ranking of the Arab States on the Human Development Index	55
4.1	Summary of Administrative Reform Proposals in Selected Arab States	73
6.1	Education and Gender of Jordan's Civil Servants	124
6.2	The Workforce in Jordan	125
9.1	Energy Consumption of Industrial Countries	183
9.2	Top Ten Countries in Oil Reserves	184
9.3	Oil Production and Revenues of Saudi Arabia	189

Acknowledgments

I would like to acknowledge the help of the Arab Organization of Administrative Development of the League of Arab States and its director general, Ahmad S. Ashour, and to extend my personal and professional gratitude to many individuals in the United States and in the Arab world. Space does not permit a complete listing, but I offer special thanks to those who left me with an enduring sense of appreciation for their help while researching this project:

During my field research in Egypt, Mr. and Mrs. Elaiwa I. Shalaby extended generous hospitality and arranged many of my interviews with senior public officials. Their help was invaluable. My discussions with Dr. Mustapha al-Said, former minister of industry and current member of Parliament, were very informative. I also benefited from my interview with Yousef Wali, minister of agriculture and secretary general of the ruling National Party. John P. Spillane, minister-counselor for economic affairs, U.S. Embassy in Cairo, was candid and realistic in his views and assessments. Professor Abdul-Wahab El-Masseery, an "Islamist-thinker" and a faculty member at the University of Cairo, is remembered for his kind reception of me in his home in Cairo, as well as for an exchange that quickly reached a dead end on all fronts—his astute use of the spiritual to dodge all earthly queries drastically limited the avenues of debate. Professor Ahmad Racheed, Public Administration Program of the University of Cairo, allowed me to review the proceedings of the program's just-concluded workshop on administrative reform in Egypt. Dr. Hussein Ramzi Kazim, head of the Central Authority for Organization and Methods, is one of many senior Egyptian officials who explained the accomplishments of their agencies.

In Jordan, Dr. Zuhair Kayed, director general of the Jordan Institute of Public Administration, was supportive and cordial. Mr. Abdullah Elayyan, president of the Civil Service Commission, was generous with his time and insightful with his remarks. As a practicing manager, Mr. Eyad Kattan's reflections on intricate aspects of management in Jordan were imaginative and informative. My contacts with various public officials and university faculty provoked sobering thoughts about the growing gap between what is officially claimed and what really has been achieved.

At the University of South Florida, Professor Tamara Sonn read the chapter on political Islam and offered thoughtful comments. Dr. Mark

Amen read the introductory chapter and masterfully used his red pencil to ask good questions and to record challenging comments. Mr. Arthur L. Lowrie's extensive experience in foreign service, focusing on the Middle East, and his teaching of the subject at USF were put to good use. Our numerous discussions and regular debates enriched my thinking as they contested many common assumptions. My students in seminars on comparative administration and my graduate assistants have been a source of helpful ideas. Mr. John Bradley read three chapters and offered editorial advice.

I am thankful for valuable comments from colleagues at other universities: Professor Robert B. Cunningham, University of Tennessee, read the chapter on Jordan; Professor Richard Cottam, University of Pittsburgh, read the first three chapters; Dr. Selwa Ismael, McGill University, read the chapter on Egypt; and two anonymous reviewers selected by my publishers offered supportive comments and good suggestions.

I must indicate that my experience with Lynne Rienner Publishers has been exceptionally gratifying, not only for superb professionalism, but also for making enjoyable the tedious work of revision. Working on this project with Lynne Rienner, Senior Project Editor Gia Hamilton, and other staff members demonstrated to me what proficient publishing can be.

My wife, Andrea, read parts of the manuscript and offered editorial suggestions; as always, my daughter, Leila, and son, Mark, are my constant inspiration and motivation.

Despite immense debts to so many people, I alone remain responsible for any and all shortcomings of this work.

J. E. J.

Part I
Introduction

1

Perspectives on National Development

A large part of human learning has always occurred through comparison.

Karl W. Deutsch[1]

The demise of colonialism after the end of World War II instigated the greatest structural adjustments of governments in history. One nation after another in Asia, Africa, and Latin America declared itself free of imperial hegemony. At the same time, these countries embarked on various plans for comprehensive societal change, even as their leaders and intellectuals were still arguing the type of political, economic, and organizational structures most favorable for the profound adjustments they were about to initiate.

It was the *performance* of the newly independent states, however, that ultimately mattered most to citizens. National independence elevated peoples' aspirations, and citizens increasingly demanded schools, roads, and health-care facilities as well as jobs and improved economic opportunities. It is not surprising, then, that many were concerned less with defining objectives and aspirations than with having the competence, the commitments, and the resources necessary for achieving them.

This study is about reforming institutions and processes of government in the Arab world. The objectives of these reforms have been linked to the creation of effective administration for executing national development plans and delivering public services. In fact, the functions of service delivery and socioeconomic development define the role of the state in the postcolonial period, a role that often appears limited only by the aptitude of political and administrative leaders, the capacities of the institutions they operate, and the availability of resources (human and material) at their disposal.

I began the examination of various administrative reforms in the Arab world with an awareness of the special influence exerted by political context over administrative process. The conventional wisdom, as conveyed in standard textbooks on government and public administration, advises that administrative institutions *implement* public policies and only occasionally

3

may actually formulate (or influence the formulation of) those policies. Classic management theories, beginning with Woodrow Wilson's famous article in 1887,[2] also stipulate a separation between policy formulation (a political function) and policy implementation (an administrative responsibility). The current view of the relationship, however, rejects the existence of a line of demarcation between the two functions and recognizes a mutual influence between the political and the administrative roles. Examining this relationship in terms of administrative reform in the Arab state reveals how absolute and personal the political control is.

Arab heads of state continue to control public policies, resources, and institutions, notwithstanding the valid observation by Roger Owen (1994, 18) that "it was usual for Arab states to embark on their independence with a constitution that called for holding of regular elections." Not all Arab states have held regular elections since independence, but all have maintained intrusive, unaccountable, and excessively centralized operations. Without any meaningful limitations on their powers, ruling leaders developed and managed accommodating, "ruler-dominated" bureaucracies.[3]

The subservience of the Arab bureaucracy is subject to various speculations and assessments. One assertion is that bureaucracy cannot be expected to fundamentally change its methods and behavior as long as rewards and benefits are not connected to professional performance. Another conclusion is that senior bureaucrats know too well that the road to power and wealth is through top political office. Appointment, advancement, and retention in a senior administrative post often depend more on the personal approval of the top leader than on the individual's job performance.

In contrast, Max Weber's conception of a modern bureaucracy presumes technical competence as the foundation for efficient service within a legal-rational political system. "The official who is not elected but appointed," Weber concludes, "normally functions more exactly" because "it is more likely that purely functional points of consideration and qualities will determine his selection and career" (Gerth and Mills 1946, 201).

My basic premise is that national development is unattainable without creating appropriate administrative and institutional structures with essential capacities for action. On this, I am in basic agreement with Esman's (1991, 20) thesis that "what most distinguishes advanced societies and their governments is not their 'culture,' nor their natural endowments, nor the availability of capital, nor the rationality of public policies, but precisely the capacities of their institutions and the skills of individuals, including those of management." In all societies, developed and developing alike, bureaucratic organizations are the main instruments for achieving national objectives.

Despite the importance of their functions and the universality of their existence, however, public organizations in the Arab world remain rudimentary in their professional competence. Various reform programs, decreed by political leaders to create administrative capacities, have proved to be inextricably linked to the proficiency of political systems that are frequently in a state of crisis. Ineffectual administrative capacity, as is the case with poor economic performance (Owen 1994, 25), is fundamentally associated with or caused by political conditions or events.

Thus, bringing the state back into administrative analysis is particularly important. Over time, the political system defines the characters of administrative structures and shapes the behaviors of individuals and organizations within them—and it is especially so in systems of command and control, such as those found in the Arab states. The role of the state is conspicuously visible and decisive in all efforts to build institutions or to form their processes.

This introduction is limited to conceptual and practical issues that have influenced the dominant intellectual discourse on development in the new nations in general, and particularly in the Arab world. With the benefit of hindsight, we know now that the developmental approaches employed by many emerging nations had little prospect of accomplishing their targets. But development is a big order. And it is not my purpose here to pursue every notion in a voluminous literature on development. Instead, I will focus on relevant issues, structures, institutions, and relationships and on how they have been contoured by their contexts. Subsequent chapters are specifically devoted to the institutional performance of the Arab state.

CHANGE AND DOMINATION: A THESIS

For the new nations, independence required substantive adjustments in all aspects of life. In a spiral mode, rising expectations fed citizens' escalating demands for improved standards of living. These demands could not be met without considerable investment in infrastructure and in social and economic development; state institutions had to have the necessary competence and commitment, in addition to such other ingredients as investment capital and coherent objectives. The state was the vehicle for coordinating all elements in a national plan to guide activities and maintain focus on strategic matters.

Conceptually, developmental perspectives that dominated intellectual discussions and exerted powerful influence during the 1950s and 1960s could be combined under two overlapping, loosely constructed frameworks: *nation building* and *modernization*. Within these two frameworks, social scientists labored to discover concepts that offered more definite prescriptions and designs for moving emerging countries from the status of subservient colonies to that of independent, modern statehood. (Ironically, the most influential theories were advanced and promoted, not from within the new states, but from the outside.)

Both concepts, *nation building* and *modernization,* have been equated with the application of rational control over the physical and social environments of people (Pye 1962; Black 1967; Myrdal 1968); to achieve such control, it is essential to effectively employ advanced technology and science. *Nation building* and *modernization* also assume the acceptance of the nation-state as the prime unit of the polity and a commitment to secularism and justice in public affairs (Pye 1962). According to this view, the implementation of societal change is most effective when administered by institutions that have the capacity to learn and to adapt their functions to reflect unprecedented advancements in human knowledge (Black 1967, 7).

By the 1970s, literature on the dominant approaches of nation building and modernization was not conveying a consensus but rather illustrating growing ethnocentric interpretations. In the meantime, strategies for comprehensive change (relying on global models or grand theories of modernization) were being criticized for lack of definite content, for being "culture and time bound" (Heady 1996), and for "not taking into account the historical, objective background to underdevelopment in the Third World" (Sayigh 1991, 44). A component of this background is the colonial experience, with its psychological legacy of suspicion of powerful, industrial nations as well as the objective political, economic, and sociocultural dislocations resulting from past colonial rule.

In brief, Western perspectives recognized the importance of building institutional capacities as instruments of the universal quest for a transformation to modernity. The apparent convergence of Western literature toward a view of modernity (commensurate with the application of science and technology to control the physical and social environment) presupposed the unfolding of these views within a liberal democratic state. Somewhat distinct from the above view is Apter's analysis, which considers modernization as "a non-economic process [that] originates when a culture embodies an attitude of inquiry and questioning about how men make choices—moral (normative), social (or structural), and personal (or behavioral)" (Apter 1965, 10). He considers choice central for the modern individual, and self-conscious choice implies rationality. "To be modern means to see life as alternatives, preferences, and choices" (10).

Again, the implications for a political system cannot be overlooked. Western writers left little doubt about the underlying political form against which all others were to be measured. The archetype is democracy, with its secular, libertarian, competitive, and multiparty structures, even though comparative political science scholarship has been suggesting alternative forms of political systems, presented in various typologies that describe existing political practices in the world. Morris Janowitz (1964, 5), for example, suggested five types: (1) authoritarian–personal control, (2) authoritarian–mass party, (3) democratic competitive and semicompetitive systems, (4) civil-military coalition, and (5) military oligarchy. Similarly, Esman's (1966) typology offers five types of regimes: conservative-oligarchy, authoritative–military reformers, competitive interest-oriented party system, dominant mass-party system, and communist totalitarian.

But these classifications are also prioritized in terms of their capacities to produce developmental outputs and maximize popular representation. Most prescriptions of Western scholarship implied the higher order of democratic norms by assuming them or by repeatedly emphasizing concepts such as equity, social justice, and participatory political culture (Luke 1990, 212; Black 1967; Apter 1965; Pye 1962).

In the end, viewing development as the application of science and technology within a democratic system presupposes two essential conditions. The first one is the presence of instrumental, rationalized administrative institutions. The second one is the acceptance of the process of change as fairly universal and not necessarily captive to or even dependent on notions of cultural and historical particularism. Thus, the solution for less developed countries, in reaching the stage of modernity, is to discover, learn, and faithfully apply the most likely ways and means that have worked for certain nations. Agreeing with such premises, in 1956 the World Bank, with considerable financial assistance from the Ford and Rockefeller foundations, created the Economic Development Institute (EDI) to offer six-month training courses in theory and practice of development for senior officials from borrowing countries (Rich 1994, 75).[4]

There are those who have profound apprehensions about this point of view. Critics maintain that Western theories of modernization have served as ideological legitimation for domination of Third World countries (Luke 1990, 212). The argument has been made that as the political and economic power of the United States expanded in the postwar period, so too did the preeminence of liberal, developmental thought in the form of modernization theory. In this, such scholars as Samir Amin, Noam Chomsky, Peter Klaren, Timothy Luke, and others see U.S. social science as the product of a collective Cold War mentality and in the service of U.S. policymakers. Academics supplied the doctrine and rationales and found their allies in the ranks of the U.S. Agency for International Development (AID), currently in search of a post–Cold War raison d'être (Klaren 1986, 8; Vitalis 1994, 46).

Those devising and adopting a strategy for development, whether such a strategy is of domestic or foreign lineage, have to contend with the impact of previously instated institutions and processes. Shortly after independence, no matter which alternative scenarios of development were being played out in emerging nations, their citizens were not an important factor.

Instead, it was the influence of the Cold War and the machinations of the superpowers that largely shaped prevalent concepts and practices.

It is no wonder, then, that both formally and informally external domination remains a recurring theme of scholarship from within developing countries and from the West. (Many of the authors expressing this point of view are cited in this study: Samir Amin, Ferrel Heady, Samuel P. Huntington, Paul Kennedy, Peter F. Klaren, Timothy W. Luke, Joan M. Nelson, Edward W. Said, Myron Weiner, and Howard J. Wiarda.) Developing countries have internalized fears of historical domination: These fears are described in a variety of contexts, such as rich countries over poor ones, Western over non-Western, and more recently North over South. Because the issue of external domination is critical for the Arab state as well as pervasive in studies of development, I briefly outline three distinct but overlapping types.

Imperialistic Hegemony

Imperialistic hegemony exists when the power of the imperial state (having a superior military force) dominates inferior political entities and reduces them to satellite status. Historical evidence conclusively supports this thesis. In modern history alone we find Spain, Portugal, France, England, Russia, and Japan acting as imperial powers at different times in relation to different geographic areas. Today, the United States is referred to as the only or the last superpower, acting as an imperial force in its relations with countries of the Third World. As Edward W. Said (1993, xvii) points out, "much of the rhetoric of the 'New World Order' promulgated by the American government since the end of the Cold War—with its redolent self-congratulation, its unconcealed triumphalism, its grave proclamations of responsibility . . . all too easily produces an illusion of benevolence when deployed in an imperial setting."

Dependency Theory

The dependency theory paradigm attempts to explain underdevelopment in terms of imbalance in global economic relationships. The core of this perspective is the notion of economic domination that results in dependency that then fosters underdevelopment. The relationship is one of domination and exploitation by a few central, industrial countries of the many peripheral, developing countries, regarded as helpless in their acquiescence and dependence (Sayigh 1991, 52). Thus, for the dependency paradigm, domination is rooted in the structure of the world economy. The restrictive policies and measures applied by industrial countries result in economic disadvantages for developing countries and perpetuate their dependencies.

Dependency theory achieved fame in academia and reached out to broader audiences in the 1960s. Economists of the Latin American Institute of Economic and Social Planning in Chile first proposed these views of development.[5] Numerous publications by Latin American social scientists—Andre Gunder Frank, Fernando Henrique Cardoso, Enzo Faletto, and others—inspired a lively debate among development economists in industrial nations as well as in the Third World.

Debates within the dependency school are as many as they are varied, but they share certain common ground, particularly the view that the force of international capitalism is setting up a global division of labor. Dependency theorists agree that under the auspices of multinational corporations, capitalism has created a world economic system binding together the globe (Smith 1985, 114). The more radical Latin American analysts, however, were more concerned with reaching a global and dynamic understanding of social structures than with looking only at specific dimensions of them. They stressed the sociopolitical nature of economic relations of production. Not surprisingly, proponents of this methodological approach—for instance, Cardoso and Faletto (1979)—found its highest expression in Marxist analysis.

Despite its explanatory value and search for an appropriate developmental strategy, the dependency paradigm has not been able to satisfy some important considerations. Foremost is the inability of the advocates to advance beyond a preoccupation with the consequences of imperialism (Smith 1985, 114). Success stories coming out of certain Asian countries also seem to provide convincing evidence of the possibilities of independent development. The progress of several Asian countries, such as Taiwan, South Korea, Singapore, Indonesia, and Malaysia, has been remarkable, despite past or present subservience to big industrial countries. A spectacular example is South Korea, which by one appraisal "has achieved more economically in a shorter period of time than any other country in modern history."[6] These cases from Asia challenge the core assumptions of the dependency theory. Finally, as Sayigh (1991, 43) asks: "Is dependence still a relevant and useful explanation of underdevelopment in our changing world, when almost all Third World countries have acquired at least the outward and formal trimmings of political independence and sovereignty, and the power of independent economic decision-making?"

Cultural Domination

Political and economic relationships, however determining they may be, do not fully account for cultural factors and their impacts on society. Cultural relations are not always symmetrical, particularly in the presence of a dominating culture. In his work *Culture and Imperialism*, Edward Said

(1993) explores European writings on Africa, India, parts of the Far East, Australia, and the Caribbean and finds depictions that are part of the general European effort to rule distant lands and people. He also notes that the Orientalist description of the Islamic world often reflects similar attitudes and assumptions.

Islamists of the Middle East, operating from a totally different vantage point, have been most vocal in the protest against Western cultural invasion of their societies. Rashid el-Ghanoushi, a leading Islamist intellectual from Tunisia, expresses such a view when he says: "I am not one who calls for closing the door to other experiences, but the bottom line is that our societies in the Islamic world are based on other values than those of the West."[7]

Certainly the resilience of cultural values and their particularistic influences on a society cannot be denied. This is why there is a need to expound approaches to development that are contextualized, that is, adaptable to cultural identity and distinction. Generally, *culture* refers to the totality of all learned social behavior of a given group; it provides standards for perceiving, believing, evaluating, and acting (Thomas 1993, 12). Culture includes knowledge, belief, law, art, religion, morals, customs, habits, symbols, and rules of discourse in a social system. As such, it is shared values and beliefs that mostly evolve and accumulate through time. As Thomas (1993, 4) points out, culture is studied not only to be described but also to be changed. Many cultural elements evolve and are maintained via institutions and structures such as the school, the family, and places of worship.

A highly deterministic delineation is the idea of culture and its impact as "the collective programming of the mind which distinguishes the members of one human group from another" (Hofstede 1980, 43). According to this idea, culture not only shapes how we view ourselves and how we view others but also translates into, and determines, a wide range of attitudes and behaviors. To demonstrate or assess the impact of culture on individual attitudes and behaviors and, indirectly, on institutions and society at large is exceedingly complex. In addition to necessary vigilance against stereotyping, assessing cultural consequences with confidence requires measurement and procedures for assigning values and significance to cultures and to their impacts (Gross and Rayner, 1985). But this is another matter altogether and not a central consideration of this study.

The Domination Thesis and Modernization Analysis

The conclusion derived from the domination thesis (whether military, economic, or cultural) is that uneven power relations, which create asymmetrical global reality, largely dictate approaches to development in less powerful countries. Believers invoke plenty of historical evidence in support of such a conclusion. European thinkers pioneered modernization analysis, and

European imperialism popularized it by dictating many of the educational and cultural norms of the former colonies. The dichotomous classification of systems as modern or traditional is itself traceable to nineteenth-century European sociologists. A prominent early illustration is German sociologist Max Weber's polar conception of the state's authority system according to legitimacy claims. In his *traditional system,* legitimacy is claimed and accepted on the basis of belief in the sanctity of traditions and the authenticity of the actions by those who exercise authority according to them. Obedience is not to enacted rules and laws but to persons whose orders are legitimized by tradition. Staff is recruited by criteria such as family kinship, wealth, and inherited personal influence, which are not connected to achievement.

In contrast, the legitimacy of Weber's *legal-rational system* rests on belief in the rule of law and the right of those elevated to authority under such rules to issue commands. Staff in a legal-rational authority system is organized as a bureaucracy. Merit, specialization, and superiority of technical knowledge are the basis of recruitment into the bureaucracy, and the impersonality of rules and procedures ensures uniformity of its decisionmaking.

The influence of such polar thinking was reflected in much of the writings of social scientists in the United States in the 1950s and 1960s about modernization. Sometimes referred to as "developmentalists," many of these scholars favored integrated, comprehensive global models that offered intellectual synthesis and comparative perspectives on development. Some examples are T. Parsons, *The Social System,* published in 1951; D. Lerner, *The Passing of Traditional Society,* 1958; W. W. Rostow, *The Stages of Economic Growth,* 1960; G. Almond and J. S. Coleman, *The Politics of Developing Areas,* 1960; L. W. Pye, *Communications and Political Development,* 1963; S. Huntington, *Political Order in Changing Societies,* 1968; and others. All viewed modernization in terms of a comprehensive, systemic process in which societies changed fundamentally from the traditional form to an approximation of a modern system.

RECONSIDERING BASIC PREMISES OF DEVELOPMENT

Views on transforming developing countries may vary on the fringes but often converge in the core. Among the core concepts are the application of scientific and technological methods to achieve growth and increase production combined with transformation of institutions and cultures to embody efficiency, orderliness, and rational decisionmaking. The application, however, is anything but constant.

Earlier blueprints of development rationality relied on central planning as a dependable medium and the state as the party responsible for overseeing the implementation of "successful planning" (Lewis 1966, 1). In the 1980s, *development* replaced *modernization* and *nation building* in the literature. Even without a universally understood meaning of the term *development* (Heady 1996, 117), in most contexts development does not require discarding the old or severing relations with the traditional. Rather it is a process of renewal through refinement and reform of the material, behavioral, and symbolic assets of society. And when it is not dependent on foreign sources but self-reliant, national development endures (Sayigh 1991).

The real test of development as a process is in the implementation that specifies not only what development should achieve but also how to achieve it. It is useful, albeit insufficient, to state that development "connotes steady progress toward improvement in the human condition" (Esman 1991, 5–6). Esman discerns five important dimensions of development: (1) economic growth, (2) equity, (3) capacity (cultivation of skills, institutions, and incentives), (4) authenticity (distinctive qualities of each society as expressed in its institutions and practices), and (5) empowerment (expanded opportunities for individuals and collectivities to participate in economic and political transactions). Other prescriptions of development criteria or objectives often bear significant similarities. They emphasize elements of rationality, planning, rise of productivity, social and economic equalization, improved institutions and attitudes, national independence, and grassroots participation (Myrdal 1968).

Perhaps the lack of controversy over objectives is a function of what may be described as the "motherhood and apple pie" syndrome. Objectives are often loosely enough stated to be able to accommodate any chosen position. Where disagreement arises is in dealing with means and methods of achieving such objectives. Consistently, evidence indicates that what matters is how development is managed and how its benefits and outcomes are distributed among people.[8] Today, the *what* and *how* of development are regularly complemented by *who* benefits by it.

From a methodological perspective, research on development encompasses three specific concerns that require resolutions. First, objectives or criteria of development are heavily qualitative and seem to defy direct statistical measurement. As a result, appraisal of development has been conducted indirectly, by using indicators that are directly measurable—number of trained doctors, literacy rate, child mortality, average life expectancy, per capita income, and even the percentage of citizens who own cars, televisions, telephones, and radios.

Second, because "no quantitative indicator is capable of exactly measuring a qualitative criterion" (Colman and Nixon 1986, 8), research is limited to approximations of qualitative levels attained in a society. Many of Myrdal's (1968) development criteria mentioned earlier illustrate this point.

Third, because development is multidimensional and defies attempts to measure it through single-factor analysis, various indicators have to be indexed in order to measure the economic, social, political, and cultural dimensions of development. Ideally, the most reliable method is to include many variables or indicators in order to obtain the most comprehensive coverage possible. In a practical sense, however, too many indicators would be difficult and costly to manage, achieving only diminishing returns. The key is to group important indicators. Particularly promising is the Human Development Index (HDI) produced annually since 1990 by the United Nations Development Program (UNDP) to define and measure progress in human development.

Compelled by pressures for relevance and persuaded by the methodological promise of more focused middle-range theories, recent literature appears less absorbed by construction of grand models of *comprehensive* development. Instead, in an attempt to improve specificity of the theory and practice of development, today's scholars loosely differentiate three types of development: *socioeconomic*, *political*, and *administrative*. Each employs its own concepts, methodologies, and disciplinary underpinning.

Socioeconomic Development

Economic development generally has been equated with growth of per capita output and income, the expectation being that economic development is served by rising productivity, growing employment opportunities, and a diversified economy. By the early 1960s, Herman (1989, 5) points out, "the physics metaphor was ascendant in economics and development became economic engineering." Also at this time, national planning was the fashion in Third World countries. This meant direct state investment in selected areas of the economy or central influence on the economy through taxes, subsidies, and regulations. In 1965, the United Nations set up a Committee for Development Planning, composed of prominent international economists, and charged it with elaborating planning techniques to share with developing countries (Herman 1989, 5). Early policies of the World Bank, too, fostered the central planning approach.

Currently, one hears very little about central planning except in the context of attempting to comprehend its failures in such areas as Eastern Europe and the former Soviet Union. The record of central planning in developing countries also is uneven. Serious trials of comprehensive development planning, often inspired by programs of international financial aid, proved to be illusory. A variety of ailments, such as poor data, lack of trained staff, inadequate political support, corruption, and poor coordination, has been cited as contributing to failure of comprehensive development planning (Heady 1996; Jreisat 1991; Caiden and Caiden 1977; and Palmer 1973). Regardless of the causes of this failure, the countries involved often managed to kindle rampant inflation, incur enormous debts, and create inflexible bureaucracies.

During the 1960s and early 1970s, the influential economic perspective of W. W. Rostow and others defined development in terms of linear stages of growth through which all countries must pass. According to this school of thought, countries need only discover the proper mix of savings and investment to enable them to "take-off" toward their cherished developmental goals. This almost mechanical sort of economic engineering was to be realized through national planning and capital investment. The futility of the stages or the linear approach gave way in the 1970s to two competing perspectives.

The first of these focused on the *structural change* that a developing country must undergo in order to succeed in generating and sustaining rapid economic growth. All that an underdeveloped economy needed, according to this perspective, was to transform the domestic economic structure from traditional, subsistence agriculture to a modern, urbanized, industrial, and service economy.

The second perspective, the *dependence model* discussed earlier, perceived underdevelopment in terms of international and domestic power relationships, institutional and structural economic rigidities, and the resulting dual societies among the nations of the world. This perspective saw developing countries caught up in a dependence and dominance relationship relative to rich countries (Todaro 1989, 68).

An economic theory with a potentially significant contribution to development economics was that put forth by John Maynard Keynes in *The General Theory of Employment, Interest and Money* (1936, 1949). The influence of Keynesian economics on perspectives of developing countries, however, has been indirect; Keynes was not much interested in the development of emerging countries. His ideas of relying on the state as the principal force in achieving economic growth (along with full employment and price and wages stability) served as a rationale for state economic activism. Thus, in congruity with Keynesian economics, governments "would establish the policy framework for development, enforce investment priorities, control abuses by regulation, operate major enterprises that the private sector was deemed uninterested in or unsuitable for, and provide a wide range of essential public services from education to transportation" (Esman 1991, 7).

Today, a neoclassical[9] countermovement in economic thought is taking hold. It advocates "structural adjustment" to free the market, privatize public corporations, and dismantle public ownership. It rejects central planning and regulation of economic activities (Todaro 1989, 82). In essence, this economic perspective seeks to minimize the role of the state in the economy by downsizing government. The ultimate faith is placed in market incentives, which proponents trust will produce greater efficiencies and better utilization of resources to achieve growth of the economy (Esman 1991, 9). The growing economic powers of the World Bank and the International Monetary Fund (IMF) are major forces behind such macroeconomic policies, which are sanctioned by large industrial systems, mainly the United States and Britain.

Despite shortcomings and inefficiencies of public sector economic involvement, advocates of the free market as the solution have not satisfied concerns over the subject of welfare economics and seem to ignore a host of issues stemming from previous market failures. History indicates that economic competition has never been perfect or fair and that government action often came to pass exactly because of "market failures" that required government to improve efficiency (Mendez 1992, 13) or attain social justice. Moreover, the private sector in many developing systems has not been prepared to assume its responsibilities as envisioned in the restructuring and privatization schemes (Corm 1995). This is certainly true in the Arab states (as argued in Chapter 10).

Typically, the choice of a strategy is based on a selection of economic assumptions and perspectives, associated with confirmed economic thinking under comparable conditions. A credible strategy usually indicates the degree of reliance on internal or external resources, specifies commitment to legitimate values and policies (equity), and takes into account existing and potential administrative capacities.

But concepts and theories of economic growth differ on methods for the measurement of results. Reliance on per capita gross domestic product (GDP) alone is insufficient to measure economic development. Per capita GDP "can easily overstate or understate poverty and mislead policymakers."[10] As a measure, GDP does not adjust for social costs of productivity (crime, urban sprawl, or safety hazards). Another important limitation of GDP is that it does not even attempt to account for ecological costs of development, such as damage to the environment. Nonetheless, per capita GDP continues to be widely used in classifying countries into categories of high, medium, or low income, as in the World Bank's annual report. Thus, the most influential indicator of economic growth is narrow—even deficient—but remains the most prevalent for measuring standards of living in a society.

Finally, the field of development economics is going through a crisis of confidence and self-doubt (Colman and Nixon 1986, vi). To a large degree the cause is the consequence of the growing influence of the neoclassical revival and the increasingly harsh criticisms of radical political economists. Whether we are witnessing the demise of development economics or its growth, serious developmental problems remain unsolved.

Political Development

Political development has to do with the ability to stimulate a process by which a political system acquires an increased capacity to satisfy old and new types of goals and demands—the ability to create organizational configurations within the administrative and political systems capable of handling whatever demands are placed upon them (Heady 1996, 119; Diamant 1966, 92). The advantage of viewing political development in terms of state capacity for autonomous action is that the discussion is freed from the perpetual compulsion of transforming traditional systems into Western-style democracies. Once we concede the possibility of different forms of political development, building various organizations, and utilizing distinct processes of managing public policies, the criteria of evaluation change. Successful development is measured then not by how similar to Western practices governing is but by how effective it is in achieving such national needs and objectives as freeing citizens from hunger, disease, ignorance, and political oppression and protecting the environment. Invariably, authentic political development requires independence of the system from external hegemony and tutelage in order to reach decisions serving citizens interests.

Linked to political development is the issue of political participation, a process that appears to be clouded by a continuing transitional definition. Joan M. Nelson distinguishes the older image of political participation from the new. The older image "reflects the intimate connection between the concept of participation and the concept of democracy" (1987, 103). Indeed, within this image participation is conceived almost entirely in democratic contexts and is deemed suspect or unbelievable in other settings.

The newer alternative image decouples the concepts of participation and democracy. Such new efforts seek to encompass broader intellectual concerns over a wider geographic and temporal range. In this image, Nelson (1987, 104) concludes: "participation is simply the efforts of ordinary people in any type of political system to influence the actions of their rulers, and sometimes to change their rulers."

Scholarship on political development of the 1960s and 1970s is in disagreement over what happened, and what should have happened, in Third World countries. As Weiner (1987, xxv) notes, adequacy assessments of the widely recognized U.S. scholarship on political development indicate an inability to anticipate or explain many of the changes in the Third World. Unable to be free of cultural and political biases and driven by predetermined methodological processes, such contributions often lost the campaign for relevance. In contrast to early economic development advocating creation and distribution of wealth rather than its aggregation, political development appears to promote aggregation of power to achieve political order and stability, democratic or otherwise (Huntington 1987, 5). In fact, authoritarian central controls became quite common, and the military in many countries happily obliged by providing such a style of governing, wanted by the people or not. The question of political development in the Arab state is so crucial and has such varied consequences that it is dealt with in detail in various chapters, particularly Chapter 11.

Administrative Development

Administrative development is an integral part of societal development and is profoundly influenced by overall political, economic, and cultural attributes. Despite ideological tendencies that discredit bureaucracy and associate with it various preconceived images, bureaucracy remains a dominant institution performing essential functions for modern society. Biased notions of bureaucracy detract from a realization of the full benefits of analysis. Certainly, it is germane to ask whether administrative development is a prerequisite of economic development and whether administrative development can be detached from political development. A profoundly revealing line of questioning is whether bureaucracy indeed exerts a hobbling effect on political development.

This relationship defies final and absolute conclusions. It is commonly recognized that administration takes place in various public or private settings. But *public administration* "is that sector of administration found in a political setting" (Heady 1996, 2). In societies with low levels of differentiation between legitimate functions and legal responsibilities, one expects overlapping, meddling, and mutual accommodations to be rampant between administrative and political structures. Despite recognition of the many distinctive operational components of politics and administration, they remain closely associated. Bureaucracy nevertheless remains a primary unit of analysis—a basic, universal structure of contemporary governments. Thus, administrative reforms aim, among other things, to build institutional capacities for making and implementing effective and efficient public decisions that serve societies' needs and demands.

At this point, one must ponder the possibility of establishing general laws from experiences examined against a commitment to what Samir Amin (1992, 12) calls "irreducible specificity." Generalizations that ignore the concreteness and distinctiveness of the case being investigated are flawed. To ensure that the relationship between the particular and the general is complementary, not contradictory, generalizations must evolve from an aggregate of particular facts that have been reliably established and verified. This is precisely why in this study I give special attention to certain public policies and decisions. Focusing on offices and the powers they assume, examining implementation of decisions and obstacles encountered, and exploring a variety of structural and behavioral elements—all are important parts in determining outcomes of reforms. Only after such analysis can overall patterns and processes be credibly suggested.

In examining and observing modes of action across political and bureaucratic boundaries, a conscious leaning toward the comparative method is apparent.[11] The comparative perspective offers many advantages. One is the attainment of higher confidence in generalizations and conclusions than in studying single cases. Another is that the comparative method serves practitioners by expanding their horizons of choice and their capacity to observe, learn, and improve performance. Also, the comparative study of institutions promotes understanding of pervasive, global characteristics; it reduces the possibility of parochial tendencies to be absorbed by culture-bound qualities.

In summary, reconsidering the promise and the reality of development since the 1950s reveals many significant changes that have taken place. Today, development is a collective effort of the society, involving the full capacities of private and public institutions in a partnership. Sustainable development is not dependent on capital infusion from the World Bank or other external sources of funding but is a self-reliant process that first interacts with and responds to community needs and demands. Also, development is not export orientation of the economy but an overall improvement in productivity and a balanced growth that does not sacrifice environmental concerns or create serious dislocations that disadvantage specific segments of the society. And, most important, genuine development is based not on a priori economic assumptions but on empirical understanding of local political, administrative, and economic realities. Finally, integral to the new development thinking is transparency of public decisions, availability of information, and accountability of public officials and institutions as well as their conscious respect of human rights and values.

THE ARAB WORLD AND CONVERGING OBSTACLES

The Arab world extends over North Africa and Southeast Asia, from Morocco to Iran (see Table 3.1). Like most emerging countries, those in the Arab world experienced colonial domination in various forms and for varying lengths of time. In Algeria, for example, the French ruled for more than 130 years before independence in 1962, directly and totally controlling the government. In Egypt, the British permitted a shadow national government that operated in collaboration with the occupying force from 1882 until the 1950s. Under the British rule the Gulf region was apportioned into autonomous municipalities, later converted into ministates ruled by "family dictatorships," as Chomsky puts it (1994, 21). The British-promoted dynasties continued to reign in each of these ministates, protected by "special relations" with the former imperial force, until the United States assumed such a role during and after the Cold War.

The Arab colonial experience is distinctive in some fundamental aspects from most countries that experienced colonial rule. The Arab region emerged from British and French colonial rule fragmented and divided into many states, most of them lacking economic, political, or military viability. The states were carved out by the imperial powers to facilitate imperial objectives in the region. In many of these states, formal independence was not equivalent to authentic self-government. In the post–World War II years, Western forces continued their meddling and interventions in the affairs of the region, primarily prompted by Cold War considerations, oil, and preservation of the state of Israel. The latter two factors continue to be important.

The immense connections between Arab external relations and internal politics are striking. During the Cold War years, for example, being pro-Soviet or pro-American meant a distinction between the type of national development attempted and the means used in achieving it. Many scholars who follow the political history of the Arabs and their current developmental policies acknowledge this connection between the external and the internal dimensions (Barakat 1993; Chomsky 1994; Hourani 1991; Said 1993; Sayigh 1991). The irony is notable in the assertive move in 1973 by the oil-producing Arab states to increase their share of the profits. Only a few years later, "what might have seemed to be a declaration of political and economic independence was in fact a first step towards greater dependence on the United States" (Hourani 1991, 419).

Nevertheless, the Arab states exhibit relatively consistent patterns, as illustrated by content analysis of seventeen master theses and eighteen doctoral dissertations in public administration completed at the University of Cairo, Egypt, between 1970 and 1993.[12] In these projects, researchers focused on issues of administrative reform, development administration, bureaucracy, and their impact on comprehensive development. Eight theses and nine dissertations dealt with the Egyptian experience. The rest of the studies covered Lebanon, Iraq, Saudi Arabia, the United Arab Emirates (UAE), and Yemen. Among the common themes in these studies are the connection between administrative reform and comprehensive development. According to these studies, administrative reform and comprehensive development are so intricately intertwined that the second will not happen in Arab societies without the first (Affendi 1994, 11). The common belief is that government's inability to plan and manage development and its tendency to micromanage the economy are largely due to weak and inefficient public institutions.

The persistent difficulty, however, is how to conceptualize reform, define strategies, and remove impediments to implementation. Surely, analysis of the Arab experience has to have a problem-solving orientation that balances abstract reasoning with knowledge of particulars. In order not to totally rely on existing literature, I gathered information from the field, so primary sources and information on real-life situations are central in this study. I conducted interviews with a considerable number of senior officials from Cairo and Amman who were involved in the process of national development and administrative reform, and, I benefited greatly from checking governmental documents, visiting operations, and observing public officials in action.

Reform measures are judged in terms of their enhancement of institutional capacity for action. Reform policies reveal internal and contextual characteristics of the system of governing that reach far beyond the immediate questions at hand. Consequently, one has to consider various aspects of a system while focusing on its institutional structures of power that provide preliminary frameworks, or "blueprints" for activities (Meyer and Rowan 1992, 23). Structures include offices, positions, rules and procedures, programs, and systems of coordination and control as well as a variety of relationships and networks of social behavior.

My initial emphasis on organizations and institutions gave primacy to levels in the hierarchy of the state below its apex. In this way the analysis includes the "lowest rungs on the organizational hierarchy where direct engagement with society often occurs" (Migdal et al. 1994, 15), the level at which state leaders impose their preferences and exercise state powers. Organizational performance produces a range of outcomes that penetrate society: regulating actions, extracting revenues, controlling or allocating resources, and rendering essential services. Eventually I was compelled to realize how much power is concentrated at the political crest. The paradox is that in the contemporary Arab state, in a manner similar to what Catherine Boone (1994, 109) found in postcolonial Africa, "patterns of political practice have worked to erode the administrative capacities and resources bases of the state."

The chapters of this book introduce the ideological setting for shaping the structure and defining the functions of the contemporary Arab state (Chapter 2); analyze issues of development administration in particular and examine specific institutional performance in several states, particularly Egypt and Jordan (Chapters 3 through 7); and investigate overall defining influences on directions of change (such as the rise of Islamism as an alternative system of governance in Chapter 8). In Chapter 9, the focus is on oil as a strategic Arab resource, a major source of revenue, and a pervasive influence on all aspects of the Arab society. In the last two chapters, I stand back again and weigh the information, ponder the analysis of earlier chapters, and reexamine the factors and the forces that shape and vitalize societal institutions. Ultimately, the purpose of the study is to identify patterns while asking again the fundamental question: Why have reform efforts not produced the anticipated results? The search for answers repeatedly brought the discussion to the critical elements of leadership, ideology, and institutional capacity considered in Chapters 8 through 11. The convergence of these elements is the imperative for any successful developmental strategy.

NOTES

1. "Prologue: Achievements and Challenges in 2000 Years of Comparative Research," in *Comparative Policy Research*, ed. M. Dierkes, H. N. Weiler, and B. Antal (New York: St. Martin's, 1987).

2. Woodrow Wilson "The Study of Public Administration," *Political Science Quarterly* 2 (June 1887).

3. In classifying regimes, Merle Fainsod uses the criterion of "the relationship of bureaucracies to the flow of political authority." His breakdown distinguishes five different alternatives: (1) ruler-dominated bureaucracies, (2) military-dominated bureaucracies, (3) ruling bureaucracies, (4) representative bureaucracies, and (5) party-state bureaucracies (quoted in Heady 1996, 312).

4. In subsequent years EDI expanded its offerings to include more practical instruction on the World Bank techniques for project appraisal and country programming. More than thirteen hundred officials participated, and many of them have risen to the position of prime minister or minister of planning or finance in their respective countries (Rich 1994, 76).

5. This institute was a UN organization that originated from the Economic Commission for Latin America (ECLA).

6. *Business Week* (July 31, 1995), p. 57.

7. *New York Times,* January 9, 1994.

8. United Nations Development Program, *Human Development Report 1995* (New York: Oxford University Press).

9. In the literature, it is also called *neoconservative* (Esman) and *neoliberal* (Corm).

10. Amartya Sen, "Profile," *New York Times,* January 9, 1994, p. 8F.

11. Fred W. Riggs says:

The term, public administration, will no longer refer just to the American practice of public administration but, rather, it will embrace the global phenomenon. Anyone writing about American public administration will need to specify this context. Moreover, there will be no need for the term, *comparative public administration,* since all serious research on 'public administration' will presuppose a comparative framework. ("Public Administration Theory: A Futurist Vision" [unpublished paper dated February 1993], p. 1).

This paper was supplied to me by Fred Riggs.

12. Atieh Hussain Affendi, "Administrative Reform in the Arab States" (paper in Arabic presented at a symposium on administrative reform, University of Cairo, 1994.

2

Ideological Setting of the Arab State

If we do not change our direction, we are likely to end up where we are headed.

Ancient Chinese proverb

National development is an all-encompassing effort that entails coordination of such various elements as defining objectives, formulating a strategy, and mobilizing resources. One critical feature of developmental processes, however, is an organizing framework that establishes the vision, guides implementation, and relates activities to each other. This organizing framework is what Heady (1996, 291) calls "ideology of development," a concept he considers crucial to an understanding of politics and administration. Ideology determines the vision for political and administrative action, "but it does not specify the exact form of the machinery for either politics or administration" (294).[1] This is why competent leaders are indispensable: They define, interpret, and articulate values and demands before translating them into plans of action.

An ideology is an integrated system of ideas and principles—associated with an influential leader, a social class or group, or a political movement—that explains and simplifies a complex sociopolitical reality (Salem 1994, 3). During the Communist control of government in the former Soviet Union, Marxist ideology expressed and rationalized the interests of the controlling socioeconomic class. Islamist ideology is a major influence on decisionmaking in the Islamic Republic of Iran.

Ideology helps people construct a more coherent, integrated, and supportable system of norms and beliefs and helps sort out their cultural values and their moral confusion, particularly in a crisis environment. Ideology becomes observable ultimately in attitudes and then in behavior. The most direct effect of ideology, however, is on political decisionmaking. Since World War II, two groups of proponents of ideology have had an important impact on the political-administrative processes of the Arab states: (1) the secular-liberal nationalist and socialist groups that have been influencing regimes for several decades and (2) the Islamists who seek control of the state and replacement of its current structures and processes (see Chapter 8).

Nationalist and socialist doctrines are not identical. Rigid separation of these two movements within contemporary Arab politics, however, is not always possible. Arab nationalists have often been socialists. At the same time, many socialists, except for hard-core Marxists, are indistinguishable from nationalists. The Arab Nationalist Ba'th Party (usually referred to as the Ba'th Party, or BP), for example, is an avowed socialist party, whereas Nasser's Arab Socialist Union has been mainly a nationalist movement.

Despite ample literature on the intellectual history and the sociological foundations of Arab nationalism and socialism, the actual linkages between ideology and management of public policies remain substantially unexplored. There are many obstacles to studying these linkages: First, Arab nationalists, and to a lesser degree Islamists and socialists, have been long on tokenism and symbolism but short on declared strategies and programmatic actions. Second, within an oppressive political order, free and open exchange of views on public issues is diminished. Research and scholarship suffer profoundly in an environment of secrecy. Critics of official views are routinely accused by their governments of being subversive or worse. Third, the gap between advocacy and achievement, rhetoric and programmed enforcement, is so vast that inconsistencies between policy formulation and implementation are commonly assumed. However, despite these impediments, to study the Arab state and its institutional development without delineating its ideological cornerstones would be an incomplete approach.

To analyze basic contemporary Arab ideologies and how they evolved is to explore meaningful attempts at shaping public policies and state institutional structures. Whether transpiring from religious, socioeconomic, or political alignments, these ideologies signify remedies to societal problems. One immediate advantage to the examination of doctrinal influences is the opportunity to appraise crucial linkages between abstract and concrete—between policy and action. Another function of ideological analysis is featuring contradictions and inconsistencies in the state's institutional arrangements and their functions.

MODERN ARAB NATIONALISM:
THE EMBRYONIC PHASE

Nationalism assumes the existence of a nation, people with common characteristics, a recognized consciousness, and a defined territory. Nationalism, Gellner (1983, 1) points out, "is primarily a political principle, which holds that the political and the national unit should be congruent." Usually nationalism is tied to a nation-state and has something to do with the nations's domestic organizational setting as well as its relations with the outside world. In the context of nationalism and the organizational configurations it produces, the shift of ideas and the apparent socioeconomic patterns are relevant material for examination. Within existing structural constraints, what do pan-Arab nationalists advocate as developmental public policies? What institutional and managerial processes have they for realizing their policy objectives?

In a notable study of Arab nationalism, Bassam Tibi (whose work originally appeared in German in 1971 and was then translated into English in 1981) outlines three distinct historical stages of Arab nationalism: (1) the Arabic literary and linguistic renaissance, during which Westernized Arab intellectuals arrived at a form of national consciousness (the *nahdha*), (2) the politicization of this literary renaissance and the transformation of cultural into political nationalism, and (3) the narrowing down of this political nationalism into the demand for a united Arab national state (Tibi 1990, xii).

Tibi's delineation reveals a dynamic process that consistently expanded and deepened national sentiments among the Arab people. The process has been accelerated by the expansion of education, the use of various modern communication tools, and the concomitant advantages of the "information revolution." These advancements have expanded and elaborated interrelations among various segments of the Arab people, despite opposite and disintegrative actions by political leaders. Indeed, during the decades following World War II, extensive mutual interests have developed across existing political boundaries.

Modern Arab nationalism, however, is not synonymous with the Arab world. Nationalism is mainly a product of the late nineteenth century, but the Arabs are people with a known history of over two millennia. Arab civilization developed and prospered at times and declined and waned at others. Arabs ruled one of the most powerful and enlightened empires in history. As George Antonius (1946, 15) states, "[U]nder their rule a brilliant chapter in the history of mankind was to unfold itself, and their real claim to greatness was not that they conquered such a vast portion of the known world, but that they gave it a new civilization." The two major dimensions of the Arab legacy, as underlined by Antonius (15), are Islamization, whereby the new faith commended itself to millions of new adherents and transformed their spiritual lives, and Arabization, both through the spread of the Arabic language and the racial Arabization caused by absorption and fusion with conquered territories by means of migration and intermarriage.

Compared to a study of the Arab world, an investigation of modern Arab nationalism is a limited and specific theme that covers only a small phase of Arab history—one traceable to the beginning of the twentieth century or shortly before. The literature provides different explanations of how and when the nationalist enterprise was activated. For Sylvia Haim (1962, 27), Abdul-Rahman al-Kawakibi (1849–1902) "may be considered as the first true intellectual precursor of modern secular Pan-Arabism." Her first reason is the clear declaration by al-Kawakibi that the Arabs must not be ruled by the Ottoman Turks and that the Arabs must have the primacy in such an association; hence, the caliphate must be restored to an Arab. Second, Haim says that despite all his preoccupations with the state of Islam, "al-Kawakibi, once he introduced the idea of a spiritual caliph, was led to consider politics as an autonomous activity divorced from divine prescription, and fully subject to the will of men" (27).

George Antonius found a different starting point for the emergence of modern Arab nationalism, tying the beginning to Christian educational establishments, mostly sponsored by missionaries, and particularly to the contributions of Christian Arab intellectuals. Antonius saw "the cradle of a new political movement" in the campaign for unity, the revival of the language, and the overthrow of barriers that separated the Arab people (1946, 53).

It is most likely that Arab nationalism developed gradually and gathered support and momentum from similar nationalist movements in Europe and other places. After four centuries under Ottoman rule, the Arabs saw that the growing emphasis on the paramountcy of the Turkish elements in the Ottoman system was bound to upset the balance between Turks and Arabs. Consequently and "by reaction Arab nationalism gradually became explicit" (Hourani 1991, 309). In the early phase, this was a movement of sentiments among some educated Muslim and Christian Arabs from Lebanon and Syria who helped to revive Arab consciousness and encouraged assertiveness that evolved from demands for administrative reform to a commitment to full independence by World War I.

The debate over the origins of modern Arab nationalism is still continuing among scholars. Some of their findings converge; others need further examination in light of new evidence and archival revelations. Research over the past few decades has produced extensive literature on the subject and attracted contributions from such scholars as Ibrahim Abu-Lughod, Aziz Al-Azmeh, George Antonius, C. Earnest Dawn, Albert Hourani, Sylvia Haim, Rashid Khalidi, Walter Z. Laqueur, Edward Said, Hisham Sharabi, and Bassam Tibi.

Despite continuing debate, there seems to be substantial agreement on several aspects of the question of how modern Arab nationalism evolved and how political forces have tried to make use of it. By the end of the nineteenth century, the Ottoman empire was crumbling. Its religious pretensions, oppressive policies, and corrupt administration dictated its failure as a system of government. Arab intellectuals and political leaders were divided in their views of the future of Arab lands under Ottoman rule.

The insiders, virtually all Muslim Arabs who served in the Ottoman parliament or occupied other official positions, advocated demands for reform in the Arab regions without severing ties with the empire, which was after all Islamic. Others, including large numbers of Christian Arabs who did not feel themselves part of the Ottoman system, demanded independence and recognition of the right of Arabs to rule themselves.

Initially, the advocates of full independence did not express their views openly for fear of state persecution. The growing Turkification of the Istanbul government deepened the disillusionment and alienation of Arab leaders, particularly after 1908 when the political group called the Committee of Union and Progress (CUP) took control. At first Arab expectations were that the ascendance of the CUP to power would bring about comprehensive reforms of the perverted Ottoman system of governing. Demands then articulated by the Arabs included decentralization of decisionmaking to provincial governors, improvements in education, the use of Arabic in schools, and the upgrading of social services. The CUP showed sympathy and support to Arab grievances until it gained control of government, when it then ruled with Turkish nationalist fervor. With the beginning of World War I, Turkish nationalist zeal reached a turning point when many leaders of the Arab nationalist movement were executed (among these the infamous hangings in Beirut and Damascus by the local Turkish governor Jamal Pasha).

As to relations with the West, despite Arab nationalists' admiration for the secular democratic political culture, they showed no interest in replacing the Ottoman privileged status in Arab lands with a similar status for Western nations. As Dawn notes, the Muslim Arab reaction to the West was shared by Christian Arabs, including most of those commonly called the creators of secular Arab nationalism (1991, 7).

The foundation period served the purpose of fermentation of ideas, but early nationalists' conceptions of socioeconomic development remained inexplicit, vague, and short of a recognizable strategy or plan of action. The main element of their platform consistently was independence: They campaigned for liberation of Arab lands and people from foreign rule. Early nationalists considered independence a prerequisite for uniting major parts of the Arab world and improving Arab standards of living. All nationalist reform agendas gave education a high priority and in particular emphasized the revival of Arabic language and Arabic literature, after a period of educational decline under the Ottoman rule. The high literary attainment of the nationalist leaders themselves may have influenced their attention to education, or they may have perceived education as the most effective medium for elevating nationalist consciousness among citizens.

The Arab revolt of 1916, led by Sherif Hussein Ben Ali, governor of the Hijaz, was the result not only of the advent of World War I but also of a process that had begun several decades earlier. The agreement that emerged from letters and pledges exchanged between the British high commissioner in Cairo, Sir Henry McMahon, and Sherif Hussein in 1915 pledged England's support of Arab independence in exchange for Arabs' assistance to the British in their war against Turkey and Germany. Six months after this agreement the British and the French divided the region between them in a secret document signed by the minister of foreign affairs of Britain, Mark Sykes, and his French counterpart, George Picot (Lenczowski 1962, 70–75).

Thus, the end of the Ottoman domination did not result in Arab independence, and the anticipated transformation of Arab society into a united and independent state took a turn that changed the Arab world dramatically and possibly damaged its national aspirations irreversibly. The new colonialists subdivided the Arab lands into British and French possessions and protectorates. To be sure, the colonial hegemony created governments headed by Arab leaders, but these were skeleton states established to serve imperial designs. As British colonial functionary Sir Anthony Parsons (1991, xv) points out:

> When World War II ended in 1945, Britain had emerged supreme in the Middle East. . . . Her old rivals in the Eastern Question—France, Russia, Germany and Italy—had been driven from the field by defeat in war or revolution at home. The mantle of the Ottoman Empire . . . had been assumed by the British Empire. Only twenty-six years later, a mere flicker of the eyelid of history, Britain too had passed from the scene.

In a complex system of political entanglements, the colonial masters installed leaders for these new Arab states as rewards for their loyalty. This was most blatant in the Gulf region, where for a long time the British discouraged integration of these municipalities into a viable political structure. Britishers acknowledge the outcome of their rule of the Gulf region, as Balfour-Paul (1991, 5) concedes: "In a sense the political fragmentation of this area [is] the outcome of Britain's nineteenth century treaties with whatever shaykhs they found locally in charge at the time, whereby their separate authority was legitimized and perpetuated."

As the new overlord of Arab lands, the British colonial administration provided staffing expertise to the ministates. They instituted and laid the foundations for compliant bureaucracies that, henceforth, expanded exponentially while fortifying their self-serving procedures. The British position in the Arab world soon became untenable. Nationalist demands forced the British out but could not eradicate their imperial political edifices in Arab politics.

The political values of the Arab nationalist movement in the interim between the two world wars were exemplified in a statement issued by the

First Arab Students' conference, held in Brussels in December 1938. Idealistic as the pledge, definitions, and manifesto may seem, the students interpreted and elaborated some fundamental principles of Arab nationalism. "Arabs constitute one nation," they proclaimed. "The sacred right of this nation is to be sovereign in her own affairs. Her ardent nationalism drives her to liberate the Arab homeland, to unite all its parts, and to found political, economic, and social institutions more sound and more compatible than the existing ones" (Haim 1962, 100–102).

The themes repeatedly stated in the students' manifesto and in various other sources before World War II expanded those that had been declared at the First Arab Conference in Paris 1913, attended by Arab representatives from Beirut, Damascus, Cairo, Istanbul, Mexico, and the United States (Al-Husary 1955, 179). The demands of the Paris conference had included fundamental reforms to be implemented by the Ottomans without delay, such as Arab political rights, decentralization of administration, and designation of the Arabic language as official in Arab lands. In the 1930s, Arab nationalists' demands continued to emphasize independence, unity, improved standards of living, and the building of viable institutions.

With the collapse of the Ottoman rule and the beginning of Western domination, the Arabs had to start another long struggle for independence against different imperial forces—this time with greater sophistication and resourcefulness. The meaning of Arab nationalism, as Laqueur (1956, 275) points out, was always clear under foreign rule: independence, home rule, and the evacuation of foreign forces. When the Arabs finally gained formal independence, it was conceded not to viable nation-states but to political enclaves, ruled by entrenched dynasties that served provincial rather than national policies. Although the Arab people had always recognized that "something significant and consolidated would somehow emerge [from independence], and not mere confusion and anarchy" (Laqueur 1956, 4), instead the area remained in a vacuum to be filled by colonial covert influence or overt intervention.

In summary, prior to World War II neither Arab nationalists nor the new Western colonialists had a specific program for socioeconomic development of the region. Nor did they provide a serious impetus for structuring the institutional mechanisms necessary for modern governing, particularly after centuries of indifference by the Ottoman rule.

POLITICAL MOVEMENTS AFTER WORLD WAR II

The political movements that prevailed during the period of Western control were intensely nationalist. Initially, Arab nationalism may have lacked Western liberal values (Laqueur 1956, 8) or may have had a "tribal nationalistic" component, but clearly this movement was embarking on the fulfillment of decisive objectives in the context of the time. Building a viable independent state was always the core of all demands but not the only one. The early nationalists also subscribed to policies of socioeconomic development, administrative reform, and a belief in the value of free and dignified living for all citizens. But in its first major test, the emerging Arab state failed dramatically.

Shortly after the end of World War II, a major disaster in Palestine in 1948 spread "a heavy cloud of disillusionment" over the Arab world (Kazziha 1975, 1). One of the consequences of the Arab failure in Palestine was a demonstrable lack of confidence on the part of citizens of many countries in their governments and in their leaders. Equally significant, Arab institutions in both military and civilian sectors had been shown to be inadequate, unskilled, poorly organized, and lacking any effective means of operation.

Traditional leaders involved in the 1948 disaster (*nakbeh*) not only were discredited but few actually survived. The prime ministers of Egypt and Lebanon, the king of Jordan, and the whole royal family of Iraq were killed at different times and by different actors. The king of Egypt and the government of Syria were deposed by their military. A new generation of Arab nationalists turned to political parties as effective instruments for change. By the late 1950s, these parties appeared to dominate political discourse. The Ba'th Party, the Arab Nationalist Movement, and Nasser's Socialist Union all claimed comprehensive doctrines rooted in the main beliefs of Arab masses. Each group also promulgated specific political platforms consistent with those beliefs. The Ba'th Party and the Socialist Union declared versions of socialism adapted to suit Arab socioeconomic conditions. The Arab Nationalist Party was one of the few political groups that did not designate socialism as an element of its doctrine. Except for the Muslim Brothers, who advocated an Islamic nation, all other political movements promoted pan-Arab unity and represented secular ideologies.

Compared to socialist and nationalist parties, Arab communist parties had smaller memberships but better organizational discipline and greater ideological control of their movements. The net effect of communist movements has been to intensify political debates throughout the Arab world, profoundly influencing the political agenda. The parties raised the level of mobilization of the masses and sharpened political objectives and ideological differences among Arab political groups. There is no doubt that Arab communist parties not only heightened demands for economic justice, but also increased consciousness of class struggle and conflict as well as resistance to Western imperialism. Over time, the political themes advanced by Arab communist parties, as Salem (1994, 147) notes, "would prove crucial in galvanizing political participation and challenging political systems that preferred to ignore such issues."

At the same time, communists, socialists, and nationalists often seemed to set forth similar policies. Together they fostered and promoted the economic and political orientation of the post–World War II era. The three political groups emphasized state ownership and direction of production, equitable distribution of income through taxation, and the provision of expanded social services. The increasing strength and appeal of these ideas were to some extent a reflection of what was happening elsewhere in the world. The blend of nationalist and socialist ideas in programs of major Arab political parties was similar to that of many parties that assumed power in the newly independent states. Socialist and communist parties in Western Europe, the growing influence of the USSR and its allies, and the coming to power of the Communist Party in China were also major historical events that influenced Arab political and economic thinking in the postwar era (Hourani 1991, 402).

Socialist culture and terminology were disseminated through mass media, education, economic planning, and general political discourse. The articulation of Marxist ideas in Arabic was primarily centered in Egypt, from which publishing houses and mass media facilities reached out to every major city in the Arab world (Hourani 1991, 402). The net effect of socialist doctrines on the state has been fundamental in terms of increasing state hegemony on the economy and its management.

The military leaders who masterminded the revolutions in Egypt in 1952 and in Iraq in 1958 and took control of Syria three times between 1949 and 1954 promised control of resources by the government in the interest of the whole society. They may have achieved the first half of the promise (control of resources), but it is debatable to what extent they served the interest of the whole society. Increasingly, military rule became entrenched and played a more significant role in the modern history of the state. The experience of Syria, Egypt, and Iraq in military governing was soon emulated by Libya, Sudan, and Yemen.

Army rule has taken different forms in the Arab states. Individual autocrats governed in Syria, Libya, and Iraq; Egypt adopted a committee structure. While concentrating all powers in the hands of the leader of a coup d'état, the military rulers almost always sought to attain legitimacy by appearing to preserve a parliamentary system. Officers who assumed power generally were younger and had lower-middle-class social origins. Their reasons for intervention varied. Usually they championed causes such as reforming the system, ending confusion, preventing anarchy, fighting corruption, and defending the country against its enemies.

No popular movement has been successful in permanently wrestling state power from the military or from traditional leaders. All serious changes continue to be decreed from above. Ruling individuals and their families, trusted associates, and relatives usually enjoy the concentration of powers in their hands and have no desire or lack the skills necessary to mobilize public support. Political movements, conversely, are not unified. They tend to split and divide over mundane arguments, perpetuating their powerlessness and minimizing their influence on public policy. More notable, however, is that these autocratic political orders disallow political parties that are not totally loyal to the command center of the state.

The three contemporary nationalist movements with uncontestable claims to nationalist thinking are the Ba'th Party, Nasserism, and the Arab National Movement.

The Arab Ba'th National Party

The Ba'th Party (BP) is the first pan-Arab political movement to have developed a significant presence throughout the world. The BP has been strongest in Syria, home of the founders but has also successfully established a strong popular presence in several Arab countries (particularly in Iraq, Jordan, Lebanon, and Syria). During the 1960s and 1970s, Arab youth regarded the BP as the premier modern nationalist party. The BP constitution is a useful instrument for understanding its ideology. Some of the provisions are:

> Unity and Freedom of the Arab Nation: The Arabs form one nation. This nation has the natural right to live in a single state and to be free to direct its own destiny. . . .
> The Arab nation is characterized by virtues which are the result of its successive rebirths . . . vitality and creativeness . . . ability for transformation and renewal. Its renewal is always linked to growth in personal freedom, and harmony between its evolution and the national interest.[2] (Haim 1962, 233–241)

Articles 14 through 21 of the document prescribe a constitutional parliamentary regime, executive power responsible to the legislative power, and an independent judiciary. Very little is said about the administrative system, except that "the Arab state is a system of decentralization."

The basic economic policy of BP is socialistic—economic wealth of Arab lands belongs to the nation. The party acknowledges that the present distribution of wealth in the Arab lands is "unjust" and that "therefore a review and a just redistribution will become necessary" (Article 27). The party declares that the law will limit ownership of agricultural lands and industrial properties and that workers will participate in the management of their factories. Property and inheritance are two natural rights. The state controls trade and employs economic planning in attaining development. Freedoms of speech, assembly, and belief as well as artistic freedom are sacred; no authority can diminish them. The Ba'th Party advocates socialism, because it is a "necessity which emanates from the depth of Arab nationalism itself." The party considers socialism the ideal social order that will allow the Arab people to realize their potential and progress materially and morally.

The delineation of major principles of the BP illustrates the scope of nationalistic thinking during and after the 1950s. The goals are independence, unity, and a future in which the state controls economic and social development as well as achieves social justice in the emerging society. Less obvious within the nationalist program are developmental and nation-building objectives and processes. The power and popular appeal of these ideas made them seem invincible until manipulation and misapplication rendered them vulnerable. The popularity of the nationalistic doctrine of the BP enhanced its appeal to many political and military leaders, who were quick to embrace its principles as a tactic for seizing power. In Syria, Iraq, Jordan, and Lebanon, military officers openly endorsed these principles. But the party organization of the BP was too weak to confront the military and too inexperienced to outmaneuver traditional politicians, who usurped power and proceeded to serve their own political agendas.

The military takeovers in the name of BP principles in Syria and Iraq proved intriguing to the party loyalists in the initial stages, particularly when these loyalists were rewarded with good positions in the new governments. The party provided legitimacy to the regimes and received their benefits in return. But the stunning divergence that surfaced afterwards and persisted over two decades between the Ba'thist regimes in Syria and Iraq became the real test of the party's vigor and endurance. Although ostensibly ruled by the same party, Hafez Assad of Syria and Saddam Hussein of Iraq became competitors with uninhibited ambitions for supremacy. Their animosity deepened as it was converted into intense personal dislike and distrust as well as political antipathy.

The break between the Ba'th parties of Syria and Iraq also pointed up the discrepancy between principles and actual behaviors of the regimes. The hostility between the two governments undermined the precept of the Ba'th constitution as it dashed hopes of unity throughout the Arab world. As an example, consider the legal and constitutional system in Iraq under the BP. A 1995 report by the International Commission of Jurists in Geneva[3] reveals unsettling conclusions. The study confirms the practical experience of the Iraqi people: The Ba'thist system offers no safeguards or protection against state violations of basic human rights or infringement of its own constitution.[4] In Iraq, as in Syria, the structure of government and the performance of its various institutions have negated the most basic elements of the Ba'th doctrine.

Accomplishments in areas of socioeconomic development and administrative reform in Iraq and Syria also have been few and infrequent. Anything but lacking, however, have been the political rhetoric of each regime and the constant rationalization of the shortage of concrete results. After three decades of military rule under the banner of the Ba'th Party, Iraq's economy is a prolonged tragedy of devastation, made more cruel by an international economic boycott that continues many years after the Gulf War of 1991. In Syria, despite moderate reforms that have been slowly introduced in the 1990s, the obstacles remain formidable. A "corrupt and sluggish bureaucracy," as the *Economist* describes it, operates by "dismal standards of management in the civil service and state companies."[5] Inferior training, low pay, and politicization of senior managerial positions continue to create a vicious circle from which the state is unable to free its institutional structures.

Nasserism in Egypt

The 1952 revolution in Egypt generated another mass movement, making the 1950s the heyday of ideology in the Arab world—a time when new ideas and objectives seemed to pledge power, progress, and prosperity (Salem 1994, 6). The euphoria and promise, however, came to a crippling end with the 1967 war with Israel and then the death of Gamal Abdul-Nasser in 1971. Nasser had articulated a set of doctrinal values that still command a significant following in the Arab world, even though these values are mainly a collection of pragmatic decisions and policies rather than a mature and coherent ideology. Nasserism evolved and was kept vibrant as an extension of Nasser's charisma and popular appeal. Today, Nasserism remains valuable more for its historical symbolism—what could have been—than for what it actually accomplished.

In articulating the role of Egypt, Gamal Abdul-Nasser envisioned three major theaters of action simultaneously (which he called circles): Africa, the Arab world, and the Muslim world. He stressed that "there is an Arab circle surrounding Egypt and that this circle is as much a part of us [Egypt] as we are a part of it, that our history has been mixed with its and that its interests are linked with ours."[6] Thus, Nasser sought to explore the latent energy in the Arab society. He conceptualized ambitiously but programmed modestly. His strategies were repeatedly hobbled, not only by external enemies but also by ineffective government institutions and inept public managers (see the section on Egypt in Chapter 4).

The Arab National Movement

The Arab National Movement advocated Arab unity and development, but without socialism. The movement attracted intellectuals who contributed some of the most profound discussions on modern Arab nationalism. They clearly differentiated nationalistic sentiments from others (such as religious), but they lacked a specific economic and administrative plan of action. Some of the spokespersons for this doctrine gained enormous respectability in academic circles for their scholarly contributions and ideological analysis. Individuals like Sati' Al-Husary, Qustantin Zurayk, and others are regarded as paragons of modern Arab nationalistic thought.

To a large degree, the Arab National Movement as an organization was a reaction to the Arab defeat in Palestine in 1948. Then Arab leaders faced accusations that ranged from outright treachery and collaboration with the enemy to neglect of duty and deliberate inaction (Kazziha 1975, 7). The self-examination that started on university campuses grew to an elaborate political movement that advocated fundamental change in the Arab way of life. The doctrine expressed commitment to the creation of a unified Arab state, economic and social development, secularism, and adoption of scientific thought and techniques (Zurayk quoted in Kazziha 1975, 9).

EVALUATING THE NATIONALIST LEGACY

"By the 1960s, Arab nationalism appeared to have triumphed. Leading Arab states vied with one another in the claim to be the purest embodiment of that idealogy" (Bill and Springborg 1990, 78). The nationalists were student leaders and cabinet ministers; they were dominant in associations of lawyers, physicians, pharmacists, and engineers. Nationalists edited numerous newspapers and journals throughout the Arab world. They were schoolteachers and university faculty members as well as military officers. With the arrival of the 1960s, advancement of Arab nationalism seemed powerful and unstoppable. Recognizing this reality, Halpern (1963, vii) wrote: "[T]he area from Morocco to Pakistan is in the midst of a profound revolution." Understanding its causes and judging its directions, however, are different questions altogether.

From the preceding brief review of three political ideologies, we can conclude that it is not easy to determine the effects of nationalistic doctrines on developmental programs and institutions. Political leaders have selectively used ideology to rationalize their actions rather than to enlighten them. As Bill and Springborg (1990, 31) note, leaders typically "pepper their speeches with ideological terms, nationalist and religious imagery, and attacks on domestic opponents and foreign enemies." Rarely does an Arab leader present an economic or social program to his people, explain a government decision, or present his policy for handling unemployment, poverty, and poor service. In formal public utterances, officials habitually deny the existence of economic problems and make general statements that defy specificity and disregard processes of professional evaluation or independent measurement.

Moreover, socialist regimes (particularly those in Egypt, Syria, Iraq, and Yemen) created economic programs instantly, often employing half-baked, urgent measures to handle each adversity. One such measure has been nationalization of financial and industrial firms considered defiant or not sufficiently dedicated to the existing political and economic order. They became public enterprises managed by government functionaries, usually without the necessary experience in the businesses they were managing. Government also took control of foreign trade in order to reduce conspicuous consumption and to protect prices of essential commodities from precipitous inflationary increases. What happened instead was that in these countries the public treasuries gradually had to increase their subsidies to such commodities until the allotments became a drain on the budget as well as on national development efforts. Scarce public funds were diverted from investment to consumption and creation of government jobs. This has been a problem for economic planning in many Arab countries, particularly Egypt.

The main drive of autocratic military and nonmilitary rulers has been survival in office. They have used ideology to justify their preconceived ideas of governing rather than to harmonize policy with public demands. Consequently, ideologies swept through the Middle East, gathering strength and momentum, then ultimately dissipating without achieving their independent objectives. In retrospect, Arab nationalist ideology only served as a transitory convenience for leaders, assisting them in seizing power, without a commitment to implement the provisions and values of the ideology. Nationalist parties attracted a massive influx of people who supported the goals and leaders of these parties, only to be ruled by self-serving autocratic chiefs instead of effective and just governments. Some of these leaders presided over successive humiliating national defeats and squandered enormous national resources. Unwilling to share power or allow public accounting of their actions, political leaders used ideologies not to institutionalize power but as political weapons to gain popular support that could be used to joust with enemies (Bill and Springborg 1990, 37).

Arab citizens found themselves living within powerful state contraptions that dominated their economic behavior without generating economic progress. The emerging powerful state turned out to be authoritarian and inefficient. Arab unity seemed increasingly faraway, given the deep-seated suspicions and rivalries among leaders. This resulted in enhancing security apparatus (*mukhabarat*) in each state at a high budgetary cost. The technical know-how and the political support provided to these organizations made them a ruthless force for the status quo and an instrument for stifling evolution toward a civil society.

"In essence," as Heady (1996, 294) says, "the distinctive quality of the development ideology is the agreement on the desirability of the joint goals of nation-building and material progress combined with a sense of movement toward fulfillment of a long-delayed destiny, underlying which [is] a nagging uncertainty concerning the prospects for eventual success." Unfortunately, over five decades, the Arab political order has had neither "joint goals" nor a "sense of movement toward fulfillment of a long-delayed destiny."

Failures and missed opportunities by nationalist rulers to effect modernizing programs and to develop institutional processes are widely recognized by the Arab people. But a different type of criticism, stimulated by entirely different causes, has dominated the literature:

1. Western literature and the mass media in the United States have generally perceived Arab nationalism as a threat to stability in the region and as a source of political extremism. These Western critics rather cynically portray Arab nationalism as a self-aggrandizing, boastful, and emotional movement that has failed in all its endeavors but does not know how to accept defeat. Images of Arabs in Western learning sources (press, movie industry, television networks, and educational systems) are replete with negative depictions. Writers and columnists have regularly sounded such stereotypical opinions, particularly in newspapers and magazines. A few examples illustrate the point.

In 1991 a cover page of the *New Republic* proclaimed in bold letters: "The Collapse of Arab Nationalism, by Fouad Ajamy."[7] Ajamy's conclusion, after "reviewing" the modern Arab national history, was: "And Reason had proved helpless in the Arab world." Many Western scholars feel the same way. Elie Kedouri (1994) argues that the political traditions of the Middle East were incompatible with and not conducive to the introduction of constitutional and democratic governments. David Pryce-Jones, a critic of Arab politics and culture in this fashion, continued in that vein when he wrote about Elie Kedouri's recent work, *Democracy and Arab Political Culture*.[8] In Pryce-Jones's opinion, Arab nationalists, such as Nasser and the Ba'thist officers in Syria and Iraq, were not "liberators" but the latest "wreckers." The reason is simple. "It was no kind of progress to foist upon the Arabs alien values which they neither could nor should adopt." Specifically, democracy is "a transplant which has already failed to take" in the Arab world. But, as Peter Mansfield euphemistically points out in another review of Kedourie's work, he is "economical with facts" and "despite the clarity of his prose, is so often evasive."[9]

Criticisms of Arab nationalism often are based on preconstructed stereotypical images that do more to bolster prejudices than to generate enlightenment. As Aziz Al-Azmeh (1995, 1) makes clear, "the Arabs are not impeccably Arab: They do not usually live up to the stereotypes after which they are cast, into which molds it is thought desirable for them to be set. . . . " Lisa Anderson (1995, 78) candidly states the issue: "Much of this social science literature treats the Arab world as congenitally defective."

2. Islamist thinkers, too, find the Arab secular nationalist thinking exhausted and outmoded. Islamist activists believe that Arab nationalism is ephemeral and transient and must be replaced by Islamic doctrine that is more deeply rooted in the minds and hearts of Muslims—Arabs and non-Arabs alike. Islamists purvey Islamic thinking as an alternative to nationalism and call for an Islamic state that gathers *al-ummah,* the nation, under one system governed by Islamic teachings. "The Arabs are changing from below. Arab nationalism is finished and the Islamist spirit is rising in places like Saudi Arabia," said Hassan al-Turabi, a leading Islamist thinker, in the *New York Times* on December 6, 1994.

3. Radical socialism also promotes critical views of nationalism in general, portraying it as a regressive movement that seeks to detract or deter the advancement toward a universal Marxist state. It is the means and the ownership of productive elements in the society, and the relations between them that make the difference. The socialist perspective is based on class struggle between the exploiting and the exploited, so that the struggle is universally tied to the battle to liberate productive workers and unite them worldwide, not nationalistically. Arab socialists, however, have often aligned themselves, at least tactically, with the nationalist camp on many public policies, particularly those aimed at issues of independence from Western colonial hegemony.

The three strands of criticisms are neither neutral nor without self-interest. They seem to underestimate certain inherent but latent strengths. Arab nationalism is not merely a category for identification, a type of passport, or an identity card; nor is Arab nationalism a creation of some political party seeking to metamorphose into a different abstract ideology, more consistent with the spirit of the age or time. Arab nationalism is a set of assumptions but also deep feelings and sentiments. In part, it is Arabs' particular fears of external aggressions and anxieties over domestic failures. At the same time, it is Arabs' aspirations derived from sentiments buttressed by common cultural, religious, and linguistic attributes. The sense of political community—common purpose—is strengthened by these collective, mutual aspects shared through long history.

Actually, one can argue that genuine Arab nationalism has not been accurately represented in any contemporary Arab political system, despite many claims by leaders who have governed in its name. To be sure, many regimes have declared, and many have been influenced by, nationalist ideologies, but in no fair measure do the military rulers of Egypt, Iraq, Syria, or Libya exemplify the authentic values of modern Arab nationalism. Egypt's rulers simply used nationalist ideology to advance narrow and self-serving designs. By the same token, the Ba'thists of Syria and Iraq are hardly considered the embodiment of Ba'thist or nationalist ideals. They seized power by military force and perpetuated it by getting rid of any opposition, real or imagined. In the Gulf states, self-indulgent dynasties are preoccupied with perpetuation of their family dictatorships and the survival of the dynasty first and foremost. Al-Magreb el Arabi (Morocco, Algeria, Tunisia, and Libya) has been conspicuously neutral on issues of Arab nationalism except when such policies serve its rulers' public relations needs.

Thus, current Arab regimes cannot legitimately claim to represent the ideals of Arab nationalism. Even the independence of certain Arab states has been seriously compromised by their leaders' submission to foreign protection. But these failures do not signal the end of the collective mission of the Arab nation, nor are they cause for the usual disparaging diagnosis of the Arab mind and appraisal of the Arab psyche. Those who take these failures as characterizing a nation or a culture as prone to failure for inherent, peculiar characteristics ignore two fundamental factors. First, citizens under autocratic rule cannot be responsible for policies they did not participate in making nor do these policies reflect their demands or preferences.

Second, Western analysts seem to apply different rules to evaluating failures of Arab public policies than to those of other systems. Arab values and culture are instantly evoked even before more relevant political and economic factors are considered, as if Arab leaders are not allowed to make faulty policy choices or to opt for bad alternatives. It is most revealing that every Arab military, political, or economic defeat appears to instigate declarations of the death of Arab nationalism or to renew the search for discovering its replacements. As if nationalism is an aberration of the human experience, Western press and writers have sought at every turn to discover the genetic defects of Arab nationalism and the peculiarities of its values that produce the assumed irrationality of the "Arab mind and culture."

Nationalism, as Cottam (1964, 3) points out, is "a belief on the part of a large group of people that they comprise a political community, a nation, that is entitled to independent statehood, and a willingness of this group to grant their community a primary and the terminal loyalty." Thus defined, he continues, "nationalism which clearly insists on independence and dignity for the nation furnishes a part, but only a part, of the value system of the individual members of the community." Arab citizens have not realized independent statehood nor have they developed institutional capacities that offer them that awaited sense of pride and dignity and the achievement of unity and economic opportunities.

Arabs view their nationalism not merely as a set of ethnocentric slogans but as a call for redefinition and renewal. The emphasis is on a vision of the Arab people by themselves and for themselves. As a value system, nationalism cannot be imposed from outside by an imperial force nor can it be permanently hobbled by traditionalists from within. Despite political failures and misuse of the ideals of ideology, Arab nationalism has been a liberating, unifying, and modernizing influence throughout the Arab societies. It has served as a force for new ideas and for some important reforms such as those in education and social habits.

Also, the ideals of nationalism are ingrained in the consciousness of the people, ready to unleash new energies when the appropriate channels are created. In a survey conducted between 1977 and 1979 of six thousand residents of ten Arab countries, 78.5 percent of the respondents said they believed in the existence of an Arab entity and 77.9 percent agreed that this entity constituted one nation; 53 percent believed that this nation was divided by artificial borders.[10]

CONCLUSIONS

Despite extensive literature on Arab nationalism and socialism, one finds little comparative analysis of institutional or developmental programs and their doctrinal background. With few exceptions, no serious effort has been made to examine political doctrines in terms of their actual organizational and managerial thrusts.

Clearly, nationalists encouraged statism in all its manifestations and supported central control of production. Also, these political movements competed for greater state involvement in the economy, usually under pretexts of achieving equity and social justice. Issues of economic efficiency or enhancement of public productivity frequently were relegated to lower status than that of creating jobs or punishing nonresponsive private capital.

On balance, an acknowledgment of certain influences of the nationalist parties is germane. Namely, they brought the Arab masses into the game of governing and were instrumental in the emergence of all sorts of organizations representing students, lawyers, engineers, teachers, and others. This was the flourishing of mass politics on a large scale, even when the roles and scopes of these associations were largely circumscribed by the political context.

Arab nationalists also battled to reconcile a liberal-democratic mode with ethnocentric or chauvinistic inclinations. During the embryonic phase, values and sentiments had to crystallize and deepen before the nationalist movement could gain popular support or achieve the doctrinal maturation that embodies operational substance. The popularity of nationalist ideologies during the intermediate phases of modernization was based mainly on the introduction of many patriotic, secular, and progressive outlooks that were then recast in nativist form and utilized for purposes of liberation and independence. With expansion of education and more experience in governing, nationalist influences could have gone on to change the politics of adulation of individual leaders to one of accountable institutional governance. That this did not happen caused a momentous disillusionment in the performance of modern Arab nationalism.

The legacy of the nationalist rule does not include significant advancements in areas of economic integration of the Arab world, democratization, the building of viable institutions, or the achievement of greater economic ability to compete globally. What does endure from the legacy is a remarkable failure of the political order on numerous fronts. Individual autocratic rule has been the norm over the past several decades, giving only lip service to the revolutionary promises to transform the Arab society and to modernize its institutions.

The process of building institutions with the capacity to govern effectively and the power to develop visionary strategic plans and implement them has been hampered by a variety of political obstacles. Thus Arab society has been deprived of the advantages of viable administrative and political institutions (including political parties and elected legislative councils) that operate programs, promote national values, oppose absolute solutions, safeguard individual freedoms, and defend communal interests.

Finally, it is worthwhile for scholars to search for causes and effects of the absence of compatibility between Arab politics and Arab national objectives (Salame 1994). It is also important to explore the possibilities of emerging principles or doctrines that will succeed the presumably "expired" Arab nationalism. Whether the replacement is nationalism by nation-state or Islamism (Khalidi 1994, 1), defeats and defaults of Arab leaders and policies are not the same as the end of nationalism. A presently dormant force may still prove that all pronoucements of its extinction are, in fact, premature.

NOTES

1. I often use *ideology* and *doctrine* interchangeably, knowing that the first is more inclusive and that the second can be quite specific—when it involves written and unwritten rules and norms in the institutional and functional contexts, as is the case with military doctrine.
2. A complete text of the Ba'th Party constitution is in Haim (1992, 233–241).
3. *Middle East International,* no. 494, (February 17, 1995), p. 19.
4. Ibid.
5. *Economist* (March 30, 1996), p. 45.
6. Gamal Abdul-Nasser, *Falsafat al-Thawrah* (The philosophy of the revolution) (Cairo, n.d.).

7. *New Republic* (August 12, 1991), p. 23.

8. David Pryce-Jones, *The Time* (December 15, 1994).

9. Peter Mansfield, *Middle East International* (March 3, 1995), p. 22.

10. Saad Eddin Ibrahim, *The Trends of Arab Public Opinion Toward the Issue of Unity* (in Arabic) (Beirut: Center for Arab Unity Studies, 1980). Cited in Bill and Springborg (1990, 43).

Part II
Administering Development

3

Managing Development
in the Troubled Arab State

*All is not well in the Arab world. For nearly a decade now, Arab
newspaper editors and publicists, social scientists and community
leaders, political activists of all persuasions as well as self-
serving emirs and* de facto *presidents-for-life have, everywhere
within the Arab world, been writing and talking with an ever-
increasing sense of urgency of an Arab impasse, of a deepening
Arab crisis, of a sense of impending dissolution and even of the
possibility of total national disintegration.*

Samir Amin[1]

The Arab people have profound similarities in culture, religion, language,
and geography as well as a collective history and common public purpose.
The geographic region known as the Arab world is globally notable for
several reasons: First, three major monotheistic religions (Judaism, Chris-
tianity, and Islam) originated in this region. Second, the area is thought to
be the cradle of the earliest known civilizations, from the Sumerians and
the Babylonians of Mesopotamia to the ancient Egyptians on the Nile.
Third, its strategic location, as the connection among three major conti-
nents, has made it a tempting setting for many outside intrusions as well as
the constant target of numerous expansionist empires. As Richards and
Waterbury (1990, 1) note in reference to the Middle East, "Geopolitical
significance draws resources and special treatment from outside powers,
but it also draws interference, meddling, and occasionally invasion."
Fourth, the Arab region contains the largest oil reserves in the world, oil
being a commodity that constitutes the lifeblood of the industrial world.
Finally, vast human resources of more than 220 million people, who manifest rising expectations, rich cultural and historical legacies, and a determination to achieve freer and more fulfilled living, reside in the area.

Following the end of European colonial rule after World War II, the
way that most Arab states achieved formal national independence was as
a collection of incompatible sovereign states with political and geographic

45

divisions mostly engineered and enforced by external forces. A complex power structure consisting of the old British imperialism in alliance with international oil companies and the intensifying influence of the United States managed to drain the new Arab independence of its substance. Imperial ambitions determined the new condition without regard to national identity, preferences of the population, or rational division of natural resources. For example, the political boundaries of the new states produced excessive differences in distribution of resources as oil-rich territories were parceled out and separated from areas with large population clusters. Many of the emergent ministates may satisfy ceremonial requirements of statehood and UN membership, but they do not possess nominal requirements of political, military, or economic viability.

The many unifying characteristics of the Arab world do not obscure its persistent diversity and conflicting attributes. Variations in size, legitimacy of leadership, maturity of public institutions, and endowment in natural resources have expanded differences in the organizational and managerial capacities of the states. Arab countries vary in other measures as well, such as literacy rate, health care, quality of education, and technological advancement. Disparity in population size is pronounced. Egypt has a population of more than 58 million. In contrast, six of the states (Bahrain, Kuwait, Mauritania, Oman, Qatar, and UAE) are ministates, each with a population of 2 million or less. In terms of gross national product (GNP) per capita, differences also are excessive. Based on statistics from the World Bank, in the mid-1990s more than 50 percent of the Arab population averaged less than $1,000 per capita GNP annually. At the same time, about 1 percent of the population, mostly concentrated in three ministates, earned an annual average of more than $14,000 per capita GNP. Moreover, the current political divisions of the Arab world have deepened old parochial loyalties and produced new ones based on regional, tribal, or sectarian identifications. These growing differences render the task of developing reliable generalizations about the Arab countries more daunting.

DEVELOPMENT POLICIES AND THEIR CONSEQUENCES

Since the 1950s, each Arab state has claimed at one time or another a major developmental initiative in the form of a comprehensive national plan or some form of public policy commitment. Accomplishing these developmental objectives, of course, would have required enormous financial and human resources. Although not all Arab countries displayed the same level of seriousness regarding such initiatives, one condition was constant:

Overall capital invested was invariably exorbitant while derived benefits were small and affected only narrow segments of the population.

One example of large capital investment in development is Saudi Arabia. The third Saudi development plan (1980–1985) was allocated 783 billion Saudi riyals (SR) (about U.S.$230 billion),[2] in addition to SR 123 billion ($36 billion) for the first plan (1970–1975) and SR 112 billion ($32 billion) for the second plan (1975–1980).[3] Planning in the 1980s was said to mark "a significant shift away from expenditure on physical infrastructure towards the development of the producing sectors of the economy, to diversify the economic base. . . . "[4] Successive plans have been less ambitious in total funding but have asserted similar policies.

Not all Arab states, however, are in the Saudi position of capital spending on development. Other states, such as Jordan, have had serious capital shortages that have limited their developmental activities. Jordan has had several five- and three-year development plans since the 1960s. Each plan was made contingent on availability of funds, which also depended on foreign sources such as loans or outright assistance. To illustrate, Jordan's GDP by expenditure at 1991 constant prices is estimated for 1997 at a scant 1,550 million Jordanian dinars (JD).[5] Another way to portray the situation is to consider the national budget of the country, in which the total capital expenditures for the seven years 1986 to 1992 is only JD 1,390 million (under U.S.$2 billion).[6]

Irrespective of capital abundance, as in the Saudi case, or capital scarcity, as in the Jordanian case, social and economic realities in the Arab societies after World War II invited government intervention, not only to generate economic growth but also to provide essential services. Public institutions became the front line of intervention, which is why their numbers, costs, and powers increased dramatically. At the same time, this expanded reliance on public bureaucracy, particularly in the implementation of development plans, exposed the bureaucracy's lack of institutional capacity and necessary administrative skills.

Arab development plans have been criticized not only for their modest total outcomes but also for their failure to generate a development momentum. Between 1980 and 1992, the average annual GNP per capita real growth rate for most Arab states was either nominal or negative: Algeria –0.5 percent, Bahrain –3.8 percent, Jordan –5.4 percent, Saudi Arabia –3.3 percent, and UAE –4.3 percent.[7] The economies of Iraq, Somalia, and Sudan in the mid-1990s are in catastrophic conditions. This situation is a conspicuous contrast to that of many developing countries that experienced significant economic growth during the same period, including Argentina, Turkey, South Korea, Thailand, Indonesia, Malaysia, Botswana, and many others. Initially, most of these countries had far fewer financial resources, educated personnel, technological means, or linkages with big industrial powers than did the Arab world.

Another criticism of Arab development outcomes is that they have not served well the cause of equity and social justice. In several Arab countries, population growth has expanded the ranks of the nonbeneficiaries of economic development, and the beneficiaries are a continually decreasing segment of the society. The advantages of development are shared by a shrinking group that encompasses mostly political leaders, landowners, wealthy merchants, owners of big construction industries, army officers, and top civilian bureaucrats. The majority of the people have benefited little or not at all. Middle- and lower-level employees, whose ranks have been rapidly expanding, have found their economic benefits dwindling in the midst of rampant inflation.

Exacerbating the disparity of wealth and deprivation among citizens of different Arab states is the burden of public debt on poor countries. Countries with the largest populations and lowest per capita GNP carry the heaviest burden of external debt, exceeding $150 billion in the early 1990s. Conversely, Arab foreign "investment" is estimated at "$650 billion, all of which is held by the Gulf's governments and ruling families, Arab banks, and investment corporations."[8] Another estimate of investment abroad is nearly $800 billion, an amount that creates a liquidity shortage in the Arab market.[9] What makes this situation so objectionable "is that only 5 percent of all surplus funds accumulated by the rich Arab states has been invested in the region."[10]

MISMANAGEMENT OF CAPITAL

Arab governments control capital supply and dominate patterns of spending through public budgets, which command considerable portions of GNP. The expenditures of the U.S. government as a percentage of GNP are about 22 percent. In comparison, the same number in Egypt is 40, in Tunisia 35, and in Jordan 31.[11] These ratios would not be damning if the states were efficient in spending their financial resources, which they often borrow at high interest rates.

Instead the staggering waste of resources because of mismanagement, destructive military conflicts, or capital flight abroad has deprived Arab markets of badly needed funds and hampered developmental initiatives. Since 1980, over $1 trillion have been consumed or destroyed in wars and eaten up by poor investments from Spain to London and New York. To appreciate the magnitude of such waste, one has only to know that the cost of these wars and just a few of the bad investments would be sufficient to pay off all known foreign debts owed by the Arab states and, in addition, grant each citizen in every Arab state over $4,000. (This is not to say that such distribution would have occurred if the funds had not been squandered.)

A dramatic illustration of destruction of states' resources is the eight-year war between Iran and Iraq that ended in 1988. The negative effects on development efforts in each state are incalculable. Only a few years later, the United States, Britain, and their allies led an attack on Iraq in retaliation for Iraq's 1990 invasion of Kuwait. The whole country of Iraq, not only the military, suffered unprecedented bombardment and destruction. The Gulf War cost the Arab countries $620 billion, according to the Arab Economic Report, an annual study by the Arab Monetary Fund, the Arab League, the Organization of Arab Petroleum Exporting Countries, and other leading institutions.[12] The report stated that the destruction of oil wells and pipelines, telecommunications facilities, roads, buildings, and factories cost Kuwait $160 billion and Iraq $190 billion. In addition, the governments of Saudi Arabia, Kuwait, and the Gulf emirates made $84 billion in direct payments to the United States, Britain, and France for military expenses. Another $51 billion was paid by Saudi Arabia and Kuwait in logistical support for the six hundred thousand American and allied troops. The report further said that the war contributed to a drop in GNP for the twenty-one Arab countries estimated at 1.2 percent in 1990 and 7 percent in 1991.[13] In 1993, the Arab Economic Report adjusted the figure on the cost of the Gulf War upward to $676 billion to include damage to the environment, suppression of economic growth, and loss of income to Arab and non-Arab workers who were employed in Saudi Arabia, Kuwait, and Iraq.[14]

As an illustration of the magnitude of destruction to Iraq alone after the Gulf War, a French author-diplomat, Eric Rouleau, wrote (1995, 61–62):

> Iraqis understand the legitimacy of a military action to drive their army from Kuwait, but they have had difficulty comprehending the Allied rationale for using air power to systematically destroy or cripple Iraqi infrastructure and industry: electric power stations (92 percent of installed capacity destroyed), refineries (80 percent of production capacity), petrochemical complexes, telecommunications centers (including 135 telephone networks), bridges (more than 100), roads, highways, railroads, hundreds of locomotives and boxcars full of goods, radio and television broadcasting stations, cement plants, and factories producing aluminum, electric cables, and medical supplies. The losses were estimated by the Arab Monetary Fund to be $190 billion.

In brief, the waste of resources caused by wars, mismanagement, bad investments, or corruption is historically unparalleled for the region. If Arab governments had simply preserved and distributed the capital they have collected since 1975 from sources such as oil revenues, foreign aid, foreign loans, and domestically generated funds, the per capita income of the entire Arab population could have more than tripled without any additional effort.

WASTE OF HUMAN RESOURCES

Managing the development of a society involves devising the best plan to deploy all available resources in order to maximize valued objectives. As the core of these resources, the skills and commitment of the workforce to policy objectives are crucial for the success of any developmental plan. Women are a central part of human resources with a determining effect on the society. Yet women in the Arab world not only have not been a major force in policymaking or implementation but have been disadvantaged by the results of these public policies. According to the UNDP's measure of participation of women in economic and political decisionmaking (Table 3.1), the Arab world as a whole is ranked lower than all other regions (Asia, Africa, and Latin America).

Although Arab women constitute more than half of the population of the Arab world, they are less than 10 percent of wage earners. Underutilization is most surprising in countries that face a severe shortage of humanpower, such as the Gulf states. The following numbers on the ratio of women in the labor force illustrate this condition: Women are 10 percent or less of the labor force in Algeria, Bahrain, Libya, Oman, Qatar, Saudi Arabia, and UAE; 10 to 20 percent in Egypt, Jordan, Syria, and Yemen; and 20 to 30 percent in Iraq, Lebanon, Morocco, and Tunisia.[15]

Certainly, the role and status of women in most developing countries are not changing in tandem with the rest of society. As U.S. Under Secretary of State for Global Affairs Tim Wirth acknowledged at the global population conference in Cairo (September 1994), "sustainable development cannot be realized without full engagement and complete empowerment of women."[16]

In health care, a dramatic manifestation of the problems faced by women in developing countries is epitomized by maternal death rates, particularly in Africa and South Asia, where the risks of childbearing are compounded by women's low economic and social status and by high fertility rates. In Africa, for example, women have a 1-in-18 chance of dying from complications during pregnancies, compared with a 1-in-500 chance in most Arab states and a 1-in-10,000 chance in northern Europe.[17]

It is true that Arab women have achieved greater improvements in education, health care, and employment, for example, than have women in several developing countries in Africa, the Indian subcontinent, or Asia.

Table 3.1   United Nations Human Development Rankings

Country	GDI Rank and Value[a]		GEM Rank and Value[b]		
Kuwait	51	0.716	Iraq	47	0.386
Bahrain	56	0.686	Syria	81	0.285
UAE	57	0.678	Morocco	85	0.271
Tunisia	59	0.641	Algeria	87	0.265
Qatar	61	0.639	Tunisia	91	0.254
Lebanon	65	0.622	Kuwait	93	0.241
Syria	72	0.571	UAE	94	0.239
Libya	75	0.534	Egypt	96	0.237
Iraq	78	0.522	Jordan	99	0.230
Saudi Arabia	81	0.514	Lebanon	103	0.212
Algeria	84	0.508	Sudan	102	0.219
Egypt	92	0.543			
Morocco	93	0.450			
Sudan	109	0.332			
Yemen	117	0.307			

Source: United Nations Development Program, *Human Development Report 1995* (New York: Oxford University Press), pp. 76–77, 84–85.

Notes: a. GDI: Gender-related Development Index, which measures the achievement in the same basic capabilities as the Human Development Index of the UNDP does but takes note of inequality in achievement between men and women. The greater the gender disparity, the lower a country's GDI. A total of 130 countries are ranked.

b. GEM: Gender Empowerment Measure, which measures the participation of women in economic and political decisionmaking. The greater the gender disparity in participation, the lower the GEM. A total of 116 countries are ranked.

Nevertheless, Arab women remain minor beneficiaries of development despite denials and rationalizations by political and religious ruling elites.

In education, although there have been significant increases over two decades in the ratio of women to men in secondary education (Table 3.2), women in most Arab states still received less education than men. The discrepancy between males and females is less pronounced at the primary level but more blatant at advanced levels such as universities. The same conclusion is true considering spending on women in health care, nutrition, and training for jobs.

In a different sense, the issue of improving overall conditions for women goes beyond what economic development can provide. It is primarily an issue of fundamental rights and of equal and just treatment throughout the society. Certainly, women cannot adequately contribute to the improvement of the political, economic, and social quality of life in a

Table 3.2   **Females per 100 Males in Secondary Schools in Selected Arab Countries**

	1970	1991
Morocco	40	69
Syria	36	71
Egypt	48	76
Tunisia	38	77
Algeria	40	79
Saudi Arabia	16	79
Jordan	53	105

Source: World Bank, *World Development Report* 1994 (New York: Oxford University Press), pp. 218–219.

society that places them in a lesser legal status than men or even excludes them entirely from the political process. The rights of women is an explosive issue in the Arab society because of the resistance by traditional and religious leaders to fundamental change. At the same time, women's rights could develop into a rallying, uniting strategy for forces of change and development.

Overall, perhaps an unanticipated consequence of development is the enlargement of the gap and thus the growth of tension between economic and social groups, nurturing already perilous social antagonism as well as augmenting the perennial problem of legitimacy of political authority in Arab states. As Hudson (1988) points out, the Arab state has not developed strength or moral authority commensurate with its enhanced technologies of control. Increasing estrangement of the people from their rulers, Hudson concludes, has often resulted in government's spending freely to develop the efficacy and pervasiveness of their policing bureaucracies.

Consequently, of all the technology transfers that have taken place in the Arab world, probably none have been as effective as those in the political security field. Establishment of electronic surveillance and the state computerization of lists of security suspects have been far more thorough and effective than anything else undertaken by the state (Hudson 1988, 30). More than any other failing, this aspect of governing in the Arab society has supplied Western critics with some of their most damaging images. One critic describes the Arab states as "fragile as sandcastles. They have produced tyrants and secret-police agencies and corrupt bureaucracies that rule over restive populations by imposing a suffocating conformity, both intellectual and political" (Viorst 1994, xii). Ironically, during

the Cold War era and after, the big powers offered many forms of technical and economic aid to defend and sustain some of those same Arab
regimes widely criticized in the West. It is not surprising that while rulers
gratefully received such aid, their citizens suspected its motives and feared
its consequences. Few political leaders govern in today's Arab states without overt or covert sustenance from a foreign power.

Governmental attempts at socioeconomic development and at improving the quality of life for the people have generally been disappointing. A
study by Yahya Sadowski (1991, 4) for the Overseas Development Council points out that despite the excessive wealth of an Arab minority, by the
1990s the real annual per capita GDP in the Arab world is less than that
of Latin America. Life expectancy, infant mortality, environmental pollution, and literacy rate—all are unfavorable by international standards. Life
expectancy in Saudi Arabia (64 years), for example, is lower than in less-
wealthy Greece (76), Sri Lanka (71), China (70), and the Dominican Republic (67).

The quality of any workforce is related to values and skills measured
by levels of educational attainment, including adult literacy rates. Education is now and will continue to be the foundation upon which certain
qualities are built, particularly the capacity to acquire scientific knowledge
and to absorb new technologies. Thus, education is a determining and
durable influence on socioeconomic development. In the Arab world, numbers of students, schools, and budgets tell a quantitative success story, but
when qualitative considerations enter into the analysis of educational development, the picture changes. Baha Abu-Laban and Sharon McIrvin
Abu-Laban (1992, 22) offer the following assessment:

> In terms of absolute numbers, the expansion of Arab education has been
> particularly dramatic at the primary level, with average enrollment
> growth rates exceeding population growth rates by a large margin. . . .
> For example, between 1965 and 1985, enrollments at the primary level in
> the eighteen most populous Arab states increased by 250%, or from about
> 10 million to over 25 million . . . this increase is equivalent to providing
> schooling for an additional 2,100 pupils every day for a period of 20
> years!

Despite such vast quantitative growth of education in the Arab world,
the balance sheet reveals impediments and substandard outcomes. Arab
educational systems have not prepared their students to meet the requirements and demands of contemporary societies. Analytical skills, sciences,
mathematics, reasoning, and ability to apply knowledge are inadequately
articulated in the curriculum and poorly taught in the classroom. Based on
outcomes, Arab educational institutions in general have not played an active role in building a sense of community or in fostering ethics of public

responsibility. Moreover, many Arab students have been deprived of formal education altogether. Internal strife in Lebanon, Somalia, and Sudan denied millions of children proper education. Also, military occupation of the West Bank and Gaza withheld educational freedom and opportunities from Palestinian children.

After fifty years of expansion in education, illiteracy rates continue to be very high throughout the Arab world, exceeding 50 percent of the total Arab population. Stressing the importance of basic education, Gary S. Becker, the 1992 Nobel laureate in economics, points out:

> Economic development cannot be sustained when a nation neglects elementary education for a sizable part of its population. Education lets young persons from poor backgrounds acquire the skills to rise in the world, and it reduces the tendency for inequalities in wealth to be perpetuated from one generation to the next. The example of the so-called Asian tigers—Hong Kong, Korea, Singapore, and Taiwan—is instructive: Early in their development, they largely eliminated illiteracy and raised the schooling of the bottom stratum to decent levels.[18]

In the past few years, the UNDP introduced the HDI as a yardstick for measuring human progress. The annual report publishes integrated data on per capita income, education, and health. To arrive at a comprehensive measure of development in 1994, the HDI ranked 173 countries by combining indicators of purchasing power (real GDP per capita), education (literacy rates and educational attainment), and health (life expectancy at birth). No Arab state is in the top fifty. According to this index, only 50 percent of the adults in Egypt are literate, 66 percent in Iraq, 82 percent in Jordan, 52 percent in Morocco, 35 percent in Oman, 64 percent in Saudi Arabia, 28 percent in Sudan, 67 percent in Syria, and 41 percent in Yemen.[19] In comparison, adult literacy rates are nearly 99 percent in most European countries and 88 percent or more in the Philippines, Venezuela, Mexico, Thailand, and many other developing countries.

Evaluation in terms of HDI, according to Sadowski (1991, 4), reveals that the Arab world as a whole is less prosperous than one might expect when compared to other developing regions. The UAE—the richest Arab state in terms of GNP per capita—has a lower HDI than do Costa Rica, Mexico, Panama, and Malta. A majority of Arabs still live in countries where the HDI is comparable to that of sub-Saharan Africa. The citizens of the low-income Arab states, representing 66 percent of the population of the Arab world, live in countries with HDIs lower than those of Indonesia, Honduras, or Botswana.

The UNDP's report lists the Arab states in three groups: high, medium, and low human development. Only one Arab ministate with huge oil revenues (Kuwait) is in the high development ranking (and this is largely due to a peculiar policy in determining who is a citizen that excludes most people born or living in the country). The largest Arab states—Egypt, Morocco, Sudan, and Yemen—occupy an unenviable position at the bottom of the medium group or within the lowest ranks. Table 3.3 lists the Arab countries by HDI and GNP.

Comparing the data in Table 3.3 to country populations indicates that only 0.8 percent of citizens live in a high human development socioeconomic system. The majority (77 percent) are in the medium levels, with heavy concentration toward the bottom of the list. Finally, more than one in five Arab citizens (22 percent) is living in societies with some of the lowest standards of human development in the world. These data are even more disturbing considering capital inflow of hundreds of billions of dollars from oil revenues and from borrowing during the past two decades.

A conspicuous incongruity of Arab development in recent decades is modest results in the midst of abundant strategic assets: The Arab world has the largest reserves and the largest exports of oil in the world (see Chapter 9). Egypt operates the lucrative Suez Canal, and Arab lands possess huge mineral deposits; Jordan and Morocco are world leaders in phosphate

Table 3.3   Ranking of the Arab States on the Human Development Index

High Human Development			Medium Human Development			Low Human Development		
Country	HDI	GNP	Country	HDI	GNP	Country	HDI	GNP
Kuwait	51	28	Qatar	56	20	Yemen	142	136
			Bahrain	58	33	Sudan	151	147
			UAE	62	10	Mauritania	158	127
			Saudi Arabia	67	31	Djibouti	163	125
			Syria	73	94	Somalia	165	172
			Libya	79	41			
			Tunisia	81	85			
			Oman	92	38			
			Iraq	96	73			
			Jordan	98	99			
			Lebanon	103	83			
			Algeria	109	72			
			Egypt	110	122			
			Morocco	119	106			

Source: United Nations Development Program, *Human Development Report 1994* (New York: Oxford University Press), pp. 129–131.

exports; Syria and Egypt are renowned for the quality of their textile industries. Vast agricultural lands produce diverse products and have the potential
of doubling outputs with minimum investment in improvements. A vibrant
tourism business operates hotels, transportation systems, food industries,
handcrafts, and many dependent businesses sustained by the existence of in-
comparable ancient sites and religious shrines that attract global interests.
These are only a few examples of the collective wealth of the Arab countries.

The record of Arab development policies is not a shining one. Public
disenchantment and distrust of government are deep. The inconsistency in
the situation is dramatized by M. H. Haykal, one of the most influential
political commentators in the Arab world today. In a lecture in Cairo on
October 27, 1994, Haykal said:

> The Arab world has wasted one of the biggest fortunes ever made avail-
> able to a nation establishing itself or even to an empire building its
> strength. Over the past quarter of a century, for instance, the Arab na-
> tion's income from its various sources, especially oil, was estimated at $4
> trillion. It can generally be said that $1 trillion was spent on Arab infra-
> structure, services and productive projects, and the second trillion on
> arms. But half of the income—$2 trillion—needs someone to look for it.[20]

BUREAUCRACY AND REFORM

As Arab governments acted to stimulate development and to provide essential public services, the role of civil bureaucrats grew. Consequently,
building administrative capacity became a component of the efforts to implement developmental plans. This is why government reform in the Arab
world has always been linked to national development efforts and why
failures of these developmental activities are often explained away as
merely failures of the public administration system.

In truth, reforms proclaimed by the Arab states since the 1950s have
not produced many radical departures from existing organizational structures and managerial processes. This is not to deny the many attempts at
change, mostly in areas of local government reorganization, personnel
training, decentralization, procedural simplification, and tinkering with
methods of public service delivery. Because these reforms have always
been at the margin of the system, the effects have been limited to timid alterations of near-term priorities—and then only to the extent that such results and processes are politically "safe."

Assessments of administrative reform efforts in Third World states in
general disclose only small successes. "More ambitious comprehensive reforms faltered and proved a great disappointment in poor countries that
had pinned such high hopes on them" (Caiden 1991, 375). This conclusion

is based on studies of African, Asian, and Latin American experiences, where administrative reform initiatives had collapsed. Reasons vary but encompass combinations of factors such as bureaucratic resistance, political corruption, bureaucratic inertia, social disharmony, lack of political support, and insulation of the public from the process.

A consistently stated thesis by Fred Riggs (1991, 485) since the 1960s suggests, however, that bureaucracy is only part of a larger system of governance. Politics and administration, he says, are organically linked, and consequently the behavior of one fundamentally influences the behavior of the other. These observations are sufficiently general to win wide support in contemporary public administration literature. However, Riggs's (1991, 504) proposition that "all bureaucracies have their own political interests and power enough to protect them" has injected a troublesome consideration into analysis and prescriptions. If this is true, then in the absence of viable political institutions in developing societies, bureaucrats become a ruling class able to flout administrative values or, by contrast, to administer well, as their own self-interest dictates. Consequently, the success of administrative reform is dependent on its utility (profitability) to bureaucratic politics, according to this view.

Clearly, political change has lagged behind the social and economic transformation under way in Arab society. Instead of managing change according to worthy strategic policies developed with citizens' participation, incumbent regimes are adept at defusing and containing crises and criticisms. Inappropriate traditional bases of authority and mistrust of the opposition have augmented authoritarianism and diminished participatory governing. Indeed, political and administrative changes in the Arab world are tolerated only if they do not tamper with the extraordinary powers and privileges of the ruling oligarchy or dynasty.

In sum, literature on administrative reform in the Arab world today is generally pessimistic (Ayubi 1989; Cunningham and Sarayrah 1993; Jabbra 1989; Palmer, Leila, and Yassin 1988; Jreisat 1989, 1990, 1991). The absence of professional management, manifested in several ways, is usually considered a major detriment to implementation of development plans. First, there are such critical managerial deficiencies as scarcity of diagnostic analysis, infrequent needs assessments, and lack of reliable performance evaluations. Poor performance of public managers is demonstrated at every level of the administrative process, particularly in defining problems, discovering solutions, or developing alternative methods of effective planning and management.

Second, citizens' input in important public decisions is a totally novel concept. Indeed, the Arab community in any state is rarely involved in public affairs and not even allowed to organize without inviting monitoring and questioning by the mighty security apparatus of the state.

Third, autocratic political leaders who exercise absolute powers have reduced bureaucracy to a tool for carrying out their wishes rather than utilizing managerial professional skills for independent rational decision-making. All substantive measures of change, before being declared, are sanitized to fit the political status quo. Radical departures that might weaken the grip of the hierarchical authority on decisionmaking are suspect and the careers of their advocates may be permanently stymied.

For public employees at the operational levels to be consulted by political or administrative leaders is a rare occurrence. Because of this, the state loses valuable expert opinion and fosters an environment of management riddled with lack of enthusiasm for any proposed change. The alienation of middle and lower management imposes constraints during the implementation of policy that check and challenge the skills and expertise of senior managers. Change requires risk taking, and Arab executives in a control-oriented system fear making mistakes. The absence of administrative change, in a risk-averse management that avoids unfamiliar tasks, is a natural consequence of rigid hierarchical controls.

Nevertheless, because of these widely publicized "ills of bureaucracy" in the Arab state, administrative reform has been universally proclaimed as a national goal of the political and administrative leadership in every country. Generally, the depictions of "bureaucratic dysfunctions" that are found in contemporary states highlight accumulated excessive bureaucratic powers that have generated numerous pathologies and few accomplishments. Hence, the search continues for remedies to these pathologies through various reform strategies.

PERPETUAL PROBLEMS OF ADMINISTRATION

Six persistent problems that have impeded administrative performance in the Arab countries can be defined.

1. Public organizations are overstaffed, employees are underpaid, and productivity is low. The Egyptian bureaucracy may be the most glaring example, but it is certainly not the only one exhibiting these characteristics. The Egyptian bureaucracy swelled from 250,000 in 1952 to 1.2 million in 1970 to more than 4 million in 1994.[21] These numbers do not include another 3.7 million working for public enterprises, known in Egypt as "public sector corporations."[22] Public employment continued its phenomenal growth even after the adoption of liberal economic policy in 1974 (Ayubi 1989, 62). During the period between 1977 and 1981, despite the official rhetoric about decentralization and local government revival, Ayubi (63) explains that the Egyptian central bureaucracy increased by 60.4 percent,

whereas employment in local government increased only by 28.7 percent. The magnitude and the type of growth in public employment indicate that (1) the bulk of expansion is at the central offices and not at the local government, (2) the growth is in "conventional" rather than "developmental" jobs, and (3) the growth tends to be proportionately larger at the top echelons of each category of the bureaucracy (63).

Overstaffing and low productivity encumber the Saudi administrative system, too. The Saudi bureaucracy, although it has grown rapidly in numbers and has assumed new obligations in formulating and administering development programs, is still lacking the basic capabilities necessary to meet demands being placed upon it (Heady 1996, 335). Overstaffing is apparent at all levels of the Saudi bureaucracy, but more so at lower levels of jobs because government is the main employer in the society. Various attempts at administrative reform, particularly in the civil service functions, have resulted in a great deal of formalism and little real capacity (Heady 1996; Osman 1978).

Except for major oil-producing countries, in most Arab states public employment is an opportunity to have a job in economic systems with a constantly high unemployment rate. The state has always been the largest employer, with its hiring practices aimed at meeting minimum standards rather than seeking the most qualified. Public employees seem more attentive to dividing benefits of the public treasury than to serving the goals of public service. Since the public treasury in these societies is chronically anemic, wages as well as expectations of productivity are kept perennially low.

2. Innovative and effective public managers are in short supply. A study by Palmer and his research associates (1989) in Egypt, Saudi Arabia, and Sudan reports that bureaucracies lack innovative skills. According to the findings, Egyptian and Sudanese officials, because of low wage structures in their respective states, were somewhat more predisposed than their Saudi counterparts to view low innovation as a problem of incentives. But in the Saudi case, where financial incentives are no problem, innovation also was low. The authors conclude that "incentives alone are unlikely to solve the problem of low innovation unless they are combined with programs that address all of the relevant dimensions of bureaucratic behavior" (Palmer et al. 1989, 25). In societies emphasizing socioeconomic development through ambitious national plans, lack of innovation within the bureaucracy inevitably has serious negative effects on the whole process of development.

3. Centralized decisionmaking and nepotism can affect even relatively successful systems. A study of bureaucracy and development in Jordan points out that in comparison with other developing countries, the Jordanian bureaucracy inspires fewer negative portrayals and sometimes even is

commended for its performance (Jreisat 1989, 99). However, efforts to professionalize the Jordanian bureaucracy were not successful in eliminating the ills of centralized decisionmaking processes that have the effect of reducing senior managers to a clerical class mindlessly enforcing higher commands. Moreover, nepotism and political favoritism in awarding senior government positions kept the level of knowledge and skills within narrow confines. In this context of a low level of professional management, all powers of decisionmaking are concentrated in the cabinet and the prime minister's office. Thus political control is maintained and with it manipulation of public resources. These and other shortcomings have been most decisive in retarding the effectiveness of bureaucracy in implementing policies of socioeconomic development (Jreisat 1989, 94).

4. Problems can spread throughout the region. A study of 140 "successful managers" from the Gulf states (Bahrain, Kuwait, Oman, Qatar, Saudi Arabia, and UAE) underscores "several troublesome issues," especially "increased red tape," "lack of authority to make decisions," "indecisiveness and avoidance of risk," and "government interference" in business affairs (MEIRC 1989, 114). These "troublesome issues" prevalent in the Gulf states are shaped and deepened in two major ways. One is the transmittal of the same ailments found in other Arab states, such as Egypt and Sudan, because they have been providing technical assistance to the Gulf countries in organization and management. The second is the consequences of the type of political regimes in power and the method of ruling through family dictatorships.

5. Corruption has been a common concern as the antithesis of reform. Although particularly tied to the act of bribery, corruption also involves misuse of authority as a result of considerations of personal gain, which need not be monetary (Bayley 1970, 522). In Africa, Asia, and the Middle East as well as in the United States, incidents of corruption are not unusual. Causes of corruption, however, cannot be definitively decided. Poor pay, inadequate fringe benefits, weak commitment to the state or to the party in power, lack of monitoring and control of public officials, and the culture of the society have all been blamed for rampant corruption in modern governments.

In the Arab states, corruption is so widespread that many public officials look at it as an acceptable and legitimate route to success (Jabbra 1989, 5). It seems that corruption does not evoke the necessary legal punishment or, more seriously, the social penalty that could have a negative effect on one's respectability in one's community. This situation is creating a vicious circle in Arab governments that seek reform. How can one expect a corrupt political or administrative leader to seriously effect reforms that prevent his self-enrichment or limit his arbitrary power? Perhaps one of the most alarming aspects of corruption in many Arab societies is that "the practices of corruption are being internalized by younger gener-ations and will become part of their value systems if no measures to stop them are implemented" (Jabbra 1989, 5). Within this context, public offi-cials place higher importance on decisions enriching them individually than on those that develop the country.

Numerous studies of the Arab governments have reported large-scale corruption. Palmer, Leila, and Yassin (1988, 33) point out that in Egypt corruption disrupts bureaucratic performance by blunting the logic of merit-based recruitment and evaluation processes as well as by undermin-ing public confidence in the objectivity and impartiality of the bureau-cracy. Moreover, Ayubi (1989, 75) reports that "corruption had to a large extent been 'institutionalized' in the seventies, partly as a safety valve for the badly paid bureaucracy, and partly as an accompanying symptom of the laissez-faire policy." In Syria, Hinnebusch (1989, 90) finds "symptoms of parasitism" that cause extractions from peasants by corrupt officials. Reports of huge bribes to senior government officials or members of the ruling dynasties in Morocco, Saudi Arabia, Kuwait, and other Gulf states are almost routine.

6. Arab administrative structures, mirroring the political context, have not adapted to the urgent need for inclusionary decisionmaking processes. This lack of inclusion has two dimensions. First, within public organiza-tions, employees have not experienced involvement and participation that energize them to improve performance. Research on group dynamics (French and Bell 1995, 94) concluded that employee participation pro-duced better solutions to problems and greatly enhanced acceptance of de-cisions. Second, citizens have not been included in deliberations on poli-cies that affect their futures. "People today have an impatient urge to participate in the events that shape their lives."[23]

The transition from centralized, hierarchical patterns of organization and management to more participatory modes of decisionmaking is more than an organizational issue. It requires different modes of socialization in the society and the commitment of forces inside and outside the organi-zation to new, inclusionary values. An autocratic political context en-courages looking upward for direction by every administrator, not side-ways, not within himself or herself, and certainly not downward to subordinates. As a result, the outcome is often skewed but not in the di-rection of the general public. To reduce resistance to change and to serve broader public interest, political and administrative leaders have to be concerned with such questions as how the community feels, what do citi-zens want, and how to move forward on issues of common interest. Con-nections with the whole community, in contrast to concentration on spe-cial interests, are imperative in order to adapt public policy to an era of collaborative governing.

OTHER ADVERSE EFFECTS ON DEVELOPMENT

This discussion would be incomplete without considering, however briefly, a host of factors, not necessarily administrative in nature, that exert a negative impact on development: population growth, urbanization, type of political setting, military cost, and the burden of public debt. These burdensome influences are significant not only for their hobbling effect on development but also because public policies have failed to control their negative consequences, let alone to reverse their effects.

Population Growth

Population growth is probably the most noticeable change. The entire population of the Arab world was of the order of 35 to 40 million in 1914, 55 to 60 million by 1939, 226 million in 1991,[24] and 240 million in 1993.[25] Werner Fornos of the Population Institute points out (1990, 3), "[T]here were less than 2.5 million Egyptians at the beginning of the 19th century; today, there are 55 million, with one million more added every eight months."[26] At the present 2.9 percent growth rate of the Arab world, Egypt alone would have to accommodate a doubling of its population within only twenty-five years.

The increase of Arab population by more than 250 percent during the past fifty years is caused primarily by a decrease in the death rate as a result of improved economic and health conditions. A major result of the rapid growth in population is that the age distribution changed. By 1960, "more than half the population in most [Arab] countries was under the age of twenty" (Hourani 1991, 373). At the political level, rapid population growth is problematic in many ways. It forces change that exceeds the coping capacity of domestic public institutions and heightens tensions domestically and even internationally.

This demographic reality alone constitutes a mammoth challenge to public policy, particularly in the areas of education, food supplies, employment opportunities, environment, and housing. Population growth unquestionably increases the pressures on existing resources and diminishes any developmental gains in many countries. The impact on the environment could be drastic enough to threaten the survival of people by endangering global biosystems and the availability of basic resources such as potable water and breathable air.[27]

Urbanization

Urbanization of the Arab world is a consequence of a general population growth as well as a decrease in population of the countryside. The increasing number of cities swelling with 1 million or more inhabitants presents many economic and social problems. In Algeria, Egypt, Iraq, Jordan, Lebanon, Morocco, Syria, Saudi Arabia, and Tunisia half or more of the citizens live in urban areas. In Morocco, for example, "by 2010, seven out of 10 people are expected to be living in urban areas."[28] This trend in the Arab world is consistent with a global population increase expected to reach a rate of 50 percent by 2025 and an absolute number of 8.3 billion. At that point two-thirds of humanity would be living in cities, according to a report prepared by three international organizations (World Bank, UNDP, UN Environment Program) and a leading think tank, the World Resources Institute.[29]

The most dramatic consequences of urbanization are felt in the decline of the quality of living and the effects on the total socioeconomic life of the society. First, according to World Bank sources, a high ratio of people in urban areas live in precarious and illegally built shacks or in somewhat better but substandard housing built without permit on unserviced land. A 1989 census in Morocco found that 23 percent of the urban population lived in such housing conditions. The ratio can be expected to be higher in Egypt, the largest Arab state. Second, shortages of water in many Arab cities are increasingly reaching a crisis phase. "Per capita water supply in the region [Middle East and North Africa] is now one-third 1960 levels and is expected to halve in the next three decades, according to a new [World] Bank report that analyzes the state of water resources in North Africa and the Middle East."[30] Further deterioration can be averted only through immediate government action and with appropriate policies. Finally, in addition to problems of housing and water shortages, urban congestion generates a host of other social ills, such as disease, crime, illiteracy, and poverty.

Type of Political Setting

The power of the Arab state in the era of independence is enormous. "The triumph of nationalism," Hourani (1991, 381) says, "may have appeared at first to be that of the indigenous possessing classes, but in most countries this was short-lived, and the victor was the state itself, those who controlled the government and those in the military and civil service through whom its power was exercised." As in most developing countries, the activities of Arab governments extended beyond the traditional functions such as maintenance of law and order, collection of taxes, and delivery of essential services. Arab governments own and manage public utilities, banks, railways, airlines, buses, television and radio stations, newspapers, universities, and hospitals as well as housing projects.

The hegemony of the state is a world phenomenon. Even in Western industrial nations, according to the World Bank's estimates, the central government's expenditure consumes a significant percentage of GNP (34.6 in the United Kingdom, 47.9 in Italy, 42.6 in France, 40.6 in Sweden in 1989). In the Arab world, ideological and nonideological factors have contributed to the dominance of the state. The ruling parties in Egypt, Algeria, Syria, and Iraq since the 1960s have advocated state ownership and/or control of critical public services. Thus, through nationalization as well as creation of public enterprises, many operations that were owned by the private sector or by foreign investors changed to public ownership. Many public services, industries, and utilities were built by the state, which kept full or partial ownership of such enterprises. Nationalization developed its own momentum in certain countries. The reasons for government intervention expanded beyond the economic rationale of stimulating productivity to include objectives of social justice in the society, as has been the case with land reform programs in Egypt, Syria, Algeria, and Iraq.

The increase in oil profits, particularly between 1973 and 1982, benefited the states extracting oil, and some benefits rippled out to segments of other countries. However, oil revenues failed to prevent fundamental structural changes in the Arab economies, and agriculture everywhere was relegated to lower importance. Polarization of social and political forces in some Arab societies was alarmingly noticeable and led to many explosions and street violence (major popular uprisings occurred during the 1980s in Saudi Arabia, Egypt, Algeria, and Jordan). Nationalist and Islamist movements emerged to correct the imbalances in wealth accumulation and to serve wider interests of the public, among other claims.

Differences among political contexts remain striking. In one group of countries—Algeria, Egypt, Jordan, Tunisia, and Yemen—many democratic and semidemocratic political processes formally exist. In all these countries, elected legislative bodies operate at the local and national levels of government. All have considerable measures of constitutional definitions of authority in the society. Their governments are differentiated and include an independent judiciary and fairly delineated executive functions to render basic services.

Is what we see in these countries only a veneer, not the substance of a civil society? Certainly, these states cannot be construed as egalitarian, participatory political systems or as bona fide democracies that have passed the institutional survival test. The fact remains, however, that their particular organizations and methods endure and reflect, however ineffectively at times, independent judgment and influence on political decisions. Despite skepticism, one still may argue that this condition is preferable to not having any such formations and mechanisms, especially if they can be made to evolve and flourish.

A second group of Arab states—Saudi Arabia, Bahrain, Kuwait, Qatar, UAE, and Oman (members of the Gulf Cooperation Council—GCC)—is radically different from the first group. The GCC countries mainly consist of small states governed by dynasties and have no constitutional traditions. In form and in substance the central authority is absolute and revolves around the power of a single family in each government. There are no definitions or guarantees of civil liberties. Positions at policymaking levels are endowed on the basis of family ties, tribal influence, and/or wealth.

In general, Arab regimes seldom reflect popular will, and their decisions as well as their authorities have been lapsing into a perpetual crisis of legitimacy. Most of these systems of government have no structures for genuine political representation. No organized political opposition may operate freely or develop consequential alternative programs for governing. Without exception, political and administrative leadership in every Arab state rules with the support of an extensive patronage system that drums up support through direct benefits to individuals and families. In the absence of any effective universal measures of accountability or transparency of public decisions, the suspicions and alienation of the public are deep-seated.

The legitimacy problem is exacerbated when rulers are beholden to foreign powers or are charged with corruption and ineffectiveness, perceived or real. Moreover, decisions on war and peace as well as on investing, armament, setting development goals, or budgetary allocations ultimately are made by one person in each state, without genuine public participation. The absence of viable political institutions, invigorated by free expression and free press, ensures continuation of oligarchic rule and insulates the public from governmental action.

Consequently, the survival of such regimes is ensured only through foreign powers' guarantees of protection. The yearnings of citizens as well as their frustrations seem to find effective expression only through the periodic violent explosions that have occurred in almost every Arab state over the past decade. The material and human costs of such outbursts have always been severe. The Arab citizen today from Algeria to Egypt to Saudi Arabia is entangled in a financial, political, and religious crisis as deep as any in recent history. Citizens who once took pride in their nation's rich cultural heritage now find themselves pushed to the margins of the global stage. Their economies are declining because of mismanagement, and their future opportunities are increasingly narrowed by population growth, high unemployment, inflationary pressures, and political corruption.

The role of Arab bureaucracies has been pivotal in the conception, design, formalization, and implementation of developmental activities. Increasing state power underscores the strategic position of bureaucracy in almost every Arab country. Despite widely recognized bureaucratic pathologies and broadly publicized explorations to remedy them, bureaucracy is the loyal servant of the political master. The political leadership relies on the bureaucracy in governing (rewarding it with more power, prosperity, and security of employment). Thus, the reform of Arab bureaucracies is not a technical act as much as a test of political will and know-how.

Military Expenditures

The heavy financial burden of military expenditures on the Arab economies is excessive. The United States is the largest supplier of weapons to the Arab world. In 1993, "U.S. sales accounted for nearly $3 out of every $4 spent, congressional researchers say."[31] Saudi Arabia, Kuwait, Egypt, and Oman were among the top purchasers of U.S. arms in 1993.

According to figures published by the U.S. Agency for Disarmament and Arms Control,[32] Saudi Arabia is the largest importer of military hardware in the Middle East region. Saudi imports of weapons reached $29.7 billion during the 1987–1991 period and increased after the Gulf War of 1991. All other Arab countries are heavy importers of weapons, thereby draining their economies of badly needed cash for investment. Also, military outlays exacerbate the problem of foreign debt in many of these countries.

According to World Bank sources,[33] at least six countries of the Middle East devoted 10 percent of their GNP to military expenditures during the 1980s. In contrast, the same countries spent only 5 percent on education and health combined. There is no doubt that military spending and the enormous financial losses military conflicts cause have undermined governments' response to long-term economic development and have penalized investment in people, their education, and their health. Overall military spending in the Arab states is a major contributor to the shortage of money to be invested in building factories, improving infrastructure, and extending essential public services to all citizens.

Public debt

The debt burden is aggravating the usual budget problems in most Arab states: uncertainty of revenues and expenditures, greater budget deficits, reduction of investment, and overall decline of economic standards. A dilemma for many Arab states is that for too long budget deficits were the main contributors to debt burden; now, debt payments are a major cause of chronic budget deficits.

In many countries the financial situation has done far more than slow economic growth and arrest socioeconomic development plans. Many Arab states have reached the stage where they cannot make interest payments on time or at any time. Accrued interests have swelled budget deficits, which also are routinely financed by nonpayment of interest. Worsening debt crises have brought in international financial institutions to recommend alternative economic policies and financial plans for Egypt, Morocco, Algeria, Tunisia, Jordan, and others.

The magnitude of the debt burden is demonstrated by the following listing of total external debt and its ratio to GNP (ratio to GNP is not available for some countries):[34]

- Egypt $40.0 billion (68 percent of GNP)
- Morocco $21.3 billion (71 percent of GNP)
- Jordan $7.9 billion (163 percent of GNP)
- Oman $2.0 billion (27 percent of GNP)
- Tunisia $8.4 billion (50 percent of GNP)
- Algeria $26.3 billion (60 percent of GNP)
- Sudan $16.0 billion
- Syria $16.4 billion
- Yemen $6.6 billion

CONCLUSIONS

As shown in this examination of comprehensive development in the Arab state, the performance of the political and administrative system is crucial. Development requires domestic reform as well as inflow of technology and capital. The domestic momentum is a function of several factors: political commitment, managerial leadership, political institutions, financial resources, technical skills, and appropriate developmental values and behaviors. Clearly, none of these internal elements is sufficient by itself, and all have to converge in the realm of public policy formulation and implementation.

Developmental decisions in the Arab states, like most policymaking, have been top-down and communicated by decree or edict. Under such conditions, three important elements are absent from the process: (1) mechanisms of accountability, evaluation, and feedback; (2) public participation and institutional discussions; and (3) employee involvement below the level of top civil servants, including an incentive system for rewarding good performance and effective implementation (Jreisat 1990, 419). Despite a considerable variation in practices among Arab states, substantive changes almost always begin and end at the top of the political pyramid. Excessive centralization and the usually undefined powers of the head of state provide a political safety valve whereby potentially disruptive ideas are vetoed and recommendations are screened to keep out those that are unacceptable. The political authority exercises control at every stage. A paralyzing conformity ensues, and innovative or radical thinking is filtered out. In fact, political leaders at the top personally, or through their trusted agents, authorize all ideas of change, approve recommendations, and control when and how implementation may proceed. Even minor changes of organization and management often require approval at the highest political levels.

Finally, as a process, development can be attempted with some measure of success only when a combination of elements and preconditions is present. Economists argue the various theories of development and debate the merits of each: classic, Marxist, neo-Marxist, socialist, capitalist, and so forth. Others attempt to offer partial explanations grounded in social or cultural factors; for instance, Sharabi (1988, 2–3) says that the attributes that characterize the Arab people lead to describing the Arab society as a neopatriarchal one that suffers social fragmentation, authoritarian organization, absolutist paradigms, and ritualistic practices. Such behavioral and cultural attributes are offered as an explanation of the determinants of development.

A totally different genre of cultural analysis, however, seeks something peculiar, if not inferior, in the cultures of other peoples that can explain their current state of backwardness. Identifying development as an economic or cultural problem can be as beneficial as it is tempting. But to achieve balanced and useful conclusions, the analyst needs to understand the limitations of these perspectives and to guard against the tendency to slide into stereotypes or to seek methodological feasibility in reductionism. To focus solely on culture in explaining national development or the lack of it, for example, is to blame citizens—in their behaviors and traits—for failings of public policies that they have neither initiated nor supported. Similarly, limiting the analysis to economic variables such as GDP or per capita income tends to divert attention from the fundamental policies themselves.

Discussion of shortcomings of existing political and administrative institutions leads to the conclusion that problems of development and reform in the Arab society are not totally economic. Evidence exists that the political and administrative structures dominate not only the core of governing but also the minute extremities of the socioeconomic order. Thus, the important question is how long these structures can continue to escape with impunity the consequences of many unsatisfied needs, both economic and noneconomic.

NOTES

1. "Introduction," in Mansour (1992).
2. The conversion rate in 1980 was about U.S.$1 = SR 3.4.

3. Kingdom of Saudi Arabia, Ministry of Planning, *Third Development Plan, 1980–1985*, p. 88.

4. Ibid.

5. Hashemite Kingdom of Jordan, Ministry of Planning, *Economic and Social Development Plan, 1993–1997*, p. 115.

6. Ibid., p. 24.

7. World Bank, *World Development Report 1994* (New York: Oxford University Press), pp. 162–163.

8. Mohammed Rabie, quoted in the *Christian Science Monitor* (April 1, 1992), p. 4; George Corm estimates Arab investments abroad at between $400 and $600 billion (presentation at the international conference, "The Arab World Preparing for the 21st Century," University of Jordan, Amman, July 24–26, 1994).

9. This estimate is from Muslim Week in Review, a service run by *Friday Journal* in coordination with *Al-Akhbar* (July 20, 1996). The Review also cites a report by the Arab Trade Fund Program that indicates (on the basis of international bank statistics) that Arab states had failed to "strengthen their position on the global economic map" despite "huge oil wealth and other resources."

10. Mohammed Rabie, quoted in the *Christian Science Monitor* (April 1, 1992), p. 4.

11. World Bank, *World Development Report 1993* (New York: Oxford University Press), pp. 258–259.

12. The report was cited in *New York Times*, September 8, 1992.

13. Ibid.

14. *New York Times*, April 25, 1993.

15. *The World Bank Atlas 1995* (Washington, DC: The World Bank), pp. 8–9.

16. Quoted by Anna Quindlen, *New York Times*, September 7, 1994, p. A17.

17. *World Bank News* 10, no. 47 (December 5, 1991), p. 1; United Nations Development Program, *Human Development Report 1993* (New York: Oxford University Press), p. 150.

18. "Economic Viewpoint," *Business Week* (May 2, 1994), p. 16.

19. United Nations Development Program, *Human Development Report 1994* (New York: Oxford University Press), pp. 129–131.

20. Haykal's lecture was published in two parts by the Palestinian *al-Quds al-Arabi*, translated by *Mideast Mirror* (October 31, 1994).

21. The first two numbers are in Palmer, Leila, and Yassin (1988, 4); the third number was supplied to me by the Egyptian Ministry of National Development.

22. *Rose el-Yousef*, no. 3450 (July 25, 1994), p. 16.

23. United Nations Development Program, *Human Development Report 1993* (New York: Oxford University Press), p. 1.

24. See Hourani (1991, 333); and World Bank, *World Development Report 1993* (New York: Oxford University Press).

25. *The World Bank Atlas 1995*, pp. 8–9.

26. By the end of 1994, Egypt's population was estimated at 60 million, with 1.4 million being added annually (according to government officials whom I interviewed).

27. University of Maryland, Institute for Philosophy and Public Policy, *Ethics and Global Population* 13, no. 4 (Fall 1993).

28. *World Bank News* 15, no. 9 (March 7, 1996), p. 5.

29. *World Bank News* 15, no. 15 (April 18, 1996), p. 4.

30. *World Bank News* 15, no. 11 (March 21, 1996), p. 1.

31. "U.S. Dominates Third World Arms Sales," *Tampa Tribune,* August 3, 1994, p. 4.

32. Reported in *Al-Dustour* newspaper (in Arabic), Amman, Jordan, April 1, 1994.

33. From a speech by Caio Koch-Weser, Vice President, the World Bank, published in *The Middle East and North Africa: Issues in Development* (Fall 1993), p. 3.

34. World Bank, *World Development Report 1994* (New York: Oxford University Press), pp. 200–201, 206–207.

4

Building Administrative Capacity

The true test of a good government is its aptitude and tendency to produce a good administration.

Alexander Hamilton[1]

Over the past several years, every Arab regime has proclaimed administrative reform as a primary public policy objective. Many of the Arab countries actually took steps toward building the institutional capacity necessary for effective management. All acknowledge the central role of public administration in national development and the inevitability of state intervention in order to make progress.

Although evidence is fragmented and analysis is scant, observers of developmental failures in the Arab world tend to agree on one conclusion: "Developmental plans have not reached their desired objectives in the Arab world because of weaknesses of the administrative apparatus in exercising its capacity to implement those plans" (Affendi 1994, 1). Surveying the Egyptian bureaucracy, Palmer, Leila, and Yassin (1988, ix) determine: "It is now apparent that the Egyptian bureaucracy is a major obstacle to the economic and social development of the Egyptian society." Hence, development of public administration and the improvement of the capabilities of those working in it have become requisites for achieving the desired comprehensive development.

In this chapter, I review administrative reform efforts in several Arab states, as delineated in official documents and as described by individuals involved in preparing those documents, in order to determine the content of and the responsibility for reform activities in each state. In Chapters 6 and 7 particularly I extend the line of inquiry to evaluate reform programs after they have been implemented by estimating outcomes and impact. I gained valuable primary information from official assessments of reform initiatives and through interviews with officials and experts in Jordan and Egypt. My visit and discussions with the leadership and staff of the Arab Organization of Administrative Development (AOAD), an organ of the League of Arab States, were most valuable in acquiring an overall picture of reform efforts in the Arab world. AOAD is dedicated to administrative development within twenty-one Arab countries.

71

When organizing a conference on administrative reform in the Arab world (held in Cairo in December 1992), AOAD requested each participating country to report on steps taken to reform its system.[2] The ensuing reports, individually and collectively, constitute a vital source of information about governments and public policies, even if they attracted only limited public debate. The reports do, of course, embody official perspectives and therefore suffer from the usual drawbacks that are intrinsic to such sources, hence the need to supplement and to verify the contents of these reports whenever feasible.

The following sections are a synopsis of the vital elements of operative concepts and strategies of administrative reform in several Arab states over recent years. My purpose is to offer a specific and authentic account of the components of various reform programs and their expected outcomes. Also, this summary helps to assess and evaluate reform activities and to determine their organizational efficacy. Table 4.1 summarizes the reform proposals that I discuss.

EGYPT

Criticisms of the Egyptian bureaucracy are rampant, and efforts to reform it are continuous. In fact, a full-time cabinet member and a host of public agencies are charged with reforming and developing the Egyptian public administration. A more comprehensive study of Egypt, the largest and most influential of the twenty-one Arab states, follows in Chapter 5. The purpose here is to define recent objectives of administrative reform and examine some critical proposals that have been authorized for implementation.

Reform attempts in Egypt may be grouped into four clusters: (1) establishing new organizations and reorganizing existing ones; (2) analyzing and describing public service jobs; (3) training and developing managerial leadership; and (4) relying on consultative assistance, either through international offices or through Egyptian entities such as the Central Agency for Organization and Administration, the National Institute for Administrative Development, and units of organization and development scattered among executive agencies.

Despite numerous claims of reform initiatives in Egypt, the results are all but inconsequential in their impact on the overall performance of political and administrative systems. Advocates of reform initiatives have been hard pressed to demonstrate substantive accomplishments in the field. Explanations offered by public officials for the lack of goal attainment are consistent with those in the literature on Egyptian bureaucracy (particularly with those presented by Nazih Ayubi and by Monte Palmer, Ali Leila, and El Sayed Yassin).

Table 4.1 Summary of Administrative Reform Proposals in Selected Arab States

	Reform Proposals	Responsible Agency
Egypt	• Reorganization • Job analysis and job description • Training and leadership development • Reliance on consultants • Information system	• Central Agency for Organization and Administration • National Institute for Administrative Development • Ministry of Administrative Development
Jordan	• Job description and job classification • Performance evaluation • Procedural simplification • Organization and methods • Development of workforce	• Civil Service Commission • Institute of Public Administration • The prime minister
Iraq	• Workforce needs assessment • Employee development • Evaluation of methods of operation • Information, surveys, applied studies • Activating academic institutions in development	• National Center for Planning and Economic Development • Ministry of Planning
Syria	• Developing suitable "doctrine" for the state • Review organizational structures • Updating laws • Training and skills development • Employees' incentives • Information gathering	• Committee for Administrative Development • Planning Agency • Prime minister's office
Saudi Arabia	• Simplification of procedures • Definition of organizations' objectives • Determining staffing needs • Improve coordination • Correct excessive centralization	• Civil Service Bureau • Institute of Public Administration • Central Organization for Administration

(continues)

Table 4.1 continued

	Reform Proposals	Responsible Agency
Tunisia	• Deconcentration and decentralization • Improve relations with citizens • Modernize procedures and methods of operation • Attention to the human side of public service	• Ministry of Administrative Reform and Public Employment • Committees of officials and citizens
Sudan	• Prepare public service to lead operations of economic development • Reorganization • Depoliticize civil service • Training and staff development • Simplification of procedures	• Special committee
Bahrain	• Review civil service rules • Simplification of procedures • Employee incentives and benefits • Develop work standards	• Civil Service Bureau
Qatar	• Improve performance • Strengthen relations of administration to development • Develop job design and content • Free public service from impediments	• Civil Service Commission
United Arab Emirates	• Reorganize agencies • Staff training and development • Information system	• Public Personnel Department • Minister of state for cabinet affairs
Yemen	• Update methods to serve economic development • Define objectives • Review overemployment • Job description standards of performance	• Civil Service • Minister of administrative reform • Prime minister's office

Sources: Information in this summary is derived from official reports submitted by official agencies of the respective governments. Several of these reports are specifically cited in the text.

Overemployment in the public sector is the foremost reason given for failure of reforms. Overemployment abounds in every public organization and at ridiculously high rates; many employees have no designated offices or defined responsibilities. Activities that could be adequately performed by two or three employees are handled inadequately by at least twice as many. Repeatedly the poor performance by the bureaucracy is explained in terms of the government's being the main source of employment, and people are given jobs as a sort of welfare handout rather than as a consequence of usefulness or merit. Overstaffing renders definition of responsibilities and processes of performance evaluation almost useless. A bureaucracy designed to absorb successive generations of college graduates is not well equipped to handle the complex task of development. As Palmer, Leila and Yassin (1988, 25) report: "The social welfare orientation of previous Egyptian governments has resulted in the severe overstaffing of the bureaucracy and has precluded agencies from implementing evaluation procedures that distinguish between productivity and slough."

Overstaffing is only one of many shortcomings and weaknesses; low salaries and low motivation are others. Additionally, leaders in both the executive and legislative branches of government point out such problems as unsuitable government buildings, poor equipment and facilities, primitive record keeping, a multiplicity of conflicting rules and regulations, poor incentives, the lack of capacity for follow-up on decisions, and ineffective training. Nevertheless, the set of reform activities with which Egyptians are struggling are so rudimentary that very few people believe they will make a significant difference even if implemented.

Lip service to reform is first-rate. Political and administrative leaders define reform objectives in a logical and convincing manner. Senior Egyptian officials (from the executive and legislative branches as well as the civil service), in formal and informal settings, provide a consistent depiction of reform ideas: They confidently proffer schemes of reorganization for public institutions and for workplace development; they present elaborate wage reviews, leadership selection methods, and training programs; and they are ready to discuss control systems and processes of evaluation of public employees. The problem is that such information, generated from interviews with many of these officials, often has little authenticity and more often consists of responses designed to impress, justify, or protect rather than to illuminate a problem or suggest a solution.

One of the main frustrations for a researcher conducting field study on government in Egypt by means of interviews with public officials is that of distinguishing between word and action. Over and over officials replied to questions by citing this law or that statement by a senior official, such as the prime minister or the president. It is difficult, for example, to make the subject of an interview consider the idea that laws do not precisely define what goes on within Egyptian public organizations or that what the prime minister said in a speech remains merely an utterance until it is actually implemented. The interviewees seem to believe that if it is said, it is done. The irony is that the gap between rhetoric and reality among Egyptian officials often seems unbridgeable.

Since 1991, with growing pressures for economic reforms and the urgency of dealing with the burden of public debt, reform objectives in Egypt have expanded. These additions include developing capabilities in public debt management, establishing structures for the study of public projects, improving entities responsible for investment activities, developing competent leaders, and modernizing management information systems.

Most of the changes made in the context of these new objectives have been initiated at the cabinet level and dictated from the centralized command. Myriad accomplishments are claimed in official statements and reports, particularly when issued to the press or in legislative sessions. Opposition political groups, independent newspapers, and some government officials, however, question most of the changes and their efficacy. Reliable information and studies about these government claims are either nonexistent or out of public view. Preliminary assessments, based on my interviews, do indicate moderate achievements in a few areas that can be credited to reform programs. Independent and systematic assessments are now essential to inform future policies and to remedy existing deficiencies. Such efforts require, in addition to resources and time, the cooperation of senior government officials and their willingness to face up to long-standing illusions and unrealistic portrayals of existing conditions.

JORDAN

A government report, "Project for Developing Public Administration in Jordan,"[3] proposed to increase the efficiency and effectiveness of government administration through four sets of measures: One set focused on what has been referred to as the public position or the individual job. Activities for reform included improvements in areas such as job description, job classification, performance evaluation, and procedural simplification. The second group of measures dealt with questions of organization and methods as they applied to the organizational structure of government. The purpose was to examine such structure in order to improve coordination and introduce additional functions designed to ensure accountability and control. The third set of measures dealt with a core of exercises and ventures that aimed at the workforce itself. Training for professional development, conferences, and labor-market assessments were the main elements of these measures.

Finally, the Jordanian public policy conceded the importance of developing institutional instruments to be entrusted with the task of reform. To this end, the government initiated various actions for improving the effectiveness of the Institute of Public Administration (IPA) and streamlining the operations of the Civil Service Commission (CSC), two institutions that are closely involved with attempts of administrative reform and play a major role in the larger scheme of administrative development. They have also relied on consultants from the UNDP for technical advice.

The period of time designated for implementing these changes was 1990 through 1993. However, most of what the leadership of IPA and CSC was able to point to in 1994 as accomplishments still revolved around reports and studies that lacked actualization. Few procedural simplification measures had actually been brought about, although a controversial organization called the Bureau of Control and Inspection had been created (it was elevated to ministerial level in 1994). This new organization was pronounced within and without the Jordanian bureaucracy to be dead on arrival because of inexperienced staff and a vague mission. In addition, the responsibilities of the Bureau of Control and Inspection, conceived and authorized by the prime minister, duplicate and overlap those of certain existing agencies such as the Central Bureau of Accounting and the CSC. (This issue is revisited in Chapter 6.)

IRAQ

In 1989, Iraq concluded its fourth decade of national planning for socioeconomic development. The beginning of the oil boom in 1950 had marked the turning point for comprehensive development planning. In that year the Iraqi Development Board was established to formulate and monitor the execution of national plans, initially funded in total with oil revenues.

The leaders of the 1958 revolution widely publicized the failures of the early policies of development, often using them to justify their revolt. New leaders charged old ones with, among other things, failing to promote rapid industrialization of the country and allowing the rich to gain a disproportionate share of the benefits of development. New leaders claimed the earlier regime had served the financial interests of British imperialists, large landowners, and the ruling political oligarchy. In 1959, the new government replaced the Development Board with a Ministry of Planning and a Planning Board chaired by the prime minister and composed of other ministries concerned with economic and financial affairs.

From the outset, inherited problems as well as new ones hindered the performance of public organizations. Lack of managerial capabilities to handle the additional complex tasks of national development was the most constraining of these difficulties. Also complicating matters were the inadequate pay and low skills of civil servants as well as the lack of reliable statistical measures of economic performance. Consequently, civil servants were free to improvise in the conduct of their duties, producing uncertainty and irregular results in the implementation of development plans and programs. During the 1960s and 1970s, necessity compelled various governments to elevate the objective of building the country's managerial capabilities to a higher priority of public policy.

In the late 1980s, a definite qualitative departure from previous plans was reached. Up to that time, Iraq had ambitious programs of administrative reform that enjoyed political support at various levels of the political structure. State policy emphasized the importance of changing the relationships of citizens to public organizations by simplifying procedures and by connecting administrative development to comprehensive national development. Public policy also dictated a commitment to achieving "greater harmony between the provisions of the national plan and the resources and needs of the society."[4]

A new program of reforms was proposed for the 1990s. The time span for implementing the reform program was 1992 to 1996. In reporting progress occurring between 1985 and 1990 related to the proposed reforms, the most noteworthy were the efforts to improve hospital and health services and to provide managerial and technical training to employees. The organization entrusted with the responsibility of administrative reform and development was the National Center for Planning and Economic Development within the Ministry of Planning.

The main elements of the proposed reform program for the 1990s were: (1) assessment of needs and available workforce; (2) development of knowledge and skills of public employees; (3) continuous evaluation of frameworks and methods followed; (4) gathering information, conducting surveys, and preparing applied studies; and (5) activating academic institutions to assume a more active role in developmental efforts.[5]

The Gulf War in 1991 and its aftermath brought such efforts to a virtual standstill. Military destruction, the international economic boycott that followed the war, and the cumulative effects of the prolonged war with Iran during the 1980s all disabled Iraq's efforts to develop and reform. The negative effects of the economic and social damage on national development are inestimable at this time.

SYRIA

The "Draft of Administrative Development Plan for the Arab Republic of Syria" outlines a long list of objectives. Before delineating reform proposals, however, the report expounds on administrative development and reform, placing these objectives at the top of public policy priorities. I translated the features of this ambitious plan for administrative development as follows:[6]

Administrative development is a conscious and purposeful operation exemplified by the capacity of the administrative order at renewal, building, and development of concepts, directions, frameworks, structures, laws, methods, and administrative processes . . . for meeting the requirements of political, economic, and social development. . . . A society that has a developed administrative system can achieve a good national development pattern whatever the size of its resources. . . . In the absence of a well-developed administrative system, economic resources and natural wealth will not be sufficient for reaching balanced development because they will not be appropriately utilized. (p. 1)

After emphasizing the crucial role of an effective administrative system "as the fundamental instrument for building the modern state" (p. 2), the plan reports numerous directives and proposals for reform. According to this plan, the proposals have been approved by the president, endorsed by the leadership of the ruling B'ath party, and sanctioned by various authorized committees and offices. Some of these sources simply confirmed suggested reform ideas, others proposed new ones.

Among the objectives discussed are establishing an administrative "doctrine" suitable to the conditions of the state, reviewing and evaluating the organizational structure of the government and the public sector (referring to public enterprises), and reviewing and updating laws. Improving employee incentive systems also made the list, along with other personnel matters such as training, improvements in communication, accounting, information gathering, and placement of staff.

The authority committed to implementing reform is the Committee for Administrative Development within the agency responsible for public planning. Syria defined the time span for achieving reform objectives as 1991 through 1995. However, no matter how well or how thoroughly they are discussed, few of the strategies for reform have been implemented.

The administrative development plan, although it soars rhetorically, suffers greatly from an obvious lack of definition of responsibility for execution. Authority is diffused. A cumbersome committee structure dominates, preventing the emergence of executive-managerial leadership entrusted with defined tasks and functions. Perhaps the most telling fact about development efforts in Syria is something the "Draft of Administrative Development Plan" explicitly recognizes:

Examining the reality of administrative development [in Syria] leads to a fundamental conclusion that is not positive. Despite clear authorization by all levels of leadership, of the directives and decisions related to administrative change, they remain without execution. There is an urgent need to concentrate on implementation within the shortest possible time. (p. 29)

Reluctantly, Syria has been searching for a way out of its inherited "statism" or local brand of socialistic policies that produced designs of price-fixing, stifling regulations, poorly executed subsidies, and other counterproductive measures. The economy has been enduring the same ailments as the former socialistic countries of Eastern Europe: bureaucratic rigidities, overemployment, inefficiency, undercapitalization, and constant apprehension over political consequences of change.

Syria's current search for alternative developmental policies has begun to reveal some preliminary features. The new overall reform strategy that is gradually unfolding has many of the globally touted, standard measures of restructuring that are being phased in by many developing countries. There is little doubt that failure of public administration reforms has forced the consideration of other policy alternatives in which the state is not the centerpiece. Definitely, the direction seems to be toward greater reliance on private initiatives. A new and wide-ranging strategy of reform is slowly taking shape, incorporating a broader agenda with these main elements:

- Reform the economy through privatization
- Reduce government subsidies
- Reform the banking system
- Reconsider and ease business regulations

The call for reform is gaining impetus and cannot be ignored by the political leadership without risks. Pressures are building up, owing to the visibility of failures of former public policies, a heavy external debt burden, rising unemployment, and the need for economic stabilization. Even though it is difficult to measure progress at this time, the perception holds that reform will carry political consequences, just as failure to reform will amplify chances of serious political risks.

SAUDI ARABIA

Saudi Arabia's official report is designated as "The Executive Program of the General Plan for Administrative Reform."[7] The report delineates specific objectives of reform that include simplification and improvement of procedures in agencies with direct relations with the public. It calls for organizing administrative units to achieve a sharper definition of objectives and more responsiveness. Also promoted is a proposal for defining staffing demands and redeploying current employees according to agencies' needs. The most serious problems facing the administrative system here are a high degree of formalism, hidden unemployment, excessive centralization, and absence of coordination and complementarity of government actions (Affendi 1994, 14).

According to this report, the government designated a "preparatory administrative committee" for preparing, defining, and monitoring the operational aspects of administrative reform. These responsibilities are executed in cooperation with the Civil Service Bureau, the Institute of Public Administration, and the Central Administration for Organization.

The administrative reform plan has many phases; each phase has a one-year span and coordinates with the fourth five-year National Development Plan (commencing 1984). A schedule of activities was prepared to specify preparatory steps as well as execution and even experimentation. Typically, leaders seeking to push administrative development and reform have called on outside consultants and have relied on internal studies to define issues needing attention. Recommendations almost always include training and/or purchase of new machines and modern technology to enhance productivity. Saudi wealth in the early 1980s influenced this choice of solutions.

The government of Saudi Arabia enjoys certain advantages in comparison with other Arab states, such as an abundance of oil revenues and a small population.[8] During the 1970s and early 1980s, the Saudi regime approached development as a commodity, one that could be purchased from abroad. The orientation was to purchase everything needed (material or otherwise), including knowledge, technology, labor, machines, and consultants to organize everything. In the 1990s, such a policy proved to be very costly and misleading. Problems persisted and seemed institutionalized. Financial difficulties forced the government to borrow and to postpone obligations of payments on purchases of weapons and other expensive imports and contracts.

Finally, the system of government in Saudi Arabia is in the grip of traditional, tribal political and religious cultures that perpetuate archaic notions of governing. A coalition of powerful dynasties and religious zealots has institutionalized self-serving political and social processes that maintain their domination and exploitation of the abundant financial resources of the country. At the same time, citizens are held under restrictive living conditions that deny them basic freedoms and rights, particularly those for women. To compensate for the failure of various political and social patterns, the government supports exaggerated methods of spending that keep the treasury under constant pressure of continuously shrinking assets.

TUNISIA

Reports about administrative reform in Tunisia since 1990[9] indicate that four principles have influenced action: (1) the necessity of deconcentration and decentralization, (2) the importance of improving relations between the administration and the citizens, (3) modernization of managerial procedures and methods, and (4) greater attention to the human element in public service.

What sets the current Tunisian approach apart from previous attempts at administrative reform is that the Tunisians profess to be more practical today than they were during earlier ventures. They claim to be particularly successful in controlling the administrative problems of public projects and in employing diverse skills to create solutions to these problems. To this end, Tunisia has employed thirty work groups of citizens, in addition to those from government, to recommend improvements. These work groups include university professors, lawyers, parliamentarians, specialists, and citizens who patronize public agencies.

The designated authority responsible for reform initiatives is the Ministry of Administrative Reform and Public Employment, in cooperation with various committees and work groups composed of officials as well as citizens. Compared to other Arab states, Tunisia appears to be tinkering with some fairly sophisticated reform concepts. The government shows greater awareness of the need to move beyond the conceptualization phase toward measures of effective implementation. Showing significant progress in readily improvable managerial functions, the Tunisians have achieved at least four goals: They have delegated substantive responsibilities within agencies, narrowed the gap between citizens' perceptions and actual performance of public agencies, improved information-sharing processes, and simplified procedures.

Some of the administrative changes introduced in Tunisia are unique and worthy of being watched by other countries; the potential of these ideas is immense.

First is the concept of *administrative mediator* (AM). This role is reminiscent of the familiar Scandinavian ombudsman or citizens' defender. According to a Tunisian law promulgated on May 3, 1993, the AM is responsible for handling the complaints people may have in dealing with the administrative system. The statute defines the authority and responsibility of the mediator, who is required to submit an annual report to the president that includes recommendations for improving the practices of public agencies, even if these require changes in existing laws.

Second, a 1993 law created an *Office of Citizens Relations* in every ministry to look into helping citizens overcome difficulties encountered in dealing with the administrative process. These offices serve several functions. They receive citizens' complaints and respond to them, guide citizens through administrative procedures when requested, and discover complications in the process and seek to simplify them.

Third, the use of *citizen supervisors* in Tunisia is a novel tactic for dealing with a perennial administrative problem. It works this way: The government assigns groups of citizens to be supervisors over the performance of public offices. These citizens watch the quality of services, how they are delivered, and how public funds are spent. The citizens are appointed by the prime minister for a year, a term renewable only once according to specific qualifications. The citizen supervisors perform their duties discreetly, after oath, and receive compensation for their efforts and for any costs they incur in the conduct of their assignments. Significantly, confidentiality is king: These supervisors are forbidden to reveal or publicize their functions.

Fourth, a *president's award program* encourages new initiatives by employees and rewards major improvements in application and research on organization and management.

The initial results of the Tunisian experience are positive. Tunisia appears to be unlike other Arab states in that it is the only one embarking upon a genuine evaluation of its reform efforts. Information derived from annual assessments and feedback is used to develop new strategies, modify existing ones, and remedy deficiencies.

The Tunisian experience also indicates important efforts to humanize governmental agencies and to placate the public by involving citizens in reform programs. It is therefore surprising that at the same time the regime has launched a campaign to silence government critics and dissidents. The landslide results of the last presidential elections, for example, heighten the dilemma of a regime that is touchy about any opposing views: The president won national elections in 1994 by 99.27 percent of the vote! Two electoral challengers are in detention on charges of "setting up an illegal party and spreading defamatory information."[10] Can a regime that is intolerant of any opposing political force abide a plurality of opinions in administering the state? It is too early to determine whether the twin strategies of the Tunisian experiment—focus on administrative efficiencies and improving public service responsiveness to citizens' needs—are adequate substitutes for a civic society. The Tunisian political leadership has not come to terms with notions of popular participation in governance, civil liberties, and protection of human rights.

SUDAN

In a government report prepared in 1990,[11] Sudan's program of administrative reform outlines the following objectives:

1. Formulate policies and strategies for improving public service and enhancing its productivity.
2. Prepare public service to lead the operations of economic development and state-building.
3. Keep public service neutral and preserve it from political influence as well as racial, geographical, and religious interference.
4. Organize administration in the context of a political structure in a federal union.
5. Train and motivate administrative leaders.
6. Develop and rationalize the financial management system.

7. Simplify procedures and review and modernize laws and information systems.

A blue-ribbon committee conducted the preparation of this reform program with the help of specialized subcommittees. No information is available on the time frame for executing the program and no information about results or accomplishments related to such reform efforts yet exists.

BAHRAIN

A report from Bahrain on "the development of rules for the civil service and public employees"[12] lists the objectives of reform in the country: Review and development of civil service rules, simplification of work procedures in public organizations, development of work standards and organization, delegation of responsibilities within public organizations, material incentives to public employees, early retirements, and employees' safety at work.

Clearly, the concerns of Bahrain are focused on the civil service and the need to update some of its processes with an interest in simplifying its procedures. Another claim made about reform efforts is that they serve the interest of public employees in regard to pay, retirement, safety, and other measures. The organization responsible for the ideas of reform in Bahrain, as in several Arab states, is the civil service establishment.

QATAR

A development plan prepared by the Civil Service Commission of Qatar[13] describes the main objectives of its proposed reform program: Improve public administration performance, strengthen the connection between development operations and administrative development activities, make the most of human resources, and develop governmental positions in design and in freeing content and services from impediments.

The report breaks down overall objectives into operational objectives that include reorganization, job description, training, decentralization, use of modern technology, information gathering, and use of public relations. The time span defined to accomplish these objectives was 1992 through 1995.

UNITED ARAB EMIRATES

The report by the civil service of UAE declared the objectives of administrative reform as:

1. Review legislation that organizes public agencies to ensure compatibility with modern administrative practices.
2. Organize ministries and departments to modernize their structures, to clarify their lines of authority, and to simplify supervision and communication.
3. Develop personnel through training.
4. Introduce information systems and employ modern equipment and techniques throughout public agencies.

The authority directing the reform program appears to be the Public Personnel Department in the office of the minister of state for cabinet affairs. According to official reports, chief among the projects so far completed is legislation regarding the civil service, including job descriptions, classification, and computerization. Other activities comprise reorganizing certain agencies, devising new training programs, and creating a National Computing Center. No information is available on the results of these claimed changes and their effects on the efficiency and effectiveness of performance.

YEMEN

Yemeni Prime Minister Haider Abu-Bakr El-Attas submitted an elaborate program of reform to the parliament (Majlis Al-Nuwaab, or Council of Deputies), which approved it in December 1991.[14] The program outlines the broad policies and the general philosophy of the modern unified country of Yemen. It discusses issues of "national construction" and "political, economic, financial, and administrative reform." The document is described as providing a clear vision of what the government of Yemen should strive for in all aspects of the society. It offers guarantees of certain levels of public freedoms and ensures openness of political and administrative decisions.

The national program for administrative development also enumerates problems to be defined and solved:

1. Administrative and financial processes lagging behind economic development and the tendency of these processes toward greater centralization and complexity.
2. Absence of precise definition of objectives.
3. Inflation of the administrative system.
4. Lack of accurate job descriptions.
5. Deficiency of standards of performance evaluation.

The authority responsible for the reform program is the Ministry of Civil Service and Administrative Reform. This ministry was created to shoulder specific responsibilities for developing the civil service system and for suggesting policies and plans for administrative reform. In fact, in 1991 a new law took effect that revamped procedures and guidelines for the Yemini civil service system.

Early in 1994, however, a violent struggle for power erupted between two rival political leaders—a struggle that endangered the four-year-old union between the north and south of Yemen. Only a year earlier, "the country's voters [had] elected their first parliament, an unprecedented exercise in democracy by the authoritarian standards of the Arabian peninsula" (*Time,* May 23, 1994, p. 43). It was one more example of the leaders of an Arab state aborting a policy decision that the citizens favored. The people of Yemen enthusiastically supported the successful coalition between the two regions of the country. Their leaders, however, were unable to avoid petty rivalries and unite to thwart destructive intrigues and meddling from outside their borders.

Lacking in statesmanship, skills in conflict resolution, and willingness to make sacrifices in the name of public interest, the leaders busied themselves with incessant bickering that they could not end short of bloody and destructive military confrontation. Although the union of the two regions appears to have been saved by the military victory of northern Yemen, the cost in human and economic terms has been high. The effect has been a substantial diversion of resources from objectives of development and reform to those of rebuilding basic infrastructure and restoring essential services in the aftermath of the north-south conflict.

COMPARATIVE ANALYSIS

The preceding summary of particulars and vital attributes of reform efforts in eleven Arab states provides an authentic glimpse of the programs and their stated objectives. One can identify common practices as well as common failures of these efforts. Indeed, what these programs of reform omitted or failed to consider is as indicative and informative as those elements specified or accentuated.

Themes of Attempted Reforms

Rationalization of the public organization. Rationalization has been a common claim as a reform objective. Issues of organization and reorganization are central themes of reform programs in Egypt, Jordan, Syria, Saudi Arabia, Tunisia, and UAE. Through reorganization, these states expressed a desire to remedy inertia, manage excessive centralization, improve performance, and clarify lines of authority and responsibility.

Simplification of operating procedures. Directly or indirectly, this goal shows up on the agenda of every reform program in the Arab states. In some cases, simplification of procedures is coupled with general notions of updating laws, reviewing methods of operation, and giving greater substance and more challenge to reform efforts.

Personnel development through training. Training is another recurrent claim in all reform packages. All Arab countries recognize the need for staff development and for training programs to help improve managerial skills. Some of these proposals single out the role of administrative leaders for special concern and design specific development programs to serve those filling these positions.

Human factors. Some proposed reform programs recognize the human side of public service as crucial for improving the performance of the public sector. Tunisia, for example, specifically calls for greater attention to human factors in examining the performance of public service. Other states, such as Bahrain, Jordan, and Syria, visit the issues from the perspective of incentives for civil servants to induce higher levels of performance. All call for skill-oriented development and training programs to improve productivity.

Information. Reform programs acknowledge the importance of information in modern management. They target the need for information and for acquiring modern tools to collect, store, and retrieve data as necessary. Specifically, Egypt plans to update information systems, particularly those used by such senior officials as the prime minister. Iraq's program calls for gathering information and survey data to help in public policymaking. Jordan established a central office for data gathering and retrieval and franchised its operation in line agencies. Other states call for greater utilization of computers in offices for faster and more accurate service.

Role of citizens. Uncommon among reform ideas is the one found in Tunisia, where citizens are taking on a significant role. Their ideas are methodically incorporated into the process of reform by means of joint committees on which citizens and public officials discuss, evaluate, and recommend managerial improvements.

Protection from political interference. Another interesting idea is the claim of neutralizing public service by protecting it from political interference that is made by government reformers in Sudan. The claim is suspect, and its achievement is even more dubious. It indicates, however, that political meddling in administration is excessive. Whatever claim is made, it cannot mean that public management can be declared independent from the political process. Politics sets many of the goals and policies that administrators implement.

Training in economics. In Egypt, a growing concern is the unavoidable economic role of bureaucracy and its implication for reform efforts. More recent reform attempts in Egypt call for training of top public managers in modern finance and in handling areas such as public debt management, investment, and management of public projects. In the midst of an environment that focuses on privatization and downsizing, Egypt's reform programs are seeking to improve the capabilities of bureaucracy in managing activities presumably slated for less government responsibility.

Omissions from Attempted Reforms

The most revealing aspect of these reform proposals is what they omit. Noteworthy is the striking absence of information about outcomes expected or actually realized. Policies are stated in general terms, devoid of measurement of results (anticipated or achieved). One can find no evaluation of programs supposedly already carried out. Reform rhetoric does not appear to differentiate between formulating a policy and implementing it—"saying it" is confused with "doing it." Consequently, the difference between perception and reality invariably expands. The determination of whether "things are right" or not with government performance is consistently reduced to perception rather than to professional and verifiable analysis of policies and their impact.

Certainly, nowhere is the seriousness of these reform proposals undermined more than in the lack of attention to the difficulties of implementation. No appreciation exists that the process of formulating reform policy is different from the process of implementing it. Thus, information on results is scarce, and the ability to correct actions when necessary is lacking. Even if those responsible for reform know what to do, the question of how to get it done remains.

Also missing in reform proposals is a policy orientation that actively resists corruption and mismanagement. In none of the reform proposals made can one find any effort to deal with the problem of corruption in government, define contributory factors, or recommend remedial actions. Reform proposals seem to focus on traditional managerial concerns such as procedures, reorganization, and training. Tinkering with procedures, organizational forms, and day-to-day operations involves few or no political or economic risks. Few dare tread in areas where power may be fundamentally altered or where privileges may be curtailed.

CONCLUSIONS

Reform programs of the Arab states, as formulated and promulgated, are unable to achieve their purported goals, let alone build a competent public service profession. Nor are any of these programs qualified to redirect existing public institutions so as to reflect the dramatic changes taking place in the society. Arab administrative systems in general have not succeeded in developing capacities such as risk taking, recognition of outstanding performance, or overall professional competency, despite all of the recent reform endeavors.

None of the reform programs reviewed constitutes a mature, coherent strategy carrying the necessary operational thrust. Each is merely a collection of proposed remedial actions that at best are stopgap measures incapable of addressing the continually worsening problems. In fact, it is justifiable to consider proposed reform remedies as a Band-Aid approach to a heavily bleeding patient. The big issues in developing professional management are continually sidetracked.

At the same time, pressures are mounting on political leaders to develop administrative systems with neutral competence and the capacity to provide disinterested advice on public policy issues. Professional expertise and ethics are missing in public agencies that make daily decisions affecting the lives of citizens. Political loyalty, family connections, social status, and old-fashioned patronage have been the determining factors in the staffing of senior government positions. Such practices have produced crippled administrative structures, inflicted with various ailments that prevent effective and efficient performance. The challenge for reformers, therefore, is to forge administrative institutions that have the capacity (skills, knowledge, and ethics) to produce developmental objectives and to execute them. The difficulty is that such a task must be accomplished at a time when it is harder to attract staff with required skills because of fiscal stress, demoralization, lack of incentives, and poor leadership.

Politically, Arab contemporary experiences indicate that any democratic trends have been short-lived. Lebanon, which had a free press, active competitive political parties, and relatively open elections before its self-inflicted destructiveness, was the exception. In the 1990s, Jordan, Egypt, Tunisia, and Yemen could point to democratic trends worthy of note, and yet Yemen seems to have stumbled into such a bloody local war between its north and south that its consequences inevitably will retard democratic aspirations. The governments of Algeria, Egypt, Iraq, and Tunisia battle their domestic opposition with repressive measures and elect their presidents by ridiculously fabricated results (often in the ninetieth percentile). The sad fact is that at the end of the twentieth century there is still no Arab state that enjoys continuous constitutional rule, a competitive party system, free press, and supremacy of citizens' power.

Finally, another approach to portraying the limitations of reform experiences of the Arab world is by relating them to an existing conceptual model of planned change. An influential framework distinguishes between transactional change and transformational change (Warner Burke and

George Litwin's model as explained in French and Bell 1995, 85). *Transactional change* variables involve creating first-order, evolutionary adaptations in which features of the organization are changed but its fundamental nature remains the same. In contrast, *transformational,* or second-order, *change* is revolutionary and fundamental; in it the nature of the organization is altered in significant ways (French and Bell 1995, 85).

In applying this model, reform efforts of the Arab states appear stuck at the first-order (transactional) change level. Generally, reform agendas are preoccupied with managerial issues of personnel, simplification of procedures, job descriptions and classifications, computerization, and a myriad of low-impact organizational tinkering. To transcend this level to that of a transformational change will require certain conditions. Foremost is that of having transformational leaders who inspire followers to transcend their own self-interest for the good of the organization and who are capable of having a profound and extraordinary effect on their followers. This need is qualitatively different from the requirements of transactional leaders "who guide or motivate their followers in the direction of established goals by clarifying role and task requirements" (Robbins 1989, 329).

Transformational leaders are not confined to established levels or preexisting standards of performance. They are visionaries who motivate their followers and inspire them to new heights of achievement by example, commitment, skills, and professional ethics. Reform efforts in the Arab states suffer from a lack of leaders who have the capacity to manage transformational change and from an inflexible political context that prohibits any serious attempt at such fundamental change.

NOTES

1. *The Federalist,* no. 76.
2. I received copies of several of these reports (in Arabic) while writing a working paper for the Cairo conference, commissioned by the AOAD.
3. Hashemite Kingdom of Jordan, Civil Service Commission and Institute of Public Administration, "Project for Developing Public Administration in Jordan 1990–1993" (unpublished report, July 17, 1991).
4. Iraq's report on administrative reform, 1993 (memo).
5. Ibid.
6. Arab Republic of Syria, Committee for Administrative Development, State Planning Authority, Prime Minister's Office, "Draft of Administrative Development Plan for the Arab Republic of Syria" (unpublished report, August 1991).
7. Kingdom of Saudi Arabia, Higher Committee for Administrative Reform, Saudi Arabia, "The Executive Program of the General Plan of Administrative Reform" (in Arabic) (n.d.).
8. Saudi Arabia's public debt increased dramatically after the Gulf War. Because of the government's secrecy, it is extraordinarily difficult to gauge the health of the Saudi economy. According to Clay Chandler, *Washington Post,* October 28,

1994, the Gulf War and lavish spending left the oil giant with limited choices. A frequently cited figure about Saudi debt is $70 billion, mostly to domestic banks.

9. Three reports in Arabic from the office of the Tunisian prime minister: "Administrative Reform Activities" in 1990 and 1991 and "Organizational Frameworks of Agencies Responsible for Administrative Reform" in 1992.

10. *Middle East International,* no. 473 (April 15, 1994), p. 11.

11. Sudan, Prime Minister's Office, "National Program for Reforming and Revolutionizing Public Service" (in Arabic) (January 1990), 42 pages.

12. Report submitted to the 30th ordinary session of the General Assembly of the Arab Organization of Administrative Development, Cairo, October 17–18, 1993.

13. Qatar, draft of the Civil Service Commission's "Program for the Developmental Plan of 1992–93 to 1994–95" (in Arabic) (June 1992), 62 pages.

14. Republic of Yemen, office of the prime minister, "Program for National Building and Political, Economic, Financial, and Administrative Reform" (in Arabic) (January 1992), 164 pages.

5

Egypt: An Exhausted System

*The Egyptian official was the oldest in the history of civilization.
. . . Even the Pharaohs themselves, he thought, were but officials
appointed by the gods of heaven to rule the Nile Valley by means
of religious rituals and of administrative, economic and organizational regulations. Ours was a valley of good-natured peasants
who bowed their heads in humility to the good earth but whose
heads were raised with pride if they joined the government apparatus. Then would they look upwards to the ascending ladder
of grades which reached right to the doorstep of the gods in
heaven.*

Naguib Mahfouz[1]

STRUCTURAL DIMENSIONS

Egypt's sense of history is evidenced in the first sentence of its 1977 constitution: "We the masses of Egypt working on this glorious land since the
dawn of history and civilization . . . " The constitution acknowledges the
authority of the people as "supreme," the "source" of all authority in society. It declares government as a republic, headed by an elected president.
The Egyptian people are part of the Arab nation, Islam is the religion of
the state, and Arabic is the official language (Articles 1 and 2).

The application of many of these constitutional principles and values,
however, is an entirely different matter. Actually, the compatibility of
constitutional principles with practices of governments in most developing nations is a predicament. Although the gap between rhetoric and reality may expand or contract from one country to another, in general it remains large. In Egypt, the problem of practicing lofty constitutional
provisions is a contentious matter within and without the political system.
To understand how this system operates, it is necessary to define its structural components and their relationships. Currently, five institutional
structures hold varying levels of power and influence over public policy
decisions.[2]

The first structure is the *presidency*. It includes the president, his advisers, and the institutional context within which they operate. This is the most critical center of authority in the Egyptian political system, which "is dominated by the president who has either been granted, or has accumulated, vast powers" (Owen 1994, 193). The president even regulates the exercise of power by all others through various direct and indirect processes of action, including the use of extensive police and security forces.

The presidential selection method in Egypt illustrates the tensions between being democratic in theory but practicing something else. After the ruling party's candidate is nominated by a two-thirds majority of Majlis El-Shaab, the People's Council, his name only is placed on ballots for public referendum. The tenure is six years, and the officeholder may succeed himself indefinitely. In fact, since 1955 only three men have occupied the presidency of Egypt: Gamal Abdul-Nasser, Anwar el-Sadat, and Hosni Mubarak. Nasser died in office, Sadat was killed while in office, and Mubarak is still in office (a term renewal in the fall of 1995 extended his tenure into the twenty-first century). No president yet has succeeded another living president. Looking at this experience, one discovers that a de facto order of president-for-life has evolved. So far, the average tenure of a president has been about fourteen years.

The *military* is the second structure. They provide the foundation for the president's power and offer the main tools for enforcing his will. Since the 1970s, presidents have tried to serve or satisfy the interests of the military without appearing subservient to them. In fact, President Anwar El-Sadat made a point of the role of the military as servant and not the master of the order. He rotated and fired his chiefs of staff as often as he could get away with it to demonstrate this point. Sadat listened to the military and served its interests but sought to keep military leaders out of political decisions and to limit their interference in nonmilitary affairs.

The presidency and the military establishment maintain a sort of equilibrium that seems to serve both interests well. This balance is the result of subtle practices and implicit policies of deterrence that have operated since the days of President Gamal Abdul-Nasser—namely, the military leaders keep out of the political fray, and the president keeps their interests and concerns at the top of his agenda.

The executive branch, the third structure, has two major allied components: the cabinet and the bureaucracy. The cabinet is headed by the prime minister and includes the political appointees of the prime minister, deputy prime ministers, ministers, and deputy ministers. The prime minister and his appointees share with the president the responsibility of initiating public policies and providing directions to ministries and executive agencies. Collectively they share responsibility for preparing the public budget, incurring debt, proposing laws, and preparing the national development plan. The president, the cabinet, and other heads of agencies rely on the bureaucracy to carry out their duties.

Bureaucracy provides continuity, information, and the expertise needed for the execution of public decisions. Relations between political appointees and the bureaucracy, however, are not always logical or harmonious in spite of their many linkages as makers and enforcers of the same policies. A differentiation is made between the executive institutions of the cabinet and the bureaucracy in terms of the origin and the legitimacy of power as well as the level of expertise in exercising it. The cabinet and the prime minister are appointed by the president. These appointments represent political interests favored by the regime. Appointees also are individuals of wealth and influence, who boast family connections, personal friendships, and above all loyalty to the president and the ruling party.

In contrast, the bureaucracy in Egypt is a historical, cumulative human force, hired and retained over the years in accordance with existing laws and regulations. The result is a huge structure extending throughout the society; its rigid routine, selective application of the rules, and reputation for corruption and mismanagement of programs are the rock upon which waves of political decisions and actions can be shattered or reduced to nothingness, and with impunity. The image of the Egyptian bureaucracy is made even worse because it is frequently used as a scapegoat by political leaders to rationalize failed policies.

The fourth structure is the *legislative branch,* which consists of Majlis el-Shaab, or People's Council, and Majlis el-Shura, or Consultation Council. Majlis el-Shaab (henceforth referred to as the parliament) is a classically weak legislative institution with all the features of a parliamentary system, at least in appearance if not in substance. According to the constitution, the Egyptian parliament legislates, approves public policy decisions, approves the budget, and exercises a watchdog function over the executive branch. Its members are elected by direct, secret ballots. The constitution provides that at least one-half of the members will consist of farmers and labor (Article 87).

The Consultation Council is a unique body that has no legislative or executive responsibilities. It consists of no fewer than 132 members, one-third appointed by the president and the rest elected by the people through a direct, secret ballot. This council provides advice to the president and to the parliament on matters such as constitutional amendments, the national socioeconomic development plan, treaties, laws, and any matter of public policy referred to it by the president.

Extraconstitutional political institutions and configurations make up the fifth structure. These include political parties, unions, the partisan

press, and commercial, industrial, and agricultural interest groups. A map
of this structure might be said to have three distinct colors:

1. One group is organizations that have the upper hand in the power
structure and are well connected with the regime. They enjoy an open door
to the government's resources, jobs, and influence. The best example is the
National Democratic Party of Egypt (the ruling party).

2. Opposition groups consist of an assortment of political organizations espousing different degrees of opposition from the right and from the
left of the party in power. The Islamists are the most formidable, having
solid "connections with the street," an Arabic idiom meaning grassroots
support. They are well organized and have been in active opposition to the
government since the presidency of Anwar El-Sadat.

But Islamists are not a monolithic movement. They range from the
conservative establishment of the Muslim Brothers to the radicals who are
waging a protracted campaign against the state and Mubarak's National
Democratic Party. Recently some of these groups have resorted to violent
acts against individuals in government and against economic sectors such
as tourism—at enormous financial cost to the economy. Among the known
organizations on the radical side are the Islamic Group and the Islamic
Jihad. "The two groups share the goal of replacing Egypt's secular government with an orthodox Islamic state, but they differ over tactics, compete for funding, and have personal rivalries" (Murphy 1994, 79).

3. Diverse guilds and professional associations represent lawyers,
physicians, engineers, writers, journalists, students, labor unions, and others. They maintain their organizational identities but align with existing
political parties on various policy questions. The regime occasionally
seeks to co-opt influential leaders from the opposition through symbolic
gestures of recognition by the president and policy concessions on mar-
ginal issues or by inclusion in the extensive patronage system of the ruling
party. Opposition leaders who patronize the regime quickly lose legitimacy
and are excluded from the ranks of the core opposition.

PUBLIC POLICY FORMULATION AND ITS CONTEXT

To understand how Egypt formulates public policy one must first understand fundamental attributes of the larger political order. Policymaking in
Egypt, as in most developing countries, involves a wide range of activities:
establishing values, allocating resources, setting procedures and rules, and
developing grand strategic designs. Generally, policymaking receives
greater attention at the macro level, where major departures or new initiatives take place. Nevertheless, the many decisions on specific programs of
limited scope underscore basic features of the political process.

To learn how reform and development decisions are made in Egypt (and to what effect) is to identify centers of power and the strategic institutions that assist the exercise of such power. It is vital to recognize the qualities that distinguish political from administrative actions and to focus on issues of implementation. It is here where the realization of reform objectives is determined by the level of managerial professionalism and the distinction of organizational responsibility.

In essence, reform and development are composed of many decisions and choices among various possible alternatives. Such decisions are ultimately linked together in a coherent strategic policy for action. In Egypt, as in all other Arab countries, the economic role of the state is usually dominant. The state assumes patriarchal responsibilities of feeding, educating, and employing the populace; increasing agricultural productivity; industrializing the society; training and equipping the military; and maintaining a semblance of order (Richards and Waterbury 1990, 2). All this is in the midst of an explosive population growth and problematic military expenditures that are often beyond the economic capacity of the country.

The republican system in Egypt is less than fifty years old. Not including General Muhammad Naguib (who occupied the office for a short period as a front-man for the Revolutionary Military Council of the Free Officers that toppled the monarchy in 1952), only three men have held the presidency during this time. Each of the three succeeding presidents left his personal mark on government: structure, overall policies, order of priorities, and the primary constituency served by public policy.

Under Abdul-Nasser, the postcolonial state assumed a mode of economic expansion and intervention. The government proclaimed socialism as its doctrine and proceeded to nationalize major industries and services. The state became the owner and manager of numerous enterprises and businesses ranging from airlines to hotels and from steel industries to telephone and electric utilities. Perhaps one of the most outstanding traits of Nasser's regime was the appeal to a much larger constituency both inside and outside the country than had been created by any other ruler in the modern history of Egypt.

After Anwar el-Sadat became president in 1970, he departed from Nasser's approach and policies in fundamental ways. He declared a new economic policy, Infitah, which was to liberalize the economy, encourage private ownership of means of production, entice foreign capital, and limit the economic power of the public sector. By design or default, Sadat's constituency narrowed considerably in comparison with Nasser's. He appeared less interested in the application of his political power to details and to small decisions. Instead, he flamboyantly pursued strategic economic and foreign policy matters. Not surprisingly, Sadat's basic support came from business interests that benefited from his policy and from elites who enjoyed the new liberal political and economic stance of the state.

The transition from Nasser to Sadat is illustrative not only of the highly personal manner in which the responsibilities of the presidency have been executed but also of dramatic discontinuities in public policy. Sadat tempered Nasser's state socialism by his policy of Infitah. He sought to replace the Arab Socialist Union with an experiment in multiparty politics. Sadat nurtured the Islamic right so as to outflank Nasserites and elements of the political left, at one time the dominant force in Egyptian politics. In the area of foreign relations, Sadat replaced the Soviet Union, Egypt's stalwart ally during a decade and a half of conflict with Israel, with an Egyptian-U.S. axis founded on the normalization of Egyptian-Israeli relations in 1978 and the dismantling of Nasser's pan-Arab policies (Palmer, Leila, and Yassin 1988, 6).

Sadat may have introduced many spectacular shifts in foreign policy, but he did little to strengthen the domestic capabilities of the Egyptian bureaucracy. In spite of the optimistic expectations of Sadat's Infitah for economic development, reliance on the traditionally lethargic bureaucracy continued, and the developmental pledge of Infitah simply did not materialize. Intentionally or not, Sadat's policies disengaged the state from his predecessor's practices of direct involvement and economic activism. Rather, Sadat favored a policy of limited and selective intervention. His policies benefited some businesses, attracted scant foreign investment capital, deepened political patronage, and continually added newly alienated segments of the population to the ranks of the opposition.

Repeatedly, Sadat blamed and attacked what he called "centers of power" that work to augment their wealth and influence. Yet his policies, particularly the Infitah, appeared to make political rather than economic sense. The government evaded any application of stringent economic reforms that might require fundamental adjustments or radical change. After almost a year of negotiations with the IMF, Egypt agreed in 1976 to implement a set of economic reform measures. Among these were cutting the budget deficit, floating the Egyptian currency, and reducing the subsidies of certain consumable items. Although it is not totally clear what these items were, it seems that the subsidies of basic staple products were targeted for elimination.

In January 1977 food riots broke out during which citizens protested a price increase on basic food items. In these violent displays, scores of people were killed or wounded. The public explosion forcefully drove home a powerful message, namely, that not only were technical decisions of economic and financial reform at stake but also conditions for the political survival of the leadership. The turn of events emphasized the political risk of advocating any change that might further deprive the poor of the essentials of living.

The following year, as a result of the Camp David accord, Egypt lost concessional lending from the Gulf states. The government managed to shore up the economy through internal actions, such as increasing Suez Canal tolls, stimulating the tourism sector, increasing the price of domestic oil, and capitalizing on remittances from Egyptians working abroad. Also, pursuant to the Camp David agreement, a U.S. aid package helped to shore up economic conditions in the short run and to open the door for more borrowing from the Paris Club countries.

But the effect of inward-looking policies of Sadat, after an assertive role for Egypt in the Arab world under Nasser, was a retreat that caused several regressive cycles. First, Egypt lost the confidence and trust of the Arab nationalist movements when it defected from the Arab consensus by signing the Camp David agreement with Israel in 1978. The vitriolic reaction of the Arab world and the expulsion of Egypt from the Arab League were watersheds in contemporary Arab history. These acts resulted in a serious slide of inter-Arab politics into a phase of acrimony, disarray, and confusion. Second, Egypt became dependent on its special relationship with the United States, which placed Egypt in the position of the enforcer of U.S. policies in the region. From a U.S. perspective, Egypt's shattering of Arab unanimity in 1978 was a courageous act; the Arab world viewed it differently, regarding Sadat as a betrayer of Arab national interests. Whatever verdict one accepts, this period must be regarded as the beginning of the current political crisis of the Arab states. The results include deeper divisions among the states, distrust among the leaders, an inward orientation of Arab politics, and a strategic decline of the Arabs' strength in all their international dealings.

Hosni Mubarak's election as president in 1981 seemed to offer a reasonable prospect of ensuring continuity of Sadat's policies. Mubarak had been a major player during Sadat's regime, as vice president and heir apparent. But shortly after his ascendance to the presidency, Mubarak faced compelling economic realities that required new initiatives. Some of the problems he faced were the burden of public debt, a chronic budget deficit, high unemployment, and overall low productivity in the public sector. At the internal level, Mubarak's policies (as those of his predecessor) proclaimed administrative reform as a top priority. He also announced changes to vitalize the private sector, encourage privatization, and continue liberalization of the financial markets and the banking system. On the external front, the Egyptian leadership continued and deepened political alliances with the United States and the Gulf countries to huge economic advantage, particularly in debt reduction.

Nevertheless, by 1990, Egypt was insolvent. When the Gulf War erupted, Egypt played a central role in supporting U.S. war efforts and the overall U.S. position, placing the largest military contingent in the field except for that of the United States. As a result, the United States "forgave" Egypt $7 billion of its debt, the Gulf states "donated" $6 billion, and the Paris club countries "waived" 50 percent of the total debt up to $10 billion.[3]

On its own, Egypt began some economic initiatives to liberalize its banking laws, strengthen the authority and independence of the Central Bank, and increase competitiveness in the banking sector. Achievements in economic reform enriched the elites and a narrow segment of the business sector, but the poor grew poorer and multiplied in numbers. Inflation and elimination of state subsidies resulted in price increases in many essential services and commodities. "Taxi fares, electricity, gasoline, cooking oil, sugar, meat, rice, and some types of bread have all risen in cost at a time when salaries have not kept pace with the cost of living and the economy is in recession" (Murphy 1994, 79).

Formal approval of reform policies is given by the cabinet. A ministry designated for public enterprises and development is headed by Atif Obeid, who is also entrusted with negotiations with the IMF. On February 14, 1994, Obeid reported to the economic committee of the parliament about progress made in the government's reform efforts. The following paragraphs summarize Obeid's report, which is considered to reflect current thinking within Mubarak's government.[4]

Minister Obeid explained how state investment historically fell into three types of organizational structures: (1) companies of the public sector that operate like business enterprises, (2) economic authorities that monitor economic activities but differ from a business company or corporation (examples: Suez Canal authority, petroleum, and railroads), and (3) service entities that are organized to produce commodities or deliver services but are not required to cover all their expenses from their own revenues. In the third group, more attention is given to service delivery than to economic value of performance. According to Obeid, the government's current focus is on reform within the first group—the public sector companies and enterprises; in the second and third types of entities, little if any change is planned.

What, then, are the proposed reforms? They are aimed primarily at preserving investments made in the first group of companies. Obeid called for caution while expressing worry that loss of such investment would negatively affect the economy, revenues, and employment level. "These investments are part of the historical savings of the country, and savings do not influence development except in a slight way," he maintained. The return on savings is added once, whereas investment has recurring returns. Return from savings is similar to the situation of a landlord who receives the rent and spends it without investing in additional economic activities.

The minister also pointed out in his report to the parliament that a population increase of 2.2 percent annually translates into an annual increase of approximately 1.5 million.[5] Also expected is an increase of 500,000 in the labor force, of which only 400,000 can be employed. Therefore, to reach full employment in 2000, Egypt must create 700,000 jobs annually. In terms of investment capital needed to reach this goal, a minimum of $4.4 billion annually (14 billion Egyptian pounds) is required.

Today, 314 companies in the public sector group are marked for reform. They have a total invested capital of about $26 billion (84.3 billion Egyptian pounds). Of this capital, 36.6 percent is owned by the state and 63.4 percent is borrowed (hence owned by someone other than the state). For various reasons, this investment is producing a very low return of about 6 percent. Reform, therefore, must aim both at preserving the capital and increasing return on investment. According to the minister, the estimated value of investment is book value, whereas market value is higher and could reach 200 billion Egyptian pounds.

Following the minister's report, discussion focused on concerns over the deterioration of industries that employ large numbers of people at low wages. One speaker criticized employment practices; complaining that "too many employees are supervising other employees and producing nothing," he cited examples such as "two of every three employees in Egypt are supervisors, while in Japan the ratio is one to eighteen." Another person referred to external pressures attempting to force privatization on the country. The advice he gave to government: "Dodge these pressures if you cannot, outright, reject them."

Evading and stalling external pressures by donors, creditors, the World Bank, and the IMF is what the government did. Since 1991, when Egypt agreed to an "economic reform" program with IMF, the World Bank, and international creditors and donors, it has made little headway in selling its public sector companies. The companies account for 70 percent of the country's industry.[6] Between 1991 and 1996, of Egypt's 314 public enterprises slated for reform, 3 were sold outright by the government, 10 were liquidated, and 10 were sold in employee buyouts.[7] The government's reluctance is attributed to fear that layoffs by these companies could swell the unemployment rate, estimated to be as high already as 20 percent.[8] With a new government in place after the November 1995 elections, expediting the privatization effort is assured.

But not all Mubarak's problems are economic ones. Theoretically and formally, the political system is pluralistic and thus political opposition groups operate freely within applicable laws and rules. Taking advantage of this during 1987 elections, the Muslim Brothers became the major opposition party. They received thirty-five seats after forming a coalition with the Labor and the Liberal parties. (After the 1984 elections they held only 9 seats.) An editorial in *Rose el-Yousef,* a liberal, influential Egyptian journal, is instructive:[9]

> April 22 is a day with special significance for millions of Egyptians. . . .
> On that day, the doors of Majlis El-Shaab will open for a new session.
> For the first time since Egypt experienced the parliamentary system, the
> opposition wins a hundred seats in the parliament. This is an entirely
> positive development. It is in the interest of democracy, which we are
> now building in our country, despite all the noise and clamor that will
> follow. What adds to the importance of this session is that we are about
> to begin the implementation of the second five-year plan of economic re-
> form. [My translation from the Arabic].

Today, opposition newspapers are replete with criticisms and protests against government policies and actions. Opposition groups regularly report stories of corruption, inefficiency, and cronyism in government. But the ruling political party, headed by the president and utilizing the powers of governmental institutions, has managed to render the opposition almost inconsequential when making policy decisions. The complete dominance of the ruling oligarchy has reduced opposition parties to political oblivion by disallowing them a role in the system, as in the November election of 1995. As Owen (1994, 194) expresses it, Egypt is a "system of controlled pluralism [which] extends far beyond that of the parties and parliamentary elections to embrace all of Egypt's associational life."

Thus, Egypt is in reality a de facto one-political-party system, under a president-for-life, within a continuing "situation in which soci-economic and religious tensions are managed by a combination of controlled multi-partyism and the use of an expanded Emergency Law" (Owen 1994, 194). Certainly, the declining economy and the growing political repression have alienated the regime and weakened its popular support. As Haykal points out with alarm, Egypt is at "a crossroads, at which we can either choose of our own free will where we head next, or failing that, prevailing circumstances will make the choice for us."[10]

With no influence over policy and without the advantages of the infamous patronage system, the opposition is driven to ever more vitriolic attacks on the regime. This situation is a far cry from a national-unity government. Egyptian opposition parties do not enjoy what Nelson Mandela described best on the eve of the election victory of his party, the African National Congress of South Africa, which won over 62 percent of the vote: "Every political party which is involved must feel that they are exercising power and that they are not expected just to rubber-stamp the decision of some other political organization."[11]

Despite constitutional and legal provisions, Egypt has failed to reap the advantages of political pluralism (*ta'addudiya*) and to prevent a single party from monopolizing power. Sharing political power within the system and permitting the emergence of different centers of power are prerequisites for accountability of power holders to elected representatives and to the public at large (Leca 1994, 49). The absence of authentic pluralism means that public policymaking prohibits one group from counteracting another and denies political representation to a variety of organized political, economic, and social interests in the society. Enjoying vast and virtually unchallenged power, the president has no requirement to abide by such values as transparency or accountability. This lopsided power division is maintained by the absence of an effective legal framework (applied constitutional provisions) that protects rights and decides outcomes through legitimate processes.

Government by the few has deepened popular disenchantment. In this regard, reaction within the Islamist movements has broken down the normal boundaries of responsible political opposition, and some elements have resorted to violence and inflicted pain on the society. Since spring 1992, Egypt has experienced an upsurge of Islamic militant violence resulting in scores of bombings, murders, and many other casualties. Even if Mubarak's regime does not seem in danger at the present, his continuation in power is totally dependent on support of the military. "But the militants' campaign has dealt a heavy blow to Egypt's $3 billion-a-year tourism industry. It has also complicated Cairo's efforts at economic reform and focused an unwelcome international spotlight on its human rights behavior" (Murphy 1994, 78).

Nevertheless, the socioeconomic context of public policy in Egypt is changing. Certain sectors of the economy and public services such as health, education, welfare programs, and public housing are in decline. As military expenditures consume more and more of the limited resources available, and the population increase continues unabated, significant improvements in these services are pushed further into the future. Public policy issues are testing the technical capabilities of the system and stretching its resources to the limit. This is most clearly illustrated in the decline of the physical environment and the uncontrollable urban concentration of population. A national agency has been established to cope with the deteriorating condition of the environment. "But government action so far has been largely hampered by the dispersal of environment policies and concerns among different sectors and ministers" (el-Sherbini 1993, 3).

Clearly, state policy has been one of solving domestic economic needs through more borrowing. Public enterprises became notorious for their dependence on easy credit. Government, too, dealt with budget deficits by more borrowing. To illustrate, in 1983 Egypt had a $700 per capita GNP and an external debt of $15.2 billion and was listed among the middle-income countries of the world. In 1992, Egypt was listed among low-income economies with a $640 per capita GNP and a total external debt of $40 billion.[12] Since 1980, total debt has regularly exceeded the country's GNP.

Since 1970, the regimes of Sadat and Mubarak have introduced only cosmetic and insubstantial changes in political, economic, and administrative systems. "To achieve the objectives of development and modernization," emphasized Yousef Wali, "there must be a clear vision, political will, and a competent administrative apparatus to realize the vision and the political will."[13] Such a vision of the future of Egypt, if there is one, has yet to be articulated and communicated, let alone carried out. Government's claims of building the administrative and institutional capacities have failed to result in notable improvements, either. And the political system remains centralized, oligarchic, and unwilling to let other groups into the policymaking process.

Perhaps the most notable aspect of Egyptian politicians is their skill in escaping responsibility and passing the blame for policy failure. The following example, however anecdotal, is expressive. On February 11, 1994, while in my hotel room in Cairo, I watched a popular television program called *Bedoun Ihrag* ("Without Embarrassment"). The program was attention-capturing not only because the guests were all cabinet members but also because of the unorthodox manner of interviewing. At the start of each interview, the guest raised his hand and repeated after the host: "I swear to tell the truth and nothing but the truth." Then the host proceeded with the interview:

Host (to the minister of public health): "The government says that health conditions are well, but half of the youth in Egypt today is unfit for military service because of poor nutrition, poor health, and disease, true or false?"
The Minister: "True."
Host (to the minister of industry): "The Production Cup is awarded to the worthy and to the unworthy *[lelli yeswa wille ma-yeswa]* true or false?"
The Minister: "True."

After each question, the respondent went on to blame a previous law or procedure that contributed to the bad situation. At no point did any of them outline a program or a solution of his own to the problem discussed.

Considering the mounting pressures and problems Egypt faces at the present, a compelling question repeatedly surfaces: How was Egypt able to muddle through thus far? The answer, perhaps, is in the ability of its leadership to manipulate a mixed strategy of reliance on outside help from various sources and initiation of reforms on the margin of the system that entail few political risks. The strategy of the political leadership appears to have two main elements.

First, to shore up deteriorating economic conditions, Egypt resorted to borrowing, which helped relieve immediate budgetary pressures, particularly in the 1980s, but meant the accumulation of enormous debt. The U.S. aid program to Egypt, especially after the Camp David agreement, as well as grants and concessionary loans from the Gulf states, helped to check deteriorating economic standards and to make up for some of the increase in population. Moreover, during the past several years, remittances from Egyptians working abroad have contributed significantly to national income.

Consequently, Egypt's economy today is more dependent on uncontrollable outside forces than on domestic productivity. Most important sources of income are exogenous: external debt, foreign aid, and workers' remittances as well as revenues from tourism, the Suez Canal, and the burgeoning oil industry. In contrast, the importance of productive sectors such as agriculture and industry has fallen sharply in recent years, according to el-Sherbini (1993, 6). Consider that both agriculture and manufacturing accounted for a combined share of only 33 percent of total GDP in 1990 (el-Sherbini 1993, 6), this despite the claims by the Ministry of Agriculture that the amount of cultivable land doubled between 1982 and 1994.[14]

Second, Egypt's political leadership appears more active in deferring solutions than in facing problems. But, as Egypt has discovered, buying time and avoiding political and economic risks do not even conserve the status quo. Egypt's experience indicates that conditions have a tendency to deteriorate rather than to remain as is. Alan Richards (1991, 1721) vividly describes the situation as follows:

> Egypt is a special case, because it offers the paradoxical spectacle of exceptionally serious economic problems receiving only a dilatory policy response. . . . A huge but relatively ineffective state confronts interest groups which are themselves too weak to impose their program . . . on the rest of the society, yet are strong enough to block or subvert reforms which threaten their short-run interests.

In the midst of such socioeconomic conditions, the perceived legitimacy of Mubarak's regime continues to erode, claims of popular support by state-run mass media notwithstanding. As Caryle Murphy (1994, 79) reports:

> Mubarak's administration and his ruling National Democratic party have also suffered a remarkable erosion of public confidence since the 1991 Persian Gulf war. Increasingly, Egyptians express anger over the arrogance, insensitivity, incompetence, and alleged corruption of government they say has been too long in power. This disaffection was most apparent during last October's referendum on a third term for Mubarak. . . . This, and the patently absurd official results of the vote [an 84.2 percent

turnout and a 96.3 percent "yes" vote] were viewed with open contempt by many Egyptians.

No search for a cure for Egypt's socioeconomic crisis will be success-ful without incorporating two fundamental features. The first is to reform the political process to be more inclusionary and to reorient public policy to be more equitable in its outcomes. This requires progressing from what Jean Leca (1994, 54) calls "facade democracy" (*dimuqratiyya shikliyya*), an authoritarian government masquerading as people's democracy, to a democracy with legal, pluralistic, representative, and power-sharing di-mensions. The second is to improve the domestic productive capacities of the state and to rationalize its archaic administrative practices. Developing professional management with neutral competence to improve the institu-tional capacity of the system is at the core of needed reforms.

BUREAUCRACY AND REFORM

Classic bureaucratic theory, as conceived by its founder, German sociolo-gist Max Weber, defines an idealized instrument of modern government that is most efficient, effective, and technically superior to any form of or-ganization and management known before. On the surface, Egypt's bu-reaucracy appears to possess all the elements of the Weberian model, such as official jurisdictions, division of labor, office hierarchy, written docu-ments, career people, rules, and training. In practice, however, the Egypt-ian bureaucracy is anything but efficient and effective or technically su-perior. It seems almost impervious to change and adversely positioned to achieve rational action and responsible behavior.

Throughout recent history, the bureaucracy in Egypt has been viewed as a major source of many societal problems and difficulties. To Morroe Berger (1957), the traditional conduct of bureaucrats appears inconsistent with organizational rationality as designated by official forms and rules. More recent critics (Ayubi 1980; Palmer, Leila, and Yassin 1988) conclude that the Egyptian bureaucracy is a major detriment to national socioeco-nomic development. Such bleak assessments abound; the issue has become not whether the Egyptian bureaucracy suffers a multitude of problems but whether it is changeable or reformable at all.

The basic bureaucratic shortcomings that seem to draw general agree-ment from analysts and observers are overstaffing, low wages, low pro-ductivity, and corruption. But administrative problems are more compli-cated than a listing of ills and defects would indicate. Some of these negatives are embedded in the structure of government and others are the effects of attitudes and behaviors that bureaucrats have internalized over generations.

No doubt, the political context has contributed significantly to many of these bureaucratic pathologies. As indicated earlier, public policy formulation is centralized and oligarchic but also fragmented. Today, Egypt has thirty-two ministries, in addition to two hundred agencies that report to these ministries. Under such a proliferation of governmental structures, fragmentation of policymaking and poor coordination in implementation are daunting realities. Many of the policy portfolios are created to accommodate special interests and to respond to political considerations rather than being dictated by common societal need. Fragmentation is best illustrated, for example, by the split up of the economic domain among four ministries that have very limited linkages (el-Sherbini 1993, 15).

Attempts at decentralization have achieved little. As an illustration, each of the twenty-nine governorates (*muhafazah*) representing the administrative structure of the country has offices and representatives from key ministries. Legally, these officials are under the command of the governor (*muhafez*), who is appointed by a presidential decree. In practice, however, the functional officials report directly to their central ministries in Cairo. This orientation toward seeking direction or approval from central offices when making decisions has often resulted in conflicts and weakened the very objective of the decentralization process (el-Sherbini 1993, 16).

Policies of public employment are antiquated and self-defeating. Two related aspects illustrate the dilemma. First is the policy of guaranteeing jobs to college graduates, which was introduced in the 1960s. Second is an unparalleled and outlandish overstaffing.

The government policy of guaranteeing employment to college graduates has flooded public offices with employees who often did not know what they were hired to do. Graduates hired by government often did not have suitable skills to meet current demands of the market nor did they know in advance what particular tasks they were to perform. The consequences of this policy have not been limited to overemployment. Automatic hiring also rendered ineffectual many modern techniques of managing human resources, at both procedural and substantive levels. Pay scale, job classification, and job analysis as well as evaluation of performance all became meaningless procedures or forms to be filled out for no definite purpose. By the 1990s, lists of applicants became so extensive that many graduates had to wait ten years before getting their application reviewed for promised jobs. Instead of repealing or revising a policy that had failed, the government simply let it atrophy. Such an official practice deepens public skepticism, and once more illustrates government's selective application of laws and procedures.

Overstaffing is a serious dilemma for other reasons. Data gathered from government studies in 1994 indicate that there are 4.3 million public service employees and 3.7 million employees of government-owned businesses.[15] Reports on privatization by specialized agencies of the government reveal incredible information, a summary of which was published in *Rose el-Yousef* in July 1994. The claim is that 1.3 million employees are all that is needed to staff government offices and to deliver public services instead of the 4.3 million employed. And only 700,000 employees are needed for government-owned businesses, not 3.7 million.[16]

Revitalization of the Egyptian economy, improvements in the public and private sectors' productivity, the development of administrative institutional capacities, and so on all seem unattainable without radical surgery to eviscerate the big bulge in the bureaucratic structure. The predicament for the government stems from the fear that massive layoffs would instigate political risks the regime could not afford.[17] Conversely, taking no action would mean continuous deterioration of development efforts. In a society with about 20 percent unemployment the choices are increasingly narrowed. Fundamental reform to improve output, increase productive investment, eliminate waste, fight corruption, and so on require political will, know-how, professionalism, and the ability to evoke alternative approaches. Prospects for the demonstration of such qualities by the political leadership are not encouraging.

The institution of bureaucracy is a frequent topic of controversy even in the West (Goodsell 1994), but in Egypt the more pressing issue is whether bureaucracy is able in any way to assume the difficult task of national development. This notion is an old view (Thompson 1964, 100) that occasionally surfaces in the literature to disqualify bureaucracy from leading in the development effort because of its "inherent" propensity toward rigidity and control as well as its preoccupation with the immediate tasks' assignment. The standard conclusion: Bureaucracy is unfit to lead national development initiatives. The common reason: It is incapable of providing needed flexibility, innovation, and attention to strategic planning.

Nazih Ayubi (1980, 50) presents damning arguments against bureaucracy on several grounds: (1) It is bound to reject all projects that might challenge its relative levels of income and its other vested interests, and hence it will handicap economic growth by either public or private initiatives; (2) bureaucracy could become even worse if corruption proved to be the only possible way of getting things done or improving the income level of those working in public offices.

Corruption leads public officials to accept money for doing what they are under duty to do or not to do. Another form of corruption may involve not cash or noncash bribery but deviation from the normal duties of a public official in order to gain status, power, or privilege. Corrupt acts include misappropriation or misspending of public funds, protecting violators of the law, and exercising influence against meritorious applicants by promoting cronyism in public employment. Unquestionably, corruption damages democratic development and destroys the legitimacy of public decisions, resulting in a crippling effect on economic development.

To be sure, many critics emphasize the ills of bureaucracy based on actual performances and practices in countries such as Egypt. It is not true, however, that the problems of bureaucracy are global or universal. In many countries, ideas of reform have emanated from offices of the bureaucracy, which manage well and with integrity. International experiences inform us that when state policymakers are genuinely committed to reform, bureaucratic resistance can be overcome and positive response can be induced.

There are clear indications, based on examples from large developing states such as India and China (Feinberg, Echeverri-Gent, and Muller 1990) and from small states such as New Zealand (Sherwood 1992), Singapore (Quah 1991), and Jamaica (Kitchen 1989), that commitment to reform by political and administrative leaders has consistently and dramatically improved government performance. Even in the United States, where criticisms of bureaucracy are widespread, various reform initiatives at national and state levels have emphasized the importance of empowering employees to get results by stressing human resources development, decentralization, and executive leadership (Sherwood 1994, 10).

Thus, criticisms based on the inherent qualities of public organizations—considering them fatally flawed tools of socioeconomic development—are overstated. They deny the potential contributions of a professional administrative system that applies ethical standards of conduct and seeks to achieve public service in its most idealized sense. The contention here is that defects of bureaucratic actions are not the consequence of some sort of mutant institutional "genetics." Rather, they are learned behaviors that are constantly influenced and even shaped by political, economic, legal, and cultural contexts. Earlier, Max Weber (1947) himself conditioned the efficiency of the bureaucratic model on the type of authority system that commands it. According to Weber, only within a "legal-rational" system of authority can bureaucracy fulfill its official mandate. Consequently, a traditional authority system, or a corrupt one lacking in legitimacy, cannot benefit by the full range of capabilities and efficiencies that the bureaucratic model could advance.

In summary, to conceptualize bureaucracy as a monolith and to deny variations of professional competence, ethics, and dedication among bureaucratic institutions is to deny a significant part of human history. Indeed, a deeper look at many of the ills of bureaucracy often leads to the political domain. As Palmer, Leila, and Yassin (1988, 25) observe: "The Egyptian political system, in all candor, has not provided the bureaucracy with either clear directions or clear priorities, a phenomenon manifest in the morass of government rules and procedures, not to mention government ambivalence on such crucial issues as the graduates policy and the interaction between the public and private sectors."

Three nefarious aspects of bureaucratic functioning in Egypt that have come to exemplify it in the public mind are overregulation, excessive routine, and cumbersome procedures. As el-Sherbini (1993, 13) points out, a recent appraisal found about fifteen thousand laws with countless bylaws, creating frequent conflict and inconsistency in regulating the same matter. Moreover, such a proliferation of regulations creates laxity of enforcement as it breeds corruption in the application. Cumbersome procedures for a citizen seeking a simple license for a project or a permit for water connection, power supply, or any of the essential services could be an ordeal. However, the complexity seems to disappear after a side payment is made to the official or a higher authority interferes to cajole or prod the street-level bureaucrat to render his official duty. A businessman in Cairo related his personal experience to me:

> I need a license to open a small factory in Cairo that will employ initially about two dozen people. My product is made of wood and will save the country hard-currency by producing locally what is usually imported. I complied with every rule, filled every form, waited numerous hours in lobbies of public buildings, paid all fees, and still after a year have not received my license. Finally, I went to a senior official, whom we know personally, and asked for his help. He did telephone the official on my behalf. But the official got upset and became threatening. He told me that I am forcing him to take an adverserial position (a subtle threat of doing everything he can to deny me a license). . . . I could have saved myself all the above if I offered to pay early on.

This anecdotal evidence does not, of course, constitute a valid generalization. One could never determine how widespread corruption is without enormous investigative power and the machinery to use it. Based on coverage in Egyptian newspapers and conversations with several ordinary citizens, however, I have no doubt that corruption at various levels of government is a serious disease. The matter is grave because rules and regulations, despite their immense numbers, are totally ineffective in ensuring control of official conduct or serving citizens properly. "Excessive reliance on rules often produces organizations that are simultaneously overcontrolled and out of control" (Thompson 1993, 314). This is the situation in Egypt, where the very proliferation of rules and regulations has rendered them obsolete, counterproductive, and unobserved.

Moreover, these excessive rules and regulations inhibit investors and delay business transactions as they frustrate citizens. Not surprising then that simplification of procedures has been a part of every government reform program. Some changes actually have been implemented. It is definitely easier to receive a passport today than in the past, as it is easier to get a driver's license. But to conclude that government procedures and over-regulation are under control would be a monumental overstatement.

It is important to briefly define here some reforms that the government either is considering or has already approved. In recognition of the importance of administrative reform, almost two decades ago Egypt established a special portfolio for a minister of administrative development. The person in this position has been a catalyst for many administrative and economic reform measures and continues to carry such responsibilities.

A great deal of government energy has been consumed in formulating a new civil service law with new provisions for recruitment, merit rating, job classification, pay scale, promotion, evaluation, and so on. How this legislation, when enacted, could change entrenched old practices is not clear (Jreisat 1995).

The president of the Central Agency for Organization and Administration proudly cites the activities of his organization: "developing the civil service system, raising the efficacy of management, ensuring justice and equality in employment, and securing efficiency and productivity, etc."[18] It is in the area of recruitment of senior management that the government is most hopeful of results. The government claims competitive recruitment procedures and has built excellent training facilities and developed appropriate curricula with the help of Egyptian and U.S. experts.

Sensing a lack of information to make accurate policy analysis on issues, the government has created a Center for Information and Decision Support with state-of-the-art hardware and software. The center's service is extended through networks established with various other government offices. The overall purpose is to assist the decisionmaking process and to provide needed data to improve the process of policymaking. Other changes have been introduced involving work simplification, "model" government service delivery facilities, and so forth.

Finally, one can clearly see that reform efforts in Egypt have been selective and fragmentary. They are weak on strategic concerns and lack reliable monitoring and feedback to ensure implementation. The commitment of Egypt's leaders to reform after the Gulf crisis of the early 1990s is questionable. The forgiveness of debts at a large scale after the Gulf War offered the current leadership the opportunity to avoid risking reform measures and to claim victory for their maintenance policies. Lacking fortitude and foresight to push for restructuring and reform, the Gulf War opened the way for Egypt's leaders to favor a go-slow policy and to change only in measured steps what would preclude any political risk. The trouble is that all of the contemplated or approved reforms, even if carefully and diligently implemented, may be neither sufficient nor timely enough to make a significant difference in the development of Egypt or in solving its current socioeconomic problems. Perhaps "the irrepressible anger" about the situation will continue to be directed against the major culprit: the state and the government. But, as Leca (1994, 77) says, "In many Arab countries, this anger has still to find an idiom which would express, trigger and control the grievances. A great tradition is available, and Islamism fights to monopolize it."

NOTES

1. Naguib Mahfouz, an Egyptian novelist who received the Nobel Prize for Literature in 1988, in *Respected Sir.*

2. My discussion of institutional structures benefited from an interview in Cairo in February 1994 with Dr. Mustapha Said, a former minister of national economy of Egypt and a current member of the parliament.

3. Interview with John P. Spillane, minister-counselor for economic affairs, U.S. Embassy, Cairo, February 16, 1994.

4. I attended the meeting at which Obeid gave this report and took notes of the proceedings.

5. Under the best efforts of family planning, the rate of increase would be 1.7 to 1.8 percent annually.

6. *Christian Science Monitor,* April 15, 1996, p. 8.

7. Ibid.

8. Ibid.

9. *Rose el-Yousef,* no. 3071 (April 20, 1987), p. 3.

10. Mohammad Hassanain Haikal, "Egypt's Moment of Truth" (remarks in Arabic at book fair in Cairo), reported in *Mideast Mirror,* January 23, 1995.

11. *Tampa Tribune,* May 7, 1994, Nation/World, p. 4.

12. World Bank, *World Development Report 1995,* (New York: Oxford University Press), pp. 174, 204; World Bank, *World Development Report 1994* (New York: Oxford University Press), pp. 162, 200.

13. Interview with Yousef Wali, secretary general of the ruling National Democratic Party, deputy prime minister, and minister of agriculture, Cairo, February 15, 1994.

14. Ibid.

15. *Rose el-Yousef,* no. 3450 (July 25, 1994), p. 16.

16. Ibid.

17. Several thousand workers were laid off in the early months of 1994 because of sales of public corporations under the privatization policy. See *Rose el-Youssef* (July 25, 1994), p. 16.

18. Interview with the president of the Central Agency for Organization and Administration, Cairo, February 17, 1994.

6

Jordan:
Surviving Economic Scarcity

Pluralism thus entails tolerance, acceptance of majority rule, limited government, and protection of basic rights. The term "democratic rules" also has a power dimension: the sharing of power within the system, the emergence of different centers of power, and the accountability of power-holders to elected representatives and to public opinion.

Jean Leca[1]

STRUCTURAL DIMENSIONS

Jordan's system of government is constitutionally differentiated into executive, legislative, and judicial structures and functions. The executive branch is headed by the king, who exercises his authority through the prime minister and the cabinet. The monarchy is the most important institution in the country. The king appoints the prime minister, the president, and the members of the upper house of the parliament, judges, and other senior government and military functionaries. He commands the armed forces, approves and promulgates laws, declares war, concludes peace, and signs treaties. The king convenes, opens, adjourns, or dissolves the parliament at will, and he may order postponement of elections (Jreisat 1989; Nyrop, 1980). The judiciary is fairly independent in settling disputes, ensuring protection of basic rights, and providing interpretations of the law—when such issues are presented to courts for adjudication.

It is the Majlis el-Nuwaab—the parliament—that has recently attracted attention and instigated excitement in Jordanian politics. The parliament came into the limelight in 1989 when it undertook an experiment in liberalization. Before that, the governing structure in Jordan was similar to the situation elsewhere in the Arab world: A strong leader held the reins of power, and a bureaucracy managed daily affairs. A midway level of political appointees served in the cabinet at the personal pleasure of the king. Such a privilege has been extended to a select few, primarily as a reward for political loyalty and/or as an acknowledgment of family influence. Only infrequently did the need for technocratic skills or the merit of the appointee determine the choice for a cabinet nomination.

Compared to other Arab states, Jordan enjoys fairly competent public sector management, but the system has not been immune to incidents of corruption and mismanagement. Rumors are rampant about get-rich-quick schemes carried out by senior officials, particularly within the ever-expanding class of current and former political appointees. Fueling such rumors is the ostentatious display of wealth by many government ministers, with their opulent mansions, expensive automobiles, and showy lifestyles that could never be sustained through legitimate government pay. Occasionally, there is a government investigation or a parliamentary debate on mishandling of public funds or a contract. Rarely, however, is an official imprisoned or even notably penalized for embezzlement, malfeasance, or defrauding government. If an investigation is conducted, it drags on until it drops from public view, and the matter is forgotten.

It is difficult to verify or document corruption in societies bent on secretive dealings in conducting private business. What prevails is an environment of gossip, innuendo, and perhaps exaggerated claims of government corruption. The press, subservient and lacking professional journalistic competence, ends up perpetuating the public's view of the authorities as engaging in coverups and being unwilling to take earnest action against perpetrators. Despite recent liberalization and diversification of opinions, the Jordanian press remains hobbled by a modest democratic tradition and the absence of transparency in government actions. The press appears to have failed to perform a key role in the political and social change under way in the society. Deficient in its informational base and lacking independence of opinion because of its close identification with ruling political groups, the press is less than it could be at this phase of development. In Lewis Lapham's words, "a sycophantic press loses the habit of candor and learns to rely more heavily on the corporate or government spokesmen, to submit more graciously to the censorship imposed."[2]

A powerless and amateur press, in addition to substandard processes of accountability to the public, enables officials to violate their official mandates as well as citizens' rights and liberties without repercussions. The security apparatus (*mukhabarat*), for example, often exceeds its mandate and operates largely unchecked (Robins 1990, 18). Political reform activists have criticized security forces for excesses in spending as well as for untoward zeal in carrying out their assignments. The *mukhabarat* has a negative reputation among many citizens and is often viewed as an instrument of oppression.

Government policies, however, have not gone without occasional dramatic popular challenges. In April 1989, violent protests erupted and quickly spread throughout the country. The uprising (also known as the bread riots) became a watershed event that galvanized popular demands and forcefully communicated to those in power the festering grievances of the citizenry. "The catalyst was an increase in the price of fuel and food, decreed by an austerity program negotiated with the International Monetary Fund after Jordan defaulted on its $8.3 billion foreign debt" (Wilson 1994, 87). Protesters demanded far-reaching changes, of which the most significant were equity and political change. People were unwilling to bear the consequences of economic austerity measures while corrupt politicians and bureaucrats manipulated, mismanaged, and misspent public money. The public demanded replacement of political personalities closely associated with the economic deterioration. To ensure equity and fairness, the public pressed for a more representative political process. During the past three decades, no incident has threatened stability more than the bread riots of 1989.

The protests of 1989 instigated many reviews of public policies and practices both within and outside of the government. One consequence of the upheaval was that it hastened restoration of democratic representation and the resumption of parliamentary processes. Six months after the April riots, the first parliamentary elections since 1967 took place. Islamists won the largest bloc of seats (thirty-two out of eighty); many nationalists, independents, and leftists also gained office. Consequently, the new parliament appeared from the start to position itself to assume an active role in policymaking and in support of the reformist momentum generated by the food riots. Calls for changes in the political system, such as resignation of the cabinet, replacement of the prime minister, and election of a representative parliament, transcended the economic issues. In a sense, the government seemed to have had little choice in attempting the belt-tightening measures that had provoked the riots and contributed significantly to the decline in Jordan's per capita income by 38 percent between 1985 and 1990 (Wilson 1994, 87).

Learning from history, it would have behooved any Jordanian prime minister to study carefully the landmark political event of 1989. But in 1996 the government decided to remove subsidies on bread and animal feed, in line with IMF prescriptions. The price of bread doubled on August 13, 1996. The next day, twenty-three deputies in the eighty-member parliament tried but failed to persuade the government to compromise; another two dozen, led by the Islamic Action Front, boycotted the session.[3] The decision was announced by Prime Minister Abdul Karim Kabariti over objections of the parliament, as part of IMF requirements for extending new credits to Jordan. The prime minister's decree of the change on his own, despite widespread objections, triggered riots in the city of Karak and other poor communities in the south and in the capital, Amman.[4]

On the surface, lifting bread subsidies was the immediate impetus for the popular uprising in Karak and other cities, requiring the use of the army to restore peace. But it is also true, as Rami G. Khouri points out in an op-ed piece in *Jordan Times*, "the price hikes had touched deep frustration among the Jordanian poor over the lack of any tangible dividends from recent developments—the introduction of limited democracy, the IMF program, and above all, the peace with Israel signed in 1994."[5] From a different aspect, Khouri argues, one can plainly see how the prime minister found it difficult to change old habits of decisionmaking. The government tends to decide without significant input from other political actors or citizens. "Jordanian governments," Khouri notes, "have exercised virtually absolute power for so many decades that they do not know how to, or do not feel the need to, engage the people in a deep, genuine dialogue of equals, for governments have neither been trained in such a process nor subjected to its political imperatives."[6]

Jordan's current economic hardship can be traced deeper to the Gulf War of 1991, which severely jolted the economy. The war itself, and Jordan's position on the conflict, led Gulf states to halt promised financial aid and to abruptly terminate over 300,000 Jordanian and Palestinian workers and professionals. Spiteful ejection of people from Kuwait, Saudi Arabia, and other Gulf states deepened the rift in intra-Arab politics and hampered all other economic dealings among Arab states, causing a lingering economic burden for Jordan.

Despite negative economic developments, certain political milestones were being achieved. On November 8, 1993, with high expectations, the Jordanian people elected their twelfth parliament. The enormous anticipation, and even anxiety, of observers outside Jordan set this election apart from others. Watchers searched for trends and potential political movements. The West and other Arab countries sought clues about subterranean political forces that might have emerged in response to the disaster of the Gulf War. Inside and outside Jordan, there was a heightened interest in these elections for what they might reveal about the electoral power of the Islamists and the resurgence of their demands, particularly after the aborted Algerian elections of 1991 and 1992.

These were the first elections in Jordan after implementation of a 1992 law authorizing formation of political parties and regulating political activities. This development followed an intensive, organized political exercise that began with the appointment of a broadly representative Royal Commission to develop a national charter for regulating the political process. After a national conference ratified the National Charter in 1991, it then served as the framework for the new Political Parties Law of 1992 and the succeeding Freedom of the Press Law of 1993. Thus, Jordanians considered the 1993 elections a test of support and commitment to the democratic process.

The 1993 elections were significant for other less obvious reasons. One is the understanding they may provide on public sentiment toward the Palestinian-Israeli Oslo accord, which had been signed only a few weeks earlier. Too, the elections forced the question of who was eligible to vote. (Many Palestinians living in Jordan were regarded as refugees wishing to return to their homes in Palestine.) Mass media and policymakers in the United States were intensely curious. They saw in these elections a test that would determine whether the upsurge of the power of Islamic movements could be tamed through democratic processes. U.S. and European pundits viewed the Arab world as "expectant," with future political and social trends open to speculation. Compared to political developments elsewhere in the Arab world, the Jordanian experience was a significant experiment in peaceful opposition and pluralistic political action.

The results of the 1993 elections may be summed up as follows: Seventy-five percent of eligible voters registered, but only slightly over half (56 percent) actually voted (Hourani 1994, 15). In 1993, 534 candidates competed for the 80 seats of the parliament, compared to 647 candidates in 1989. Of those nominated in 1993, 478 were Muslim men, 46 were Christian men, and only 3 were women (one of whom was elected). More than twenty political parties nominated candidates in the 1993 elections, but only ten won representation in the new parliament. The largest bloc was the Islamic Action Front (IAF), which won 16 seats. Independent Islamists received 6 seats. Hence, the total for both Islamic groups was 27.5 percent of all seats.[7]

The excessive fragmentation of political parties denied any of them a significant influence on public policy. Six of the political parties each gained only one seat; the largest group, Islamists, could claim twenty-two votes. Conservative and traditional political groups, when joined together, constituted about thirty-two votes. The remaining seats were dispersed among advocates of nationalist, liberal, and leftist political ideologies.

Political parties in their current configurations have failed to attract significant grassroots support. There are twenty-two announced political parties in Jordan today; one person or a handful of individuals dominates most of them. Loosely organized around these commanding personalities are small numbers of committed members. Half of the known parties have fewer than one hundred dues-paying members. In terms of doctrine or the articulation of alternative national strategies for the future, the individual and collective influence of these parties is almost negligible.

Heads and chiefs of political parties have neither demonstrated notable leadership skills nor elevated their rhetoric and actions beyond narrow, self-serving posturing. Their levels of competence and their amateurish styles of operation have not improved their overall impact on public policy. Debates on public issues, ranging from economic inflation to budgeting or public safety regulations, usually evoke endless speeches praising or criticizing the government. Rarely do they present independent, researched, or reasoned policy recommendations.

Political parties in Jordan continue to face a most intractable and unyielding problem: how to earn public support and interact with government effectively. Even among the educated class, parties are recognized or differentiated from each other by the names of the dominant individuals. The public's cynicism derives from the fact that most of these parties have been established by former politicians or rich persons jockeying for prominent positions in government. In an interview I conducted in February 1994 with a senior government official, he was scornful of political parties for being divisive (appealing to religious and tribal prejudices) and corruptive (attempting to politicize the administrative machinery of government). To be sure, fragmented and opportunistic political parties have not gained the trust of citizens or the confidence of the bureaucrats, but the political authority makes certain that they stay that way.

Clearly, political parties have been unable to seriously affect the political landscape of the country. To what extent politicians and bureaucrats of the executive branch vie to impede the efforts of a functioning pluralistic party system in Jordan is a difficult question to answer. Preliminary indications are that a rivalry is emerging, which could evolve into more of a test-of-will exercise than an honest political competition for initiating the most rational public policies.

Authors of the National Charter claimed to lay the foundation of a liberal political system by promoting wider political participation and by defining processes for protection of freedoms and civil rights. Nevertheless, several years later, central political control has not diminished. The executive branch of government (king, prime minister, and cabinet) exercises total control over policy and allocation of resources. Cabinet positions proliferate, with jobs often doled out as personal rewards. In June 1994, the assembled cabinet of Prime Minister Majali had thirty-one ministers, exacerbating fragmentation and complicating policy coordination. The succeeding cabinet of Prime Minister Zeid Ben Shaker (January 1995) also had thirty-one-members, including seventeen deputies of the lower house of parliament. Two women were appointed to this cabinet—one of whom held the portfolio of minister of planning and the other minister of social development.

The large number of deputies in the cabinet in 1996 was an obvious attempt by the Kabariti cabinet to improve its chances of getting a vote of confidence from an increasingly restive parliament. The selection of so many individuals to cabinet posts, especially those with upper-class socioeconomic backgrounds, has heightened public skepticism of the government's commitment for reform. Political elites seem entrenched and generously rewarded with positions and power while the rest of citizens endure severe austerity measures, high unemployment, high inflation, and a huge burden of debt.

In the end, whether Jordan continues on the road to democratization, stability, development, and secure relations with neighbors will depend more on what happens outside the country rather than inside. Actually, Jordan's internal and external contexts are often linked or combined, particularly in economics. Dependence on foreign aid, borrowing, and the economic conditions of Arab oil-producing countries have gripped the internal economy. At the same time, development will not continue without comprehensive reforms that involve the political process, administrative capacity, economic justice, and corruption.

DEVELOPMENT POLICY AND ECONOMIC REALITY

Jordan is a country with 4.25 million people and a foreign debt of about $7 billion, exceeding 117 percent of GNP.[8] Jordan is ranked 98th among 173 countries in the UNDP Human Development Index—ahead of Morocco (119), Egypt (110), Yemen (142), and Sudan (151), and behind Syria, Libya, Tunisia, and the Gulf states.[9]

Economically, the country has limited natural resources and suffers from a severe shortage of drinking water and from inadequate rain for viable agricultural life. Less than 20 percent of wheat consumed is locally produced, and only about 10 percent of the land is arable. Improved methods of agriculture, however, have been useful in achieving self-sufficiency in fruits and vegetables, with some surplus for export. Despite a few small-scale industries and some limited exports (phosphate, potash, fertilizers, pharmaceuticals, cement, and refined oil products), Jordan is neither an industrial country nor a viable agricultural one. The country's greatest asset is its educated and trained people, many of whom work abroad, particularly in the Arab oil-producing countries, and remit savings back home.

Inherently, the economy of Jordan is precarious and has endured chronic budget and trade deficits, in addition to incurring a huge foreign debt and an expensive military institution. Investment in the productive capacity has been anemic; private capital has shifted mainly to nonproductive conspicuous consumption or to prestige projects such as upscale housing and rental properties. Infrastructure needs and military demands put severe pressure on public funds. Thus, productive and job-generating investments have been insufficient to match labor supply or to generate economic growth that can provide essential revenues to balance the public budget.

Devoted to national planning since the 1950s, Jordan has created various instruments to formulate central plans for socioeconomic development. National plans have traditionally consisted of lists of development projects to be carried out when the government procures funding from one external source or another. Funding such plans has been almost exclusively dependent on foreign economic assistance and on borrowing. Thus one cannot realistically describe these plans—these national wish lists—as well integrated, with rational priorities and choices.

Nevertheless, the results of the meager developmental investment have been as impressive as those of countries with more plentiful funding. For more than forty years, Jordan's national planners appear to have succeeded in identifying basic infrastructure needs and responding to them with specific developmental projects. In Rodney Wilson's words (1991, 1): "Jordan is a remarkably resilient state, both economically and politically." Today, the country enjoys facilities and public services that are relatively adequate, compared to those in other developing countries. Jordan's roads, Amman International Airport, the Aqaba seaport, postal and telephone services, hotels, public transportation, and so on all function well despite underfunding and a shortage of skilled operators.

A sense of resignation and realism pervades the introduction to an early development plan, "Seven Year Program for Economic Development, 1964–1970." The document states that "Jordan is convinced that flexible long range planning is necessary for the achievement of its economic and social objectives."[10] The plan acknowledges Jordan's constraints of a small domestic market of 1.8 million people (with 45 percent under fifteen years of age), a high annual population increase, and limited natural resources.

Before the end of that seven-year plan, Israel occupied Jordan's West Bank in the June 1967 war, ending what was until then an impressive development with outstanding economic results. In the period 1959 to 1966, for example, the average annual growth rates were 9.1 percent for agriculture (including crops, forestry, and livestock); 16 percent for industry and mining, electricity, and water supply; 10.3 percent for construction; and 7 percent for services.[11]

Before 1967, Jordan was cited by the president of the World Bank as one of a small number of countries that had doubled their GNP in less than a decade.[12] With an average annual growth rate of 10 percent and a development policy that invested in human resources as well as in economic projects, Jordan appeared on the correct developmental path. The expansion of productive capacity, completion of the East Ghor Canal, and the increase of phosphate production all appeared as indications that the country finally was on its way to self-sustaining development. Additional positive signs included a high degree of monetary stability, a healthy increase in domestic revenues, and a significant reduction in budget deficit. Jordan's economy appeared positioned for takeoff.

The 1967 war changed everything for Jordan. Annual growth rates of various economic sectors declined to less than half of the pre-1967 period. The government had to meet the basic needs of a new influx of 400,000 refugees from the West Bank and Gaza Strip. Defense expenditures surged at the expense of economic development projects. At the same time, unemployment increased and earnings from tourism declined significantly. Uncertainty led the private sector to reduce its capital investments, and the budget deficit expanded alarmingly.[13] In sum, the period between 1967 and 1972 was troublesome, both economically and politically. The country faced declines in almost every major economic indicator, including a drop of 3 percent in per capita real GDP.[14]

On the political front, the idea of retrieving the West Bank, occupied by Israel since 1967, dominated Jordan's public policies. Despite its economic handicap, Jordan extended substantial financial help, amounting to nearly $760 million, to the West Bank during the 1970s and 1980s (Diwan and Squire 1993, I:6). Simultaneously, Jordan pursued numerous negotiation schemes proposed by the United States and others, only to be disappointed and frustrated by a lack of progress or any tangible results. Finally, on July 31, 1988, King Hussein renounced all administrative and legal ties with the Israeli-occupied West Bank and actually transferred responsibility to the Palestine Liberation Organization (PLO) so that the Palestinian people could decide their own destiny. This initiative proved to be a turning point in Middle East politics: What had been the Arab-Israeli conflict became the Palestinian-Israeli conflict (Al-Madfai 1993, 1).

By the late 1970s and early 1980s, Jordan's economic fortunes turned around and began moving in a positive direction again. By 1981, the country was in the midst of an economic boom, thanks to an abundance of financial remittances made by Jordanians abroad and to foreign aid from the Gulf states. Jordan registered an annual real growth in GNP of between 9 and 10 percent, gold and foreign reserves increased sixfold, and capital formation increased elevenfold (Satloff 1986, 8).

But Jordan's economy became increasingly vulnerable in the 1980s because of a growing reliance on the Gulf states for economic assistance and employment, a situation that caused greater uncertainty and less control over the direction of domestic development (Jreisat 1989, 96). Events of the early 1990s and the aftermath of the Gulf War proved the risk of excessive reliance on outside funding. The Gulf states withheld economic assistance and closed their markets to Jordan's labor and products, inflicting financial damage and disrupting the Jordanian economy. In fact, an economic slowdown was noticeable in Jordan even before the Gulf War as a result of declining world oil prices (which meant decreased economic aid from the Gulf states).

Several years after the Gulf War, Jordan is still searching for ways to compensate for its economic losses and to manage the added burden of hundreds of thousands of workers who lost jobs in the Gulf states. These returning workers pushed unemployment up to a politically unacceptable level of 20 to 30 percent. Meanwhile, the debt service burden has been pulling the economy downward through an annual payment of nearly $400 million, mostly paid by new borrowing. An austerity program, coupled with measures such as rescheduling of debt, more borrowing, and cutback management, offered a temporary reprieve.

Today, Jordan's strategy for socioeconomic development seems to be going through a subtle but unmistakable transformation. The government is exploring new avenues of economic reform and fiscal stability. The main elements so far pertain to narrowing the budget deficit, decreasing the external debt, stabilizing the fiscal position, and creating conditions suitable for resumed economic growth. It appears that the government is accepting a change of role from direct responsibility for economic growth to a facilitating one. In other contexts, this change might have been designated as privatization or a switch to a free-market economy, except that "Jordan has traditionally been viewed as a free-market economy, never having joined in the Arab-socialist or state-capitalist experiments of the 1950s and 1960s of a number of its neighbors" (Brand 1992, 170).

At present, the Ministry of National Planning seems to view its role as a study group that suggests policy and does not issue a binding development plan or monitor its implementation. Instead of maintaining the developmental momentum through a national plan, the Ministry of National Planning issues a "policy paper" that "complements" other developmental programs and decisions and "offers a comprehensive view."[15] Jordan touts its democratization process as further evidence of a new policy of economic liberalization, anticipating a greater role for the private sector in resuming economic improvement.

In July 1994, the Jordanian government signed an agreement with Israel that ended the state of belligerency between them that had existed since the establishment of Israel in Palestine in 1948. The agreement settled a few of the lingering problems between the two states and began a process to deal with the remaining questions. The questions in need of solutions include land and water issues, compensation for or repatriation of Palestinians in exile, and self-determination for Palestinians under Israeli occupation.

One immediate economic consequence for Jordan was forgiveness of $720 million of debt over three years, improving the prospect of easing the terms of debt held by certain European governments. In fact, the U.S.

president sent a letter on August 5, 1994, to the leaders of Germany, Britain, France, and ten other industrialized nations urging them to grant debt relief to Jordan, whose overall government-to-government debt totals $6 billion.[16] Jordan is counting on its recent peace agreement to relieve some of the foreign debt burden. None of the measures has so far been adequate, however, to generate meaningful benefits to citizens enduring high inflation and unemployment.

The conclusion is that the pattern of economic development in Jordan has been inconsistent and even erratic. To a large degree, the on-again, off-again economy is the result of heavy reliance on outside sources over which Jordan has no control, a dependence deepened by the paucity of natural resources and sudden influx of displaced Palestinians in several waves (in 1948, 1967, 1991, and 1992). To solve the unemployment problem and to resume economic growth, the country needs an independent, innovative strategy for development and reform. This strategy has to incorporate objectives of additional inflow of investment capital and implementation of fundamental domestic reforms. Although external policy options are limited, Jordan's domestic reform programs promise immediate benefits to all citizens. Building the institutional capacities of the country remains most urgent as the initial phase of a comprehensive reform strategy.

PUBLIC ADMINISTRATION

The connection between efficient and effective public administration and socioeconomic development is an article of faith for Arab states. "No achievement in planning and socioeconomic reforms is possible," declared the prime minister of Jordan in 1992, "if the administrative structure required to implement them is undeveloped, sloppy, or without incentives."[17] Therefore, he announced, the administrative "problem" is at the top of the agenda for the government to deal with. Unfortunately, this has proved easier said than done.

In Jordan, as in the rest of the Arab world, pressures are mounting to develop an administrative system with neutral competence and the capacity to provide professional and ethical advice on public policy issues. Numerous dysfunctions have rendered administrative units incapable of leading efforts at socioeconomic development. The reformers' challenge, therefore, is to forge administrative structures that have the capacity (skills, knowledge, and ethics) to identify developmental objectives and to plan for achieving them. The trouble is that fiscal stress, poor leadership, and general institutional weakness have rendered this urgent task much harder to realize than expected.

The civil service of Jordan is very small compared to, say, that of Egypt. The ratio of citizens to public employees is much lower than in

Egypt: Jordan has approximately 34 public employees per 1,000 people, whereas Egypt has 125 public employees per 1,000 people.[18] In 1993, total employees of the civil service (ministries, departments, and public enterprises) reached 133,643.[19] Those in top leadership positions (1,729 employees) are divided into about 92 percent men and 8 percent women. In terms of educational qualifications, 64 percent of the group have more than a bachelor's degree and 15 percent have doctoral degrees (see Table 6.1).

Administrative problems in Jordan are diverse and even contradictory. Some are rooted in financial scarcity; others are products of factors connected to political attributes and historical organizational and managerial traditions. A memo by a staff member of Jordan's Institute of Public Administration[20] describes problems of administrative organization in four categories: (1) increasing number of public agencies, (2) expansion and growth of departments and divisions inside ministries and agencies, (3) lack of clear objectives, and (4) poor coordination.

Consequently, the author of the memo contends, other difficulties have surfaced. A primary one is duplication of activities, which leads to conflicts and serious contradictions among agencies; a second is a consequence of duplication that wastes human and material resources. In fact, because of proliferation of units and agencies and growth of their managerial structures, there are not enough qualified, skilled people to staff them. Although costs of today's management are much higher than before, qualified managers are hard to find. The common effect, the memo concludes, is that one problem creates another, and collectively they lead to deterioration and corruption of public service.

This diagnosis treads softly in the political domain and ultimately seeks substantive structural alterations. The irony is that practices of the

---

Table 6.1   Education and Gender of Jordan's Civil Servants

Educational Achievement	Females	Males
Below secondary level		4
Secondary level		5
Diploma (community college)	4	12
Bachelor of Arts (B.A.)	63	540
Diploma (higher studies)	33	444
Master's degree (M.A.)	33	339
Ph.D.	12	240
Total	145	1,584

Source: Based on information from Jordan's Civil Service Commission, Amman, February 1994.

Jordanian government often seem to be heading in the opposite direction. As noted earlier, the cabinet now numbers thirty-one ministers, the largest ever. Under conditions of scarce resources, creating a new ministry or operating an existing one is an expensive undertaking that requires compelling justification. In addition to increasing the costs of government operations, the growth of administrative units is a fertile ground for turf wars, continuing duplication of activities, and difficulties of coordination among units with narrow mandates.

In a 1994 reshuffling, the prime minister introduced new cabinet-level units without legislative debate or approval. Oversized and overlapping in jurisdictions, the newly formed cabinet comprises a peculiar configuration of political positions that defy coordination and effective decisionmaking. The shuffle resulted in the prime minister's retaining the position of minister of foreign affairs, although there is another person named minister of state for foreign affairs. The cabinet has a minister for legal affairs and a minister of justice, a minister of state for education and a minister of higher education, and three ministers of state without portfolios—a euphemistic term for no defined responsibilities. It is worth noting that the announcement of the new cabinet "quickly sparked a controversy in the lower house of parliament" for lack of consultation. Several members of the parliament demanded that the government submit to a new vote of confidence.[21] To prepare for such contingency in 1996, the prime minister included a larger number of deputies in his cabinet.

Government remains the main employer in the society. Almost 57 percent of employed Jordanians are working for the public sector (see Table 6.2). It also appears that almost all those currently seeking jobs are registered with the Civil Service Commission (CSC) (96,765 applicants), which normally recruits candidates for working in government offices.

Table 6.2   The Workforce in Jordan

Total	859,300
Employed	763,000
Public sector	434,806
Private sector	328,194
Services	129,754
Mining	91,086
Other	107,354
Unemployed	96,300

Source: Information from Jordan's Department of Statistics, published in *Jordan Times,* July 31, 1994, p. 12.

Public sector dominance in employment, spending, and administrative controls is noteworthy. Hence, the impact of improvements in managing public affairs reaches large segments of the society. The 1989 agreement on management development between Jordan and the UNDP offers specific ideas on administrative reform. The main objective, as stated in the agreement, is "to assist the country in updating and strengthening the public sector in Jordan by enhancing the effectiveness and efficiency of public administration entities." Administrative improvement is to be accomplished by increasing the responsiveness of public organizations "in handling changing demands of national development and in assisting the recovery process of current economic and financial difficulties according to a set of priorities extending through the three-year period of the project."[22]

Understandably, UNDP efforts do not address fundamental, structural issues. Instead they outline relatively familiar and politically neutral problems. They focus on job description and classification, performance appraisal, and simplification of procedures. These initiatives do not take aim at systemic characteristics such as rigid hierarchical control, the proliferation of administrative units, patronage, and official corruption. The targets selected by UNDP personnel are limited, narrowly focused, and open to alteration by modest increments.

Although debates within the government over the objectives of administrative development are continuous, they have at least resulted in agreement on what needs to be done in the search for more efficient and effective administrative performance. In December 1991 the king directed that administrative development serve the following objectives:

1. Review and update all statutes
2. Streamline and simplify procedures
3. Affirm tasks of monitoring, evaluation, and incentives
4. Foster decentralization and activate the roles of administrative (local) governors
5. Concentrate central departments on functions of planning, overseeing, and managing

After discussing these objectives, the two chambers of the parliament responded with their own list. They reiterated three of the objectives as they appear in the king's address and slightly modified two others:

1. Review the organizational structure of public administration apparatus
2. Simplify procedures
3. Foster decentralization
4. Develop local administration
5. Promote the concept of public service

Soon after the parliament's debate, Prime Minister Z. Ben Shaker summarized his government's policy on the matter. He forwarded his orders to the Civil Service Council in January 1992, outlining reform targets:

1. Review of the organizational structure
2. Focus on the need for an institutional base for administrative development and the absence of coordination among such structures concerned with administrative development
3. Simplify procedures
4. Provide more effective management of administrative centralization
5. Ensure availability of reliable data
6. Establish comprehensive plan for development of human resources
7. Develop public laws that correspond with growth of the state and its obligations

No major differences divide the three institutional perspectives; legislative and executive views seem to fundamentally converge. But to paraphrase a colloquial expression, the devil for the Jordanian program of administrative development is in the details of implementation. A report published by the Civil Service Commission, "Administrative Development 1992–93," enumerates accomplishments reached in response to the prime minister's 1992 directive. The report lists:

1. Activation of various councils and committees to improve coordination
2. Analysis and simplification of procedures in fourteen ministries and agencies
3. Establishment of a central office for information gathering and retrieval with capabilities generated at departmental levels[23]

Other changes cited by the report deal with local authorities' attempts to enhance decentralization and delineate programs for development of human resources. These programs consist mainly of garden-variety training activities.

Most highly touted by public officials and government documents are certain structural changes that the government has introduced in the 1990s. One is the institution of a Civil Service Council set up to suggest policies of administrative reform and to monitor the implementation of those policies. Within the council, a subcommittee is assigned responsibility for developing organization and management in government. Membership of this subcommittee consists of representatives of entities closely associated with the same function: Civil Service Commission, Department of Accounting, Institute of Public Administration, and the newly created Department of Control and Inspection. The mandate of the subcommittee is the overall execution and monitoring of administrative development programs.

To aid in the process, an office established within the Civil Service Commission is now responsible for the implementation and evaluation of all administrative development activities. This structure is franchised to government agencies, each agency is allocated a unit specialized in administrative development. Forty-five of these units are already operating. A publication of the Civil Service Commission acknowledges the efforts of these units,[24] mentioning, among others, the Administrative Development Unit of the Ministry of Finance.

To find out about the actual impact of this unit, I made an unannounced visit to its office in the Ministry of Finance. A modern, multistory building on a busy street houses the Ministry and the Budget Department. At the door of one office is a sign: Administrative Development Unit. I entered a large room, where I encountered three employees at three separate desks: One man was talking on the telephone, the second was socializing with a visitor from a neighboring office who was standing and looking out a window, and the third, who was sitting at a clean desk, did not appear to be doing anything in particular. All the men were in their twenties or early thirties. One greeted me politely with the equivalent of "What can I do for you?" I introduced myself and briefly explained my purpose: collecting information for a research project on administrative development and reform. Then I asked if he could explain to me the main functions of his office. All three of them interrupted whatever each was doing, or not doing, and looked in my direction. The answer to my question came not from the person I directed the question to but from another. The respondent was a little older than the others and perhaps was higher on the civil service ladder.

Answer: "The director of the unit is not here at the moment. You need to direct your questions to her. If you return in about two or three hours she will be back in her office."

Question: "I would like to know from you about the activities *you* perform in this office. . . . "

Answer: "The only person who can answer such a question is the director and she is not here at the moment."

Question: "What do you do personally . . . what are your own assignments?"

Answer: "Sorry, I cannot tell you. First I am new on the job. Second, my assignment is whatever the director asks me to do."

Question: "Let me explain one more time. No names will be mentioned in my work. No direct quotes. I simply need to know the nature of tasks assigned to a unit like this from its own operators. Even if the director were here, I still would appreciate your input."

Answer: "Sincerely regret . . . she is the only one who knows and can answer such questions."

On another floor in the same building, I visited the budget offices and had a discussion with a senior man who heads a department and has the title "doctor" before his name on the door. This visit, too, was fruitless. At my request, he took me to see the so-called library. He tried to sway me politely by indicating that it was not what the title implied. There was nobody managing it, and it seemed to contain only old books on management and some files. Its total collection was no more than what might be found in an average office of a college professor in the United States. There was nothing special in it to qualify it as a library for a national department of public budgeting.

Finally, a visit to what seemed the proper place to get a real perspective on substantive issues of public management and budgeting in Jordan: an office designated for "studies and research," headed by an economist with a doctorate from a British university. The answers received may be summarized: The office is newly established and has not conducted any studies or analysis of the budget or any aspect of it. The director and his staff are consumed by day-to-day routine and calculations. Essentially they are a line operation performing mundane tasks. Bored, the director would like to receive training in budgeting in the United States.

Discussions with senior government officials in Amman, some of them closely associated with reform policies, reveal serious misgivings and frustrations. They agree that progress on reform is very slow and sometimes even imperceptible. "We suggest, we report, we lecture, but ultimately it is the prime minister who decides what can be done," said one senior official. Obviously, the prime minister's centralized control remains intact despite all claims of decentralization. The problem of excessive centralization permeates management of government organizations at all levels.

Abdullah Elayyan, president of the CSC, assumes a leading role in the whole scheme of improving the capacities of public organizations. He identifies specific problems that he feels are hobbling desired reforms. The following narrative is my summary and translation of his thoughts:[25]

We pursue two paths for reform, simultaneously. One through statutes that regulate administrative action. The second consists of various efforts that focus on individuals in positions of managerial leadership. In this regard, issues vary; they range from pay to performance appraisal to team building. The fact remains that the bulk of activities performed by the civil service are mainly advisory.

The head of the CSC underscores his responsibility for monitoring implementation of existing laws dealing with various civil service processes to discover violations and to take remedial action when necessary. He notes that his system offers very little in terms of incentives for good performance. In the following translation of his discussion, he illustrates the type of dilemmas he faces when introducing change:

> The 1966 civil service law was secretive and even oppressive on the issue of employee evaluation. The more open 1988 law includes pay incentives, right of appeal on evaluation of individuals, and other progressive elements. What happened in implementation is revealing. Under the 1966 law, only 10–15 percent of employees received an excellent rating by their superiors. Under the 1988 law, which opened up the process and granted the right of appeal, 60–65 percent have been rated excellent. In one ministry, 86 percent were rated excellent. Thus, the evaluation process lost meaning.

The president of the CSC underscores two problems that he considers particularly vexatious in dealing with issues of administrative reform. One is high turnover of the cabinet: There have been five cabinet changes in four years,[26] and each prime minister is a school of thought unto himself. The Civil Service Council is chaired by a deputy prime minister and four to five ministers are members, so rapid changes in political leadership make a stable and consistent policy all but impossible to maintain.

Second, the CSC president considers weak administrative leadership at the high levels of government a major complication. Recruitment of these individuals is highly politicized, they are badly evaluated, and there is too much political and personal consideration in the selection.

All government officials interviewed for this study acknowledged that the administrative system of Jordan suffers from heavy political influences, sometimes crudely applied, on appointments of senior public administrators. A study by Cunningham and Sarayrah (1993) points out how *wasta,* a conspicuous form of intervention in the conduct of public affairs in Jordan, influences these appointments. The authors indicate that *wasta* continues even when a system is in a transition from traditionalism to modernity. In one form, *wasta* means seeking the help or influence of a person who possesses an economic, social, or political advantage to skew a decision in one's favor—irrespective of merit. Powerful politicians, senior military officers, even close friends and members of the family of the official making the decision are asked to intercede. Frequent transactions of this type add up to a national plight that prevents honest, efficient, and fair decisions. The process epitomizes the incompatibility of administrative and political values; it has a detrimental effect on any reform of public management. A centralized, politicized, and self-serving oligarchy is inherently incompatible with notions of building neutral competence and instilling professional values in administrative units.

My discussion with an experienced Jordanian manager is instructive. Iyad Kattan, director of the Royal Cultural Center in Amman and a former member of the National Charter Committee, recognizes stifling contradictions in the system that must be resolved in order to resume progress. I translated and summarized his response as follows:

> We speak of decentralization, yet we are constantly strengthening central control and creating new mechanisms to do it. An example is the recent establishment of a central department for control and inspection. We seek to raise morale yet whenever there is a vacancy at the top, it is filled from outside, often by somebody who may not be knowledgeable about the job. A ministry never had a general secretary promoted from within, and thus all its senior employees feel stymied. Promotion of one of them to the top position will positively affect fifteen senior employees. Instead, they feel demoralized and stagnant in their careers.[27]

What complicates matters, according to Kattan, is that the executive authority is able to initiate programs and create agencies without referring to or consulting with any other authority. Creation of a new department (which may distort a good idea and mismanage it) happens without any input from the legislative branch. The parliament does not object to this; members of the parliament are ignorant of their role, authority, and responsibility as legislators. There is an absence of "parliamentary culture" because of the legislators' limited knowledge and limited experience with the process. A parliamentary culture emerges by efforts of the ruling party, the "culture of opposition," and the "culture of accountability to the opposition."

In his analysis, Kattan provides insightful explanations of certain behavioral elements that influence governing as he sees it:

> Our citizens still look up to the leader to sustain their livelihood. This is the culture of what I call a "shepherd society." The shepherd takes care of his flock. People look to leadership for grants and for gifts. The leader has free access to public assets. There is the old saying "El-miri Halal." That is, stealing from the government is fair. This is part of the government culture. The leaders of the executive branch give themselves exceptional powers even to go beyond the law. Notice in the bidding system, the minister has the right, for whatever reason, not to accept the lowest bidder or the bidder recommended by the committee within certain limits. The result is that all sorts of pre-arranged schemes can be concocted between politicians and suppliers.[28]

From all this, one concludes that Jordan has not yet solved the problem of developing true leaders at the program and agency levels. The leaders needed—people of commitment and ability—will not be found through political patronage. The current practices have produced a cadre of professional political loyalists whose relations to political leaders are the only basis for holding their jobs. Thus, political patronage and tight central control have created a profound impediment to building the necessary administrative capacity at the pinnacle of public organizations. Within this environment, managers have become little more than obedient clerks who have the skills to handle routine tasks and manage existing problems (Jreisat 1989) but do not possess the wits to anticipate risks or to divert the organization from potential rough waters that lie ahead (Cunningham 1988, 21).

Although the administrative capacity of today's organizations is determined by the competence of its leadership, to exclude consideration of other staffing needs is to invite serious risks to proper organizational functioning. In Jordan, as in most countries, demand for the services of technicians trained to operate the tools of the digital information age[29] is rapidly growing. The increasing use of new technologies for advanced decisionmaking processes requires judgment and skills often unavailable in the labor market. Repairing and operating telecommunications equipment, interacting with the public in a more liberal political environment, facilitating research and scientific developments—all require preparation of a special workforce. Increasingly, in the midst of high white-collar unemployment, there is a crippling shortage of individuals trained to be computer programmers, draftspersons, library technicians, emergency medical operators, science technicians, and so forth.

A stifling central control is often justified by the prime minister and cabinet as necessary to maintain control of scarce resources under conditions of a heavy debt burden and a relatively small country. Such an attitude allows frequent interference in and dominance of decisionmaking by the center. Actually the prime minister and cabinet are unable or unwilling to adjust their decisionmaking methods or behaviors to ensure that dividends of government accomplishments are shared by the population at large (Hawatmeh 1994, 8). The cabinet has acted in a way that excluded open parliamentary debates on critical national issues such as taxes, peace with Israel, creation of cabinet-level positions, lifting subsidies, or reorganization of public agencies. Some of the decisions caused confusion over policy, as they appeared to violate the preferences of the country for strengthening the democratization processes (Hawatmeh 1994, 7). The irony is that government credibility suffers when it continually flaunts claims of commitment to decentralization and to developing managerial capacity but makes no genuine efforts. The discrepancy between actions and formal policies undermines the government's reformist claims; hence, another vicious cycle of cynicism ensues, preparing the grounds for more violent popular outbursts.

The conclusion is that the government's policy of developing administrative capacity by creating central structures or refurbishing existing ones has failed. Successful change in this situation cannot be dictated from outside or decreed from above. Jordan needs to build the internal capabilities of public agencies. To do so largely depends on several conditions, including (1) appointment of administrative leaders on merit, (2) less control by central offices over every aspect of decisionmaking, and (3) evaluations and rewards related to actual performance on the job.

NOTES

1. Jean Leca (1994, 49). Leca is professor of political science at the Institute of Political Studies in Paris.
2. Lewis Lapham (lecture at the University of South Florida, Tampa, March 30, 1994).
3. *Economist* (August 17, 1996), p. 37.
4. *New York Times,* August 21, 1996, p. A3.
5. *Jordan Times,* July 23, 1996, p. 6.
6. Ibid.
7. All numbers are from tables in Hourani (1994).
8. World Bank, *World Development Report 1995* (New York: Oxford University Press), pp. 200, 206. Wilson estimates Jordan's debt at $8.3 billion in 1994.
9. United Nations Development Program, *Human Development Report 1994* (New York: Oxford University Press), pp. 135, 136.
10. Hashemite Kingdom of Jordan, "Seven Year Program for Economic Development 1964–70," p. 1.
11. Hashemite Kingdom of Jordan, National Planning Council, "Three Year Development Plan 1973–75," p. 2.
12. Ibid.
13. Ibid., pp. 6–7.
14. Hashemite Kingdom of Jordan, National Planning Council, "Five Year Plan 1976–1980," p. 13.
15. Hashemite Kingdom of Jordan, "Economic and Social Development Plan 1993–1997," pp. 1–4.
16. *New York Times,* August 9, 1994, p. A3.
17. An address to Civil Service Council, January 12, 1992, contained in the Civil Service Commission's monograph, "Administrative Development: Outlook and Legislation 1992–1993," p. 22.
18. For comparison: Japan has 45 public employees per 1,000 people (Heady 1996, p. 241); the United States has 10.7 employees per 1,000 people (Richard Nathan, *Public Administration Review* May/June 1995, p. 305).
19. These numbers were supplied to me by Jordan's Civil Service Commission, Office of the President, in February 1994.
20. A two-page internal memo in Arabic, signed by Dr. Ahmad Bashaireh (February 18, 1991).
21. Jordan Information Bureau, *Jordan: Issues and Perspectives* (Washington, DC, May/July 1994), p. 1.

22. A report on accomplishment of Management Development Project of Public Sector in Jordan (1990–1993), November 1993.

23. Hashemite Kingdom of Jordan, Civil Service Commission, "Administrative Development: Outlook and Legislation 1992–1993" (in Arabic), 110 pages.

24. Ibid.

25. Interview with Abdullah Elayyan, president, Civil Service Commission, Amman, Jordan, February 7, 1994.

26. Two more cabinet shuffles occurred in less than a year after this interview. By 1996, Jordan had had eight different cabinets in less than six years.

27. Interview in Amman, Jordan, March 30, 1994.

28. Ibid.

29. *Fortune* (July 22, 1994), p. 56.

7

A Comparative Analysis
of Common Problems

*Keep the capitalist busy defending what he has got, and the very
activity enforced upon him makes him a better citizen and more
considerate a neighbor and employer. Capitalists resting secure
behind the fortifications of ancient and obsolete, or modern, cor-
ruptly obtained laws, become vicious, arrogant, and harmful alike
to themselves and the community.*

E. W. Scripps[1]

Developing countries are typically less systematic and methodical in their
decisionmaking than Western countries. The Arab states, in particular, lack
relevant and reliable information about policy decisions. In the absence of
citizen representation and professional institutional input, governmental
decisions are often made on the basis of personal preference of the top
leader. Consequently, it is difficult to determine with certainty what considerations or what reasoning entered into a specific policy action, let
alone to hold public officials accountable for such actions.

Further complicating the decision process is the personal nature of actions within the Arab state. For example, senior administrators with strong
ties to powerful political leaders, seem to operate beyond the institutional
norms and to enjoy a form of protection from facing the consequences of
their inadequate performance. Although the following comment specifically addresses the case of Lebanon, it is descriptive of a larger picture:
"Men of Providence come and go . . . but they never seem to be able to
reform the political system they have come to save: as men above the system, they are little inclined to work through its institutions, thus further
contributing to the latter's atrophy and further undermining the foundations of the state."[2]

In addition to lack of documentation and the personal features of governing, the methodology of scholarship on Arab institutions and administration
makes comparative analysis difficult. In the absence of reliable information,
scholarly discussions are often rooted in ideological or religious interpretations.

Credible knowledge of the Arab domestic scene, as for all developing countries, hinges on the development of an empirical base, which is always a demanding and painstaking process. Thus, scholars of comparative politics and administration in developing countries largely tend to either congregate intellectually in the safety of issues of international conflict or foreign policy decisions or to develop global, overgeneralized, and impressionistic models about societies about which they know little.

As if comparative analysis is not complex enough, the literature on developing countries often reflects a temptation to emphasize dramatic events or to let plentiful consulting money create instant expertise and sketchy analysis. To be authentic, comparative scholarship must be the result of focused attention to specific societies or regions over long times. It requires a knowledge of history, familiarity with language, an understanding of culture, and a genuine interest in the country's problems and aspirations.

The critiques of Jordan and Egypt in this chapter offer a close view of the inner workings of the two governments. The issues addressed are basic and illustrate profound attributes with far-reaching effects on the performance of these two governments. The approach is a hybrid of a case study with an ethnographic bent. Instead of merely reporting events and carefully charting all related developments, I stand back, watch events unfold, do some investigation, read news coverage from various perspectives, and talk with informed people about these operations. The results are like snapshots: focused pictures of the process that can offer a deeper understanding not only of what transpired but of larger questions and more obscure qualities of the systems under consideration. Such knowledge, in my view, forms the building blocks for relevant and comprehensive comparative analysis.

This type of specific information, which recognizes patterns and perceives similarities and difficulties of public organizations, has been in short supply in the comparative administration literature. In part, this lack is also why it has been difficult to confirm many middle-range theories or, for cross-national research, to develop concepts and generalizations of utility or problem-solving value.

JORDAN: THE PROBLEM OF IMPLEMENTATION

Enforcing Regulations Without Political Resolve or Institutional Capacity: The Malhas Case

Living in a society of scarce resources, Jordanians are used to facing periodical shortages of one commodity or another. Gasoline, meat, sugar, or coffee have occasionally disappeared from the market. Drinking water, too, has been rationed or made available only on certain days of the week. The price of bread more than doubled overnight in 1996 when the government decided to cease its subsidy. In this context, the warning at the end of a workshop in Amman (February 26, 1994) was not particularly remarkable: A statistical bulletin issued by the Ministry of Agriculture and the UN Food and Agricultural Organization warned that Jordan's food security was endangered by the current population growth rate of 3.4 percent (Jordan's population of 3.9 million is expected to be 5.3 million by the year 2000).[3]

This news of the inevitability of a food shortage did not create a stir comparable to that unleashed by Minister of Health Abdul Rahim Malhas, M.D.,[4] in a January 1994 interview by a sensational tabloid newspaper.[5] The front page had a spread of two large words—Malhas Gate—a reference to the infamous U.S. scandals of Watergate and Irangate. Accompanied by several photos of the urbane, modishly dressed minister, the report said that merchants of drugs were reaping profits reaching 300 percent and merchants of food feeding the public "trash." The minister also told the reporters (and later the country through a speech to the parliament) that he had ordered the destruction of more than six hundred tons of spoiled meat in six months and had discovered embezzlement of public funds amounting to more than JD 150,000 (over U.S.$225,000) in two months.

These revelations mesmerized the society and absorbed its political leadership for many days, not only because the safety of food and medicine affected every citizen but also because Jordan was a net food importer and food prices were too high. Thus, it was understandable that the public reacted intensely to the news, expressing disbelief and anger and blaming the government and its wealthy allies. Emotions erupted in conversations, and press coverage was extensive. The country seemed to split into three camps: Most citizens agreed with the minister's portrayal of the merchants as "sharks" and people "without scruples." A smaller group of pro–pharmaceutical industry apologists and the association of pharmacists were displeased with the minister's statements and accused him of sensationalism. This group wanted to know why the minister did not use law enforcement agencies to deal with violators instead. A third group, particularly some columnists, editorial writers, and bureaucrats, raised specific objections against the "approach" and the "contents" of the minister's statements.

One columnist wrote that loopholes and malpractice exist everywhere. That is why strict laws are enacted to deter potential violators, he pointed out. The minister is specifically charged with the responsibility of finding these violators and bringing them to justice, but the minister had generalized and so implicated honest merchants. The writer claimed that exports of food and medicine had been hurt as well as the tourism sector, so the image of Jordan was tarnished. Thus, "it is not right for a responsible minister, with full authority to correct the wrong and to put the record straight, to create a sensation by going public and generalizing."[6]

For two weeks the national debate concentrated on the issue of food, medicine, and corruption. One civic leader went so far as to associate increased cases of cancer in Jordan with food quality and imported medicines. Merchants were not passive either; some threatened not to provide the market with its needs and to terminate imports. The press reported fierce pressures on government, regulatory offices, and laboratories, in particular, to alter their findings about spoiled or unhealthy imports.

Members of the parliament were not immune to this controversy. In a meeting of the parliament on February 2, some speakers criticized the minister and demanded evidence or proof of his allegations. Others accused him of failing to use whatever authority was at his disposal to ensure safety of food and drugs sold to the public.[7]

In his interview with the weekly tabloid, the minister was quoted as saying that existing legislation governing the sale of food and medicine was deficient. He described the merchants of food and medicine as "mafia" trying to "feed us the garbage of the industrialized world."[8]

The press made no serious effort to develop independent examinations of the issues raised, to verify the allegations, or to inform the public about what all the contention meant. The few attempts to look into some of the statements made were opinionated and lacking in specifics and demonstrated a low level of journalistic competence. By no means was coverage of public affairs by the Jordanian news media within Lewis Lapham's vision of an "infinite number of mirrors walking on an infinite number of roads." Their interests in events were too sparse and too compliant to be influential assertions.

Al-Dustour, the second-largest daily newspaper in the country, devoted a full page to investigative reporting on the Malhas story. The coverage included letters from hospitals and physicians reporting peculiar side effects to drugs supplied by certain distributors; the use of these drugs had been terminated when such results were noticed. The newspaper's report began with the statement: "Is it not strange when one stands before a pharmacy looking at medicines and not being able to buy even a headache drug without fearing that it is spoiled or contaminated?"[9] On a different page, the same paper had a column by a senior government official who wrote about food and medicine and the business-investment environment.[10] He defended the business leaders and described them as hardworking and self-made instead of "sharks," as the minister of health said. The writer continued by pointing out that unemployment was a critical problem facing the society and that the government's policy had been devoted to supporting job-creating export industries such as pharmaceuticals, the fourth-largest exports in Jordan.

The parliament devoted a whole session (February 2) to the issues of food and medicine in light of the declarations made by the minister of health. Some referred to the session as the "meeting on Malhas accusations." The spectators' space in the chamber was crowded with merchants and manufacturers of food and drugs. The prime minister and his cabinet were in attendance, too. The minister spoke for one hour and forty minutes, and his speech was fully reported in the newspapers and covered by the Jordanian television.

The minister's presentation to the parliament referred to official documents, quoted from reports, and offered dates and other specific information on imports of medicine and food. He informed the listeners about imported drugs that had expired and food that had spoiled, which he had ordered destroyed. He concluded that widespread corruption was on the increase. He further disclosed that he and his predecessors had been subjected to relentless pressures by importers who sought permits to distribute their goods even if to do so would mean the spread of a variety of ailments and uncontrolled disease.

Most unusual about the minister's allegations and the enormous coverage they received in the mass media is that not a single name of a transgressor was revealed. Names of offenders were always omitted without explanation. Even when evidence was definite and no question existed that goods must be destroyed, the importer's name was never announced. These omissions created a wave of rumors and gossip in the community. The absence of information stymied the public in any effort to express disapproval via a boycott and spared companies the shame that public exposure brings.

Nor did independent, aggressive digging by professional journalists bring to light the identities of the perpetrators. Why? Neutral competence and professional training are lacking among most Jordanian journalists. Moreover, owners of major newspapers and their editors are in league with the political and economic oligarchy that wields decisionmaking power. In this context, reporters merely transmitted what everybody said, rarely carrying out independent verification or offering trustworthy conclusions. Neither journalists nor public officials, in this case, offered the public the whole truth about the story.

The minister's presentation to the parliament continued and perhaps even deepened the divisions within the ranks of the representatives. He discussed excessive charges for drugs and the ministry's recording of no fewer than sixteen thousand violations of rules and standards during 1993. Spectators and representatives applauded enthusiastically. Then a clamor rose up from the chamber as representatives shouted requests for copies of the documentation and the evidence to which he had referred. The president of the parliament intervened, saying he would release what he considered appropriate, owing to the huge volume of material. In a dramatic gesture, the minister stepped down from the podium leaving behind a stack of papers and files. "I leave them for you all," he said. Significantly, the secretariat of the parliament refused to distribute any of the documents to the press. At a later date, some selected parts of the documents were released.

In the first session of the parliament, forty-five representatives asked to speak, but time was allotted in that meeting for only six. Those who spoke registered responses ranging from welcoming and applauding to questioning the minister's motives and focusing on legalities of his allegations. Still others requested that the whole matter be referred to a public prosecutor.[11] In three sessions devoted to the subject, thirty-seven representatives took the podium; nearly three out of four praised the minister for what he had done and asked the government to follow up with preventive measures.

The controversy continued to dominate news coverage during the first two weeks of February. A weekly review by Elia Nasrallah of selected columns from local press is illustrative:[12] One columnist proposed a national conference on public health, noting that such a conference would be timely and of paramount importance to citizens. It would tackle questions related to food, drugs, civil defense, and matters of citizens' safety in its larger context. Another columnist wrote that the minister's allegations were bound to receive support because they were directly linked to every person in the country. The writer called on the minister to adhere to his stand and provide the parliament with all the backup documents.

Still another columnist pointed out that Malhas was not the first minister to disclose corruption in his department, noting that a former minister of agriculture did the same thing. The writer acknowledged that "whoever dares to disclose anything that might endanger the interests of the so-called sharks and manipulators would be facing trouble. This is obvious from the ongoing fight against the minister and his statements, if the sharks have their way."[13]

Nasrallah reported that another columnist pointedly wrote in the largest daily newspaper that the minister's accusations resembled a shell that exploded with a loud noise but with little effect at the official level. The writer said that the minister's actions and words resulted in the formation of government committees but not in forthright movement. After all, the minister possessed all the incriminating documents against accused individuals.

Citizens undoubtedly knew all too well the lack of effective regulation and control over food and medicine. Laboratories of the University of Jordan Hospital had more than once proved that mothers' milk was polluted by the poisoned vegetables they were eating and that imported frozen meat had little nutritional value. Thus, one paper wrote that irrespective of the correctness of the minister's allegations about merchants' malpractice, the government should tighten restrictions on manufacturers and importers to ensure that public interest was safeguarded. A suggestion was advanced for the government to strengthen the Protection of Consumers Society, which can help the government maintain control over quality of products.[14]

Where were the political parties in this fray? They were totally ineffectual. Their actions were limited to issuing statements or writing articles in their own publications, which had very limited readerships. In other democratic systems, political careers have been made or destroyed over such hotly debated issues, and in Jordan the enormous popular concerns and passions expressed could have been the right stuff for demands by the political parties for public participation and effective measurable actions. None of this was forthcoming, and the government was not willing to do anything that it did not have to do.

Even the IAF, Jordan's largest political group and the most doctrinaire, was targeted for criticism for remaining "uninvolved" in the case.[15] Possibly the IAF was unable to take a stand because a large percentage of its constituency is made up of the pharmacists and food traders whose interests were targeted by Malhas's charges. And yet the president of Jordan's Pharmacists Association, who had been elected on an Islamist platform, swiftly published a letter dismissing the minister's call for updating and enforcing legislation in order to provide tighter control over the quality of food and medicine in the country. Islamists were not pleased with the minister for other reasons. Earlier he had taken positions against strict social laws sponsored by the Islamists and had repeatedly sided with progressive, liberal policies.

Political groups on the left called on "the masses to move against corruption" and applauded the minister's declarations. The headline in the tabloid of the Jordanian Communist Party said: "Corruption is the worst oppression."[16] The paper discussed the real dangers of corruption to the health, security, and well-being of citizens as well as their psychological comfort. The tabloid called on the people to organize and demand protection from fraudulent practices and uncontrolled profit chasing. The paper also reported that a group of women had collected signatures that demanded action from the president of the parliament to protect citizens' health and safety, to uncover the culprits, and to punish them to the fullest provision of the law.

The prime minister addressed the parliament on February 6 to outline government action in response to the food and medicine crisis. His solution comprised three elements: (1) All papers and documents related to food and medicine would be forwarded to the public prosecutor for investigation and appropriate action. (2) The prime minister and the cabinet would enact laws and establish an administration for food and another for medicine, each with full autonomy. (3) The ministry of health would be re-organized and various departments would be created for improving regulatory capabilities, updating laws, and checking unreasonable increases in prices. Thus, the prime minister's solution appears to have been anchored in suggestions for reform in the administrative and legislative areas as well as in commitment to fighting corruption.[17]

Beyond the Particulars. Why is this case pertinent and what does it indicate about the political and administrative system of Jordan? What public policy lessons can be learned from it? What does it indicate about administrative-political capacities of the institutions? And what does it say about the press, about the public, about public decisionmaking?

On the positive side, a responsible, open, mostly candid discussion did take place on an issue of great importance and sensitivity. The government took some action as a result of the debate and the demands put forth by representatives in the parliament. The debates dramatized citizens' concerns opening up the possibility that things will not be the same from now on. Overall, it is not far-fetched to claim that a young democracy operated as effectively as a democracy can operate within such a context.

The parliamentary debates were representative of the public mood and sentiment, which was mostly critical of corruption and the malpractice of merchants. In a political system that was not used to exertions and demands of accountability and that had strained to explain public policy decisions, the performance was impressive. Judgments were made and opinions expressed, resulting in a public give-and-take, both among public servants and between them and the citizenry. Optimistic onlookers believe that beyond enhancing accountability, the exercise of such national debate may have deepened the practice of open exchange on issues of public interest.

But the debate also underscored serious deficiencies and weaknesses that must be addressed if the democratic process is to function or if the old ways of doing things are to be reformed. Confusion over responsibility and authority was rampant; ignorance both about which laws were applicable and about what a specific law did or did not provide was apparent. The debate seemed to stay at a rhetorical level all the time, as if nobody was able or willing to come up with specific, empirical information that could settle anything. All statements and declarations were made up of general, vague, and unverifiable charges and countercharges. The process of adjudicating reported infractions was not well defined, perhaps because it is not frequently applied to matters of this type. Another explanation may be that doing business with government officialdom usually is dependent on personal relations and influences, *wasta*. In this case, it was too late for *wasta* to function effectively because of wide exposure and the many parties involved. A statement by Rami G. Khouri is instructive. He said: "The bad news, I would suggest, is that the whole controversy sparked by Dr. Malhas' interview never really touched the main point that underlies the food and medicines controversy and others like it that probably await future exposure. That main point is the capacity of our public sector to play the quality control, supervisory and watchdog functions that are its legal and moral obligation."[18]

In brief, understaffed and underfunded public institutions and ill-equipped, inadequately trained, and poorly motivated public servants are unable and unwilling to confront powerful interest groups. The preconditions for public employees to administer the regulatory functions effectively and efficiently are woefully lacking. Therefore, to control illegitimate acts by influential centers of power requires at least the availability of institutional capacity and political support.

In times of privatization and the touting of the virtues of free-market competition, developing countries must learn the lesson of this case. That is, governing a society means also the legal protection of its citizens and the building of the required administrative capacities for ensuring it. Government is responsible for regulating, monitoring, investigating, and setting standards of conduct under whatever type of economic order is present. Simultaneously, government must guard against excessive regulations and controls that can become a bureaucrat's dream and a citizen's nightmare. To guard against such an eventuality, government must build neutral competency and professional norms among the regulators and shield them from the whims of political patronage.

The Perversion of a Promising Idea

In December 1990, the government of Jordan published the National Charter, which had been drafted by the Royal Commission representing diverse political views to be a document of governance that supplemented and extended existing constitutional provisions. The most important segments of the forty-page document concern the rule of law, political participation, the right of citizens to form political parties, guarantees of basic freedoms, and commitment to principles of equality and justice.

The second chapter of the charter, titled "A Government of Law and Political Plurality," defines Jordan as "a democratic government that is committed to the principle of the supremacy of law and derives its legitimacy, authority, and effectiveness from the will of the people. . . . "[19] The charter then develops operational concepts to be implemented in order to institutionalize various designated goals and principles. The following is a case study of the implementation of one such proposal specified in the charter.

The charter recommends the "establishment of an independent entity named Diwan el-Mazalem through a special law, to assume responsibilities of administrative inspection, monitoring administrative performance, and overseeing the behavior of individual administrators."[20] The charter also stipulates that the new entity shall report to the parliament and the cabinet in accordance with the constitutional and applied legal principles and without infringement on the independence or functions of the judiciary.

Authors of the charter seem to have had a clear idea about what this provision should mean and achieve. They were interested in creating an instrument of accountability that would be independent of the all-powerful and dominating executive branch. In fact, in subsequent sections of the charter, other items were introduced that aimed at the same objectives of checking executive power and activating those of the legislators. One such item is the establishment of a constitutional court to interpret the law and to resolve conflicts over constitutional and legal provisions. A latter article actually takes away from the executive authority certain functions under the constitution and restores them to the legislative branch.

An explicit preference in the charter is for the creation of an independent instrument of action, outside the direct control of the executive branch. Nevertheless, and despite the existing immense powers of the executive branch, the prime minister and the cabinet moved swiftly in 1992 to establish the Bureau of Control and Inspection (BCI) to perform some of the tasks designated in the charter for Diwan El-Mazalem. The method, timing, and stated rationale as well as claimed benefits from establishing the BCI were met with skepticism and even some disbelief for several reasons.

First, the new bureau was established as an executive agency and by an executive order without consultation or approval of the legislators. Second, the prime minister retained the power to appoint the head of the BCI and its staff, who became subject to the same rules and regulations as the rest of the civil service.

Third, the person appointed by the prime minister to head the BCI is an academician with an undistinguished record of achievement and without any relevant practical experience. The appointee, however, is closely connected to the Muslim Brothers, the largest organized political-religious group in the country. (A relative of the appointee was elected to head this Islamist group in July 1994.)

Fourth, within the executive branch itself, many existing organizations saw that the BCI would duplicate their efforts and interfer in their own domains. Thus, opposition to the decision and skepticism of its motives and results were strong from the Bureau of Accounting, which performs budget audits, the Civil Service Commission (CSC), and the IPA.

As they practiced their trade, the staff of the BCI were not enthusiastically received within executive agencies. Of course, those who represent notions of "inspection" and "control" will hardly be hailed or cheered in any bureaucratic settings. But this reception could only get worse when the BCI staffers proved to be inexperienced, pretentious, or arrogant in performing their duties. One senior administrator related the following episode:

> I have twenty-five years of experience in government. I can honestly say that I worked with dedication and commitment throughout my career. I am considered by many of those I deal with as knowledgeable and even "expert" in what I do. Imagine one day two young college graduates, representing BCI, walk into my office unannounced and begin interrogating me about my work. The purpose of their questions was to ensure I am doing my job properly. My response to them was in the order of: Sons, when you have any experience in or knowledge of what I am doing I'll be happy to respond to your questions. My honest feeling, however, was that I wanted to throw them out of my office.

To further put this matter in perspective, I interviewed Iyad Kattan, who served on the Royal Commission that authored the National Charter. He was philosophical about the BCI and the original ideas in the charter. My translation and summary of his thoughts are valuable in explaining this development:[21]

> The idea of Diwan el-Mazalem for monitoring administrative actions, as envisioned in the National Charter, is steeped in Arabic history. Historically, such structure had high authority and is staffed by individuals with eminent knowledge of the law and administration. Individuals with grievances against anybody in the government can seek justice through this office. It is reported that common people received rulings against the Sultan himself and actions by powerful officials were corrected by rulings from this Diwan. This is the image we had when we wrote the Charter. Now we see "midgetization" of a great idea by creating a small, distorted department within the executive branch such as BCI. This has no relationship to what we contemplated in the Charter.

Actually the National Charter's prescription is a hybrid of a historic Arab-Islamic structure and the modern Swedish ombudsman. The idea of an ombudsman is that of a nonpartisan public official who investigates people's complaints and disseminates information about government officials and agencies. In Sweden, the parliament appoints officials who serve as ombudsmen to ensure that judges, civil servants, and military officers obey the laws. Thus, ombudsmen are intended to protect citizens from illegal or incompetent use of power by the government. The ombudsman may either initiate investigations or respond to a complaint by a citizen. Japan, several European countries, and some U.S. cities and states have ombudsmen.

In Jordan, the prime minister and his cabinet did not consult the parliament nor ask for a legislative action when they created the BCI. According to Iyad Kattan, the legislators did not even protest the decision by the prime minister. One reason is that the executive branch has the authority, on its own, to create any administrative structure it wants. A more important reason, perhaps, is one I have already disscussed—that the parliament does not understand its duties and responsibilities and that members of parliament are generally ignorant of their authority and the limitations on it.

Iyad Kattan's observations are insightful and evocative. He describes the situation as follows:

> There is a shallow parliamentary culture and limited experience in Jordan. To work well, a parliament needs the culture of organized opposition and how the opposition can ensure accountability. Instead, they act like chiefs of tribes in performing their duties. In the absence of good investigative reporting and professional journalism the parliament gets even weaker. Thus, the executive branch gets away with actions like distorting a great concept as in this case.

In 1994, a sudden shuffle of the cabinet portfolios resulted in the elevation of the BCI to ministerial status. The mandate of the BCI was expanded to become the Ministry of Administrative Development, with the chief of the BCI becoming the minister of the newly created ministry. In the cabinet shuffle in January 1995 a different minister was appointed for this portfolio, but the organization itself seems to have survived the change.

Only the king and the prime minister can determine what to do with the concept of Diwan el-Mazalem. They must decide whether its potential effect on democratization and its protection of citizens from abuse of power are within the zone of tolerance for changes in the system. This consideration of Diwan el-Mazalem must fit into a system in which they carefully screen and slowly consider fundamental reforms that have balancing effects on the distribution of power and benefits in the society. Reforms can only follow certain paths, which must be carefully evaluated by the top political leaders before a decision is made and its implementation started. Appointing of a person to a post and designating the organization responsible for carrying out a task are seldom sufficient to ensure actual implementation, because administrators rarely embark on enforcement until they have a clear indication from the the prime minister or the king as to their seriousness in making a proposed change. Intended or not, such a pattern is the direct consequence of centralization of authority and traditional habits of management that have been constant, despite claims of reform programs seeking a reversal of the practice.

EGYPT: CENTRALIZATION IS NOT CONTROL

Raids on Public Property

"Wasted Property Despite Watching Eyes of 9 Monitoring Agencies" was the headline in *Al-Ahram,* the largest newspaper in Egypt and, for that matter, in the entire Arab world.[22] A probe into the dealings of an Egyptian billionaire from Nasr City, a suburb of Cairo, had opened the door on large-scale negligence and an outrageous absence of any coordination among public agencies that had caused the government huge losses of property and revenue. Investigation by public prosecutors revealed infringements on government lands by wealthy developers who exploited the absence of a definition of responsibility and authority through elaborate schemes of fraud, deception, and graft.

The publicly known facts of this case may be summarized as follows:[23] Although the Egyptian government is a big landowner, its land holdings are managed by various public agencies. Some of the lands are under the jurisdiction of local authorities and some belong to the Department of Agriculture; still others are allocated to the land reform program. Certain lands "cannot be touched" without the approval of the Department of Antiquities. One category of land is owned by the state railroads, and others even belong to the armed forces.

Developers, such as the one from Nasr City, know all too well about the confusion surrounding authority over public lands and take advantage of it. The Nasr City case revolves around a wealthy developer who built numerous buildings on public lands, then sold them at great profit to unsuspecting buyers. He was able to secure documentation of ownership through complex schemes that involved falsification of papers, bribery of officials, and manipulation of legal loopholes and the gray areas of public policy. In one neighborhood, twenty-five buildings were found to be constructed in violation of laws and in defiance of various codes. The loss of revenues to the state was estimated in the tens of millions.[24]

Who Is in Charge?

Another major problem of managing public property is illustrated in the following case, the particulars of which became well known after the ownership of a piece of property became the subject of a disagreement between Al-Mansourah University and an influential member of the parliament. The specifics known about the case are that the Ministry of Agriculture granted the university a piece of public land on the Nile Island to be managed by the university's college of agriculture. At the same time, the Ministry of Public Works granted the same piece of property to a member of the parliament who is also the president of a sports club. The conflict started when each party claimed a legitimate right of ownership to the real estate.

Two questions need to be answered: Which government agency was authorized to dispose of this public property? Why did such a dispute occur in the first place? No clear answers were offered in public discussions, and none were forthcoming from interviews with public officials. Government investigations, however, revealed other crimes, including forgery of public documents, falsification of public records, and payoffs to officials. Were these cases discovered by means of the diligence of public institutions entrusted with control and monitoring, by sheer accident, or by informers? Why were most cases detected only after it was too late to affect the outcomes?

In 1993, state attorneys investigated fifty-six thousand such cases involving crimes of embezzlement, defrauding the government, graft, unauthorized use of government property, "negligence that causes grave damage," and personal crimes.[25] Indeed, the general sentiment among Egyptians as reported by newspapers and citizens is that corruption is so rampant that investigations serve only public relations purposes.

Is corruption becoming a way to life for public officials in Egypt? How can citizens use legitimate means to overcome the maze of bureaucratic controls that discourages, even frightens, citizens and investors? Government officials and private sector businesspeople, not to mention taxi drivers in the streets of Cairo, acknowledge this uncomfortable situation. It is becoming a behavioral pattern with serious negative consequences for the system of government as well as for programs of economic development.

Relating These Cases to Administrative Anomolies

The Egyptian managerial experiences suggest several challenges to administrative theory. Public administration in Egypt is highly centralized, completely regimented with rules and regulations, and burdened by several lethargic agencies for control and monitoring. Additionally, there is an astonishing absence of coordination among various agencies, as indicated in these cases of public land use.

Classic administrative theory (administrative management), as explained in standard textbooks of public administration, postulates that when activities are organized in various departments the need for coordination is imperative. This coordination is to take place at the next-higher level of authority in the organization. Thus, the common wisdom is that the administrative management theory has a bias toward control and centralization. In fact, a major justification of its excessive centralized control is to ensure coordination.

But few systems of government anywhere have a greater leaning toward centralization and control than the Egyptian bureaucracy. The anomaly is that, despite centralized control, very little coordination takes place at higher levels or at any level in the hierarchy. This may explain, in part, the mismanagement of state lands. Lack of coordination is also a factor in explaining failures of the numerous agencies that are entrusted with control, audit, and monitoring yet have little impact on corruption and graft in government.

Accounts of corruption are numerous in the daily newspapers, as are stories of poor management practices by public agencies. Today, corruption news probably is the topic most talked about in the Egyptian society, and very few would deny the alarming prevalence of corruption. Although incidents of corruption are present in most existing governments—East or West—differences in Egypt are compelling in certain respects: (1) the magnitude of corruption and its spread in public activities; (2) the effectiveness of efforts to discover, investigate, and take corrective action; and (3) the public's perception of the problem.

In Egypt, and in most Arab states, the scope of corruption is as extensive as it is troubling. Even sincere government reactions to it are feeble and inept. No strong and independent agencies exist that can monitor corruption by mounting their own investigations from beginning to end. Other instruments of accountability, such as independent financial and performance audits, are either nonexistent or overburdened with their own routines and mundane tasks. Government leaders are unwilling to establish a broad mandate with subpoena powers and administrative capabilities to fight corruption. Government muddles and the lack of resolve to fight corruption have intensified the already menacing crisis of public confidence in leaders and institutions.

Not surprisingly, the proposed solution to the problem of corruption by opposition groups is simply to bring down the government or to replace the whole "warped" system. Thus, the debate often has been transformed into a battle for survival rather than a negotiation for improving formulation and implementation of public policies. In fact, some of the opposing groups have already resorted to violent actions as the method for change. The huge socioeconomic disparities among Egyptians, added to the corruption of public officials, are fertile ground for violence and loss of social peace in the society. It is this political eventuality that Mohammad Hasannain Haykal underscores when he says: "There is a yearning for change that has gone beyond discontent to the verge of rebellion."[26]

The debates among scholars, writers, and columnists in Egypt on the subject of corruption are regular and considerable, and proposed solutions vary. With an interesting metaphor, Mustafa Amin, editor of one of the most influential (progovernment) publishing houses, imaginatively suggests the following:

It is the duty of every citizen in every country to fight corruption and to uncover it whether small or large. Silence about corruption is a major crime against the country. Corruption destroys nations, ruins governments, and overcomes peoples. Only democracy prevents corruption. The meaning of democracy is turning on the lights. Lights make the job of the thief more difficult. . . . More corruption in a country means more hunger, poverty, and deprivation. . . . It is in the shadow of individual rule that corruption prevails and thieves and robbers multiply. . . . No danger exists to a state from thieves as long as the state uncovers them, apprehends them, reveals their identities, and does not cover up for them.[27]

CONCLUSIONS

The incidents discussed here represent common managerial problems in Jordan and Egypt (and, in various degrees, the rest of the Arab world). Each incident addresses different political-administrative difficulties and underscores certain obstacles to building desired institutional capacities. In Jordan, the institutions responsible for regulating the private sector are stressed out to their limits in the face of unrelenting and corrupting pressures from food and medicine importers. In Egypt, nine monitoring agencies have been unsuccessful at preventing developers from fraudulently acquiring state lands and selling them as theirs, making huge profits for themselves and causing large losses for the public treasury.

In Jordan, the dominant executive authority is jealously guarding its power and prerogatives against any efforts to create checks and balances in the system of government. This leads to skepticism about the ceaseless claims by prime ministers that they are pursuing decentralization; in fact, they are seen to be tightening their grips on decisionmaking.

In Egypt, as in Jordan, the executive branch invariably stymies attempts to empower representative institutions of any type, whether municipal councils or national parliaments. Even the development of an independent, professional press is resisted. Distrust, indeed fear, of opposition by officeholders is epidemic. True, now and then some opposition groups and certain news organizations have acted irresponsibly or have been suspected of serving outside economic and political interests. Such unethical or illegal activities, when proven, require exposure, self-regulation, and accountability—prosecution through an independent judiciary is the answer and not the imposition of censorship, intimidation, or greater central control. Punitive actions are most effective in an environment that encourages self-evaluation and, yes, allows greater freedom. Oppressing the institutions of political opposition and the public information trade, without adjudication, is a sure way to perpetuate a lack of accountability by public officials.

Whatever the ideal, corruption remains an overarching problem of governing in the Arab state. Like a cancer eating the body of public institutions, it is also damaging the morale of citizens. Corruption is the immortal enemy of legitimacy of public authority and its decisions. The significance of corruption in developing countries, Myrdal (1970, 229) points out, is highlighted by the fact that wherever a political regime has crumbled, a major and often decisive cause has been the prevalence of official misconduct among politicians and administrators. Generally, such behaviors entice the spread of unlawful practices in the business sector and by the general public as well.

To control the negative effects of corruption, political and administrative leaders must accept a policy of transparency for their actions. They need to endorse and deepen the culture of responsibility and accountability to the public within governmental organizations and programs. To operationalize these values and to implement them, leaders have to develop institutional mechanisms that ensure accountability by continuous monitoring, measurement, and evaluation of public decisions.

Throughout recent history, from the Ottoman empire to Western colonialism, and even during the postcolonial era, the concept of government accountability to the people has not been embraced or practiced. There has been a total lack of checks and balances on executive authority. Moreover, as Kohl and Shue (1994, 322) found in several cases, "Growing disjuncture between the state and society . . . appears not to release but, rather, to reduce a state's ability to reach into and across society to effect change."

There is little doubt that for Arab leadership to regain legitimacy requires accountability, checks and balances, and the recognition that all powers in a society cannot reside forever in one person or in one office. Economic reform requires predictable and reliable decisionmaking processes in which accountability of public officials is assured. By the same token, administrative reform demands political liberalization as well as more effective use of modern organizational and managerial techniques and principles. An administrative system with enhanced capacity is able, for example, to use the budget for setting goals and objectives and identifying organizational weaknesses. Competent financial management generates useful information and improves the coordination and integration of activities of numerous offices and subunits within the bureaucracy. Moreover, competent management requires analytical capabilities that make it possible to gather valid information, define the problem, and then seek solutions for it. Finally, credibility of the public authority depends on having just and equitable laws equally applied to punish violators of any social and political strata, not just the poor and the powerless. It seems the essential change is definable but the unknown remains: Is the political leadership up to it?

NOTES

1. E. W. Scripps, *I Protest* (Madison: University of Wisconsin Press, 1966), p. 232.

2. Michael Bacos Young, "Hariri or Chaos," *Lebanon Report* (January 1995).

3. *Jordan Times,* January 27–28, 1994, p. 3.

4. Malhas is a physician from a wealthy Jordanian family that owns a hospital in Amman and includes many medical doctors.

5. *Shihan,* January 1, 1994.

6. Fahed Al-Fanek, *Jordan Times,* February 6, 1994, p. 4.

7. *Jordan Times,* February 3–4, 1994, p. 1.

8. Ibid.

9. *Al Dustour,* February 2, 1994, p. 10.

10. Ibid., p. 12.

11. *Al-Rai,* February 3, 1994, p. 10.

12. *Jordan Times,* February 5, 1994, p. 4.

13. Ibid.

14. Ibid.

15. Ibid.

16. *Al-Jamaheer,* February 1, 1994, p. 1.

17. *Al-Rai,* February 7, 1994, pp. 1, 25.

18. Quoted in *Jordan Times,* February 8, 1994.

19. Hashemite Kingdom of Jordan, 1990 National Charter, (2:2-A), p. 17.

20. Ibid.

21. Interview in Amman, March 30, 1994.

22. *Al-Ahram,* February 14, 1994.

23. This summary is based on reports in *Al-Ahram, Al-Akhbar,* and *Rose el-Yousef* (February 13–20, 1994). The main elements of the cases were also confirmed by senior Egyptian officials who did not wish to be named.

24. *Al-Ahram,* February 16, 1994, p. 3; *Rose El-Yousef,* no. 3425 (January 31, 1994), p. 7.

25. *Al-Ahram,* February 14, 1994, p. 3.

26. Mohammad Hasannain Haykal, "Egypt's Moment of Truth," *Mideast Monitor* (January 23, 1995).

27. Mustafa Amin, *Akbar el-Yom,* no. 2571 (February 12, 1994), p. 20.

Part III
Assets, Obstacles, and Choices

8

Political Islam and
Matters of Governing

So choked is the official and academic United States with "fun-
damentalist" projects and books, pamphlets and endless studies of
the Islamic threat that there can be no real dialogue between
Islam and the West. Either we produce caricatures of each other
or stress the "strategic" concept by which Islam is looked at as a
contender for power, and therefore now better courted surrepti-
tiously, just in case one of the militant parties does come to
power. Could it be that addressing the large number of secular, or
at least nonextremist, Muslim Arabs is not so palatable for us pre-
cisely because it would require a dialogue of equals, whereas we
want outright servants like Marcos, Sadat, the Shah, outright ene-
mies like Khomeini or Saddam Hussein?

Edward W. Said[1]

In this chapter, I focus on Islamic political movements in contemporary
Arab societies and their aspiration to build an Islamic state in the Arab
world. My specific objectives are to identify reasons for the current
resurgence of Islamism, to examine factors that could enhance (or impede) achievement of the Islamists' goal, and to define the claims and
promises of this Islamic option. Of particular interest are the economic,
political, and social programs advocated by Islamists for their promised
system of government, so I will define some fundamentals of the Islamic
doctrine that relate to the management of their political and economic
programs.

It is important to emphasize, however, that this is not a study of Islam
as a religion or as a political force in history. The literature is rich with
works on these topics. Instead, my purpose is to examine the Islamist
resurgence and the proposed programs for Islamist governing, just as I attempt to delineate values and programs of secular political movements.
The literature employing social science perspectives in the study of this
subject is limited.

155

ISLAMISTS AND THE CRISIS OF THE ARAB STATE

Recognizing the increasing problems facing Arab societies and the inability of current regimes to solve them, the Islamists have accelerated their quest for responsibility to govern and to correct the course of the Islamic nation (*al-ummah al-islamiah*). It is in the context of the current crisis that Islamic resurgence finds its relevance and gathers its momentum.

Islamists have already pronounced secular nationalist and socialist political movements dead or bankrupt. This is quite a different conclusion from that reached by scholars of the early 1960s who reported "a profound revolution" in progress, one that was led by nationalists attempting to transform the entire Middle East and North Africa. As a result of this revolution, Halpern (1963, vii) points out, "A way of life that endured nearly 1300 years is being destroyed by challenges for which, as a system of faith and action, it was entirely unprepared." Today, the nationalist order that was to produce a new social system, with new values to replace the traditional religious ones, is itself being pronounced dead. In fact, Islamists blame Arab nationalists and socialists for many of the afflictions of today's Arab society. Hasan Turabi, a leading contemporary Islamist thinker-activist, describes Arab socialism as "a very important slogan, but there was no content to it" (Lowrie 1992, 17). For Arab nationalism, Turabi reserves these views: "The nationalist movement aspired simply to national independence. This just meant changing a British administrator by putting in his place a Sudanese administrator. Once independence was achieved, these movements looked bankrupt. They were not prepared for anything else" (Lowrie 1992, 17).

The Islamists' popular appeal is multidimensional. Islam extends a new identity to the alienated individual in an increasingly secularized and urbanized society. Secularism often is inattentive to, if not entirely derisive of, rituals and symbolisms that comfort and reassure people raised and socialized in traditional cultures. Too, contemporary economic systems and urban living produce their own economic and social inequities. Turbulent environments and constantly changing relationships among individuals and groups foster a need for psychological stability and certainty in people's lives. The Islamic doctrine is suited for such a role as it provides reassurance to the adherents.

Since the setbacks of secular Arab nationalism in the late 1960s, other factors have been reinforcing the rise of Islamism. First, the Islamic doctrine draws on a rich moral content that regularly dispenses prescriptions for almost all aspects of individual and community existence. Islamic principles regulate family life, relations among people, and relations with God.

Second, by facilitating frequent contacts among the faithful, the role of the mosque, where Muslims meet and worship, has been vital. In the

Arab-Muslim world, the mosque is described as the "mightiest power," and it is said that "governments tremble before it."[2] Mosques serve numerous functions such as education and indoctrination, in addition to being places where the community gathers and worships. This is made easy because mosques in the Arab world are also numerous; almost every Muslim is in proximity to one.

Third, over decades of colonial rule, Islam served as a powerful ideology of resistance and proved to possess "immense capacity for mass mobilization" (Banuaziz 1994, 2). From the fall of the Ottoman empire in 1918 to the independence movements of the 1950s, Islamic ideology influenced and shaped resistance to the encroachments of imperialism in the Arab world. As Rami Khouri says,

> The roots of today's populist, politicized Islam lie deep in the many nationalist, anti-colonial and anti-Western struggles in the modern Middle East that relied on Islam as a rallying cry to seek freedom from foreign subjugation, to forge national entities from tribal alliances or to reform and revive their stagnant societies in the 19th century, from the Mahdi in Sudan and the Wahhabis in Saudi Arabia to Mohammad Ibn al-Sanousi in Libya and Abdelqadir in Algeria, among many others.[3]

Finally, Islamic political movements enjoy a twofold advantage over any other political party. One is the continuous indoctrination of its followers with the word of God, as the Islamic religious establishment (the *ulama*) interprets it. As is true of other major religions, the faith, rather than reasoning and agreements among individuals, dictates basic decisions. Varied individual experiences and perceptions are subordinated to the rules and authentic interpretations of the dogma. Thus, Islamic doctrine has a harmonizing and unifying effect on its followers, who must adhere to the finest print of the text, without exegesis. This unifying influence of Islamic teachings transcended ethnic and cultural differences, tied them into a single connected system of roles within fixed patterns, and provided them with a universal language of words and symbols.

Contemporary Islamists also have another advantage—of great practical and visible results—over other political movements. This is the collective ownership of an elaborate infrastructure of services (schools, hospitals, charities, publications) funded by levies (*zakat*) from members of the Muslim community. The services to the membership are so substantial that they often rival, even exceed, those of the state. An example of this could be seen in Lebanon during and after the 1975–1989 civil war.

It would be misleading, however, to conclude that the Islamists' current appeal is totally the result of factors intrinsic to the doctrine. In fact, the Islamic doctrine has been a dominant influence in Arab lives for over thirteen hundred years, and its current resurgence cannot be explained totally in terms of its inherent constants. A leading Arab journalist and secular thinker, M. H. Haykal, emphatically rejects the notion "that the Islamists are anything more than a vast oppositional and protest movement."[4] In Egypt, Haikal contends, the Islamist resurgence is "the result of an almost unimaginably corrupt and mediocre Government." Similar conclusions are reached by other analysts of the rising tide of Islamism. As Michael Field states, "Islamist movements draw strength not from any surge in religious zeal among Middle Eastern peoples but from political failure—brutal government, military defeat, economic mismanagement and corruption."[5] The conclusion is that an explanation of the resurgence of Islamism in the Arab world today requires one to look beyond innate characteristics and consider contextual factors. As we approach the twenty-first century, Arab political leaders have managed to plunge their countries into the worst crisis of their modern history. The enormity of the crisis and its consequences reach all dimensions of the society and extend far beyond the difficult issues of regimes' legitimacy and malfunctioning developmental institutions. Arab regimes are enduring the repercussions of political and economic fragmentation and petty feuds among Arab leaders that have reduced them to global insignificance. Such political and economic marginalization is further deepened by excessive foreign influence over Arab decisionmaking processes and control of their markets and resources, particularly those of the oil-producing states.

To complete the depiction of the crisis, add the mounting problems of unemployment, inflation, population growth, and poverty that have been discussed in previous chapters. During the 1980s and the 1990s, Arab economies experienced a loss of developmental momentum and suffered a decline in GNP and deterioration of human development efforts in education, health, and social welfare. Between 1975 and 1993, the average annual percentage change in GNP per capita among the twelve largest Arab states was –2.5, the worst performance among all regions of the world.[6]

Beholden to foreign powers for their security and protection, isolated from their own peoples, and lacking in vision and values, Arab leaders are generally viewed as corrupt, ineffective, or brutal. These leaders, Said (1993, 65) charges, "are kept in place partly because the United States gives them so much support" in order to sustain the rule of their regimes and dynasties.

Although many other developing countries have been experiencing wrenching political, economic, and social problems, the case of Arab states seems a little more stark and much more complex. Failures of domestic public policies, for example, are intertwined with bungled strategies in foreign and military affairs, as the Iraqi and Kuwaiti leaders discovered after 1990. Conceivably, citizens could have forgiven some deficiency of domestic programs had their leaders been more effective in foreign and military policies. Success of foreign policy is measured by results, such as finding better solutions to Arab grievances and more capably asserting national rights and interests.

The Gulf War of 1991 is an example of the grievous conditions of Arab foreign and military policies. On the surface, the United States collaborated with Arab regimes in a military attack on Iraq, after its invasion of Kuwait. But the end results of this conflict have victimized Arabs on both sides of the battle, deepened feuds among Arab leaders, and illustrated once more the ineffectual performance of these leaders. As I indicated earlier, the financial losses alone to Arab countries from the 1990–1991 Gulf War have been authoritatively estimated at $676 billion, a shocking waste for any economy and a steep price for the absurdity of any leader.

A central issue in the analysis of contextual influences on Islamic resurgence is the Palestinian-Israeli conflict, festering for over sixty years. This conflict epitomizes various ailments of Arab political and military systems. Arab leaders have been completely ineffective in dealing with Western partiality against the Arab side in this conflict or in presenting a genuine and impressive deterrence to Israeli encroachment on Palestinian legitimate interests. Policies of the Palestinian leadership have also vacillated among acts of desperation, determined popular resistance as in the *intifada,* or spineless political ploys by the PLO.

Even after the 1993 peace accord in Oslo, which was followed by summit meetings in Washington between the contending parties, many Palestinians continue to perceive these agreements as sacrificing their legitimate rights and not ending the occupation. Naseer Aruri (1995, 4) suggests that "Israel's non-recognition of the Palestinians as a sovereign people is the single most important obstacle to a genuine peace." Long after the Oslo Accord, Edward W. Said remains the most consistent critic: "With Oslo, the peace process entered a new and much more destructive phase. Far from bringing peace, it brought greater suffering for Palestinians, the main victims of the mess, and a much greater threat to the long term interests of Israeli people."[7]

The most organized opposition to the accord has not been by secular groups; it has come from Palestinian Islamists, who have emerged as opposition leaders and have been mobilizing popular support to their views throughout the Arab world. Who are these Islamists? Followers of the Islamist political movement are not limited to recruits from the unemployed and dispossessed or to what a Tunisian diplomat called a "constituency of despair."[8] Islamists are also recruited from the ranks of influential and powerful figures throughout Arab and Muslim societies. Nearly five hundred Islamist and nationalist figures from the Arab and Muslim world published an advertisement in *Al-Hayat,* a Saudi-owned pan-Arab daily published in Beirut, to express support for the Palestinian Islamic Resistance

Movement and its struggle for liberation. The ad, titled "Statement of Support and Solidarity," appeared on two full pages for the second consecutive week on Friday May 5, 1995, and was signed by *ulamas,* scholars of religion, intellectuals, Islamic leaders, pan-Arab nationalists, trade unionists, and representatives of political groups. The signatories of the document affirm, among other principles, that the Palestinian cause is central and that the Arabs and the Muslim nation "are duty-bound to assist the Palestinian people with all available means and support their legitimate rights to liberation, repatriation, and self-determination."[9]

For a variety of reasons, then, "political Islam is now the principal voice of opposition . . . to individual leaders, individual regimes and individual states" (Farsoun 1995, 13). Islamists have been successful in galvanizing citizens' dissatisfaction into a wave of overt and covert political protests. They appear to be the only viable political movement to lead the opposition to current Arab regimes. As a result, Islamists have seen their popular support as well as their numbers grow dramatically in recent years. The demise of the Marxist camp and the disarray of Arab nationalists have significantly benefited this Islamic political resurgence.

In the context of modern Arab history, there appears to be a continuous popular struggle against one foreign attempt after another aiming at control and domination. In an almost dialectical evolution, after the passing of each foreign encroachment, communities have managed to survive and occasionally flourish. This time, says Samir Amin, "It seems realistic to start from the bold observation that capitalist development and imperialist conquests have created the situation" of Islamic resurgence (quoted in Abu-Rabi' 1994, 14). On the same theme, Hisham Sharabi (1988, 64) argues that Islamic fundamentalism moved to the center of the political stage as a reaction to imperialism. He notes that Islamism not only criticized colonialism for religious alienation and cultural dependency but also assisted neopatriarchal structure and discourse in modern Arab society.

Even though the thesis that imperialist conquest caused Islamic resurgence has wide appeal, an irony in the situation is worth pointing out. During the Cold War years, the West—the United States in particular—fomented Islamic activism against communism. Many Islamic organizations were created at the behest of the United States to form a buffer against communism. The Pan-Islamist Congress called by Saudi Arabia in May 1962, which instituted an Islamic League, was intended primarily to counter Gamal Abdul Nasser's nationalist movement in Egypt and socialist influences in the Islamic world (Halpern 1963, 26). And it is the United States that trained and armed the mujahidin in Afghanistan, calling them freedom fighters, to battle the occupation by the former Soviet Union.[10] Now, some of the same elements, using U.S. military training, have been resisting Israeli occupation of Arab lands as well as fighting

U.S.-supported Arab governments from Amman to Riyadh and from Algiers to Cairo.

In conclusion, Islamist political resurgence is rooted in the current crisis of Arab regimes. "No doubt," Sonn (1990, 226) notes, "the Islamic activist movement that so influenced Arab politics during the past two decades was a reaction to previous political failures." Islamists have become the single most important manifestation of contemporary Arab political, social, and economic discontent. Growing disparities of wealth and rampant corruption at all levels of government are sinking the foundations of the state. The dilemma of the regimes is made much more complicated by the absence of a common positive vision of the future. The effectiveness of already weak political and administrative institutions is vitally imperiled by the lack of a legitimating ideology from which a strategy, a framework, promises a sense of direction as well as an imminent prospect of operation by trusted and competent public managers and leaders.

OPPOSING IS NOT GOVERNING

The basic Islamic precepts are stated in the Quran (the sacred text for Muslims), complemented by Hadith (sayings of the prophet Mohammad). Next are the interpretations of the *ulama* (Islamic clerics) of principles in either of these two sources or through the doctrine of *ijtihad,* derivation by reasoning. For the faithful, the Quran and the Hadith are unassailable; they are the articles of faith. Interpretations and derivations, however, are human judgments by knowledgeable people (generally the *ulama*) who offer their own translations and explications of what was meant or not meant by the established precepts of the faith.

Although many aspects of the faith are constant, they do not explain why, when, or how Islamic political radicalism was activated. It is not actually possible to fix an exact date for the origin of contemporary Islamist resurgence, although some general manifestations of its evolution are recognizable. One thing is clear, however: Current Islamism is a recent growth and a reaction to a multiplicity of modern developments and conditions. As Abu-Rabi' (1994, 13) explains, some Muslim scholars argue that modern Islamism is part of an overall Islamic historical pattern known as *tajdid* (renewal) and *islah* (reform), utilizing the process of *ijtihad* to generate the needed dynamism for renewal and innovation.

Generally, the literature dates Islamic revivalism from the beginning of reformist efforts by religious leaders such as Jamal al-Din al-Afghani, Muhammad Abduh, Rashid Rida, and others who resisted orthodox theology. These nineteenth-century reformists (often referred to as the Salafis) exhorted fellow Muslims to rise against foreign domination and to accept greater compatibility between faith and reason. They sought to open the door of religious dogma to rational and scientific interpretations through the processes of *ijtihad*. But the subsequent changes were only minor; reformers could not achieve fundamental change without the support of the more rigidly orthodox traditionalists.

Perhaps the 1920s can more realistically be said to signify the beginning of contemporary Islamic political movements. That is when Hasan al-Banna of Egypt created the Muslim Brothers, "a new movement of thought that endeavored to define Islam primarily as a political system, in keeping with the major ideologies of the twentieth century" (Roy 1994, viii).

Despite these earlier roots, the contemporary resurgence of Islamism is mainly a post–World War II phenomenon that gained momentum in the 1980s and 1990s. Today's Islamists proclaim far more than what was urged or aspired to by the Salafis or advocated by the Muslim Brothers, notwithstanding the many common notions among the three movements. Contemporary Islamists assume no less than reaching their clear objective of governing the nation (*al-ummah*).

Not all Islamists are devout Muslims committed to traditional beliefs and values or attached to the doctrine of the *shari'a* (Islamic law). Many of the members and supporters are former nationalists, socialists, liberationists, and veteran anticolonialists—all disenchanted with their former associations and disillusioned with current public policies. They are linked together by distrust of existing governments and by their apprehensions of what they perceive as imperial designs to reassert hegemony over Arab and Muslim lands.

Thus, the unifying factor of Islamist opposition is primarily a negative one—disappointment and dissatisfaction with the status quo. This is different from an appeal based on achievement or a contribution to improving socioeconomic and political conditions, real or potential. Moreover, Islamist doctrinal ideas continue to be only general policy statements, critically in need of operational thrust. Islamist doctrine has not been defined proficiently to identify the type of state Islamists seek, the political and administrative institutions they require, or the public policy processes they will employ.

Even less clear is the Islamist response to issues of leadership and leaders' succession in their prospective state. Widespread concerns about individual rights, women's rights, and civil liberties frequently have received guarded answers from Islamist activists and intellectuals rather than unambiguous, consistent ones. In a roundtable discussion with Hasan A. Turabi (a leading Islamist), Mark Tessler (a scholar of Middle East studies) asked a question that helps to elucidate the issue. Tessler requested elaboration on whether the Islamic state would or would not interfere with those who do not follow certain practices, citing as an example accounts that Palestinian and Algerian women who do not follow strict dress codes are being harassed and made to conform (Lowrie 1992, 35). Turabi's response affirms that "segregation [of women] is definitely not part of Islam." But for dress, he agrees that Islam does prescribe what is to be covered for a moral reason. His answer is prefaced by this clarification:

> In the Algerian case, there are two currents in the Islamic movement: one, *salafi,* which looks to the Saudi Arabian social model; and [the] current which definitely you would call more liberal with respect to women. The leader, Abbasi Madani, was asked again and again about this, and he preferred to be ambiguous because the movement is very new. It is an affiliation actually, a federation, and he, perhaps, didn't want to put off any particular sector until he had brought about some unity (Lowrie 1992, 35–36).

Political and socioeconomic uncertainty in the Islamic doctrine may turn out to be merely symptomatic of formidable challenges and, perhaps, lingering lethal vulnerabilities. Actually, Islamist power still may prove to be fickle and ephemeral. Membership may dissipate, thinning out the ranks just as happened to the Marxists and the Ba'athists earlier, in the post-1967 debacle. Developments in the Islamic Republic of Iran, as well as conditions within the Algerian Islamic movement, underscore the Islamists' dilemma.

The case of Algeria is particularly germane. The Algerian Islamist movement is in fact a coalition of twelve groups who agree on the goal of toppling the ruling regime but not on much else. Excessive violence against civilians has been committed by factions in this movement. "The plague of terror," as the *Washington Post* called it,[11] began after the army took over in 1992, in order to preempt the Islamists' imminent electoral victory. Scores of journalists, other professionals, and foreign visitors have been murdered. One of the dozen groups fighting the government within the Islamic front is the radical Armed Islamic Group (GIA), which has been quoted as saying: "Those who fight us with the pen shall die by the sword."[12] But not all Islamic activists subscribe to GIA methods, as Islamists are far more diversified in their goals and the means to achieve them than most people have acknowledged. Nevertheless, when, and if, the Islamists' objective of seizing power (or ousting the ruling regime) is achieved, their ability to handle the challenges of sustained management of the state is in doubt.

To say the political power of the Islamist movement is spasmodic or exaggerated is not to conclude that hard-core Islamist faithfuls will precipitously abandon ship or part company. Rather, those who joined more to oppose current regimes than because of belief in the Islamist program may not maintain their affiliation or allegiance when conditions change. It is my opinion that the decline of Islamist movements most likely will begin with one of two conditions.

The first of the two—the emergence of a genuinely secular, liberal political movement with a viable program—is the missing alternative in Arab politics. Such a movement has the potential of rallying and uniting discouraged, fragmented reformist forces. A successful national program of economic and social change would certainly attract significant popular support away from the Islamists. With effective leadership and proficient institutions, a reformist government would be able to revive citizens' confidence.

The second likelihood is an actual Islamist takeover that would convert the oppositional coalition into a ruling party. If this situation materializes, Islamists will face the responsibility of meeting inflated public expectations and demands for tangible outcomes. Their gain of state control will be the crucial test for implementing underdeveloped, overpromising, and untested theological teachings of political and economic principles. The problem, as Edward W. Said (1996, 28) says, is that "political Islam has generally been a failure wherever it has tried to take state power."

If Islamists do take over governments, it is plausible to expect that they will be overwhelmed. Governing introduces an entirely different accountability and contrasts sharply with posturing from the sidelines as an opposition political party. More precisely, it is doubtful that a governing religious fundamentalism, offering religious arguments to current political issues, would be successful in mainly secular and increasingly global political and economic systems.

The riddle in need of a solution is what synthesis will emerge to organize and manage Arab society after its current upheaval and confusion. Evidence seems to indicate that the Islamist option is very much a part of any future political order in the Arab world. The challenge is to determine what aspect of Islamism and how it will be incorporated into the structure of power. In fact, many Arab states already claim in their laws and constitutions that they are Muslim societies and that Islamic law is the main source of their legislative rationale. "Thank God, Egypt is already an Islamic state," declared Sayed Tantawi, appointed by President Mubarak in March 1996 to head Egypt's one-thousand-year-old Al-Azhar University.[13] Although an Islamist may view this constitutional process as that of regaining a pre-given right, nationalists and secularists see the accommodation as entirely inappropriate (Al-Azmeh 1994). In any case, legitimate concerns and basic questions can be expressed.

First, enforcing Islamism through violent means is not a realistic strategy at this time. To do so would certainly cause a deep polarization in the society and place Islamists against the ruling elites, the military, and a significant number of national-secular groups. Moreover, Islamists themselves are deeply divided over this issue. Violent clashes in Algeria between militant Islamists (GI) and the Islamic Salvation Army, for example, have already been reported.[14] A violent Islamist strategy would also create conditions conducive to more oppression, brutality, and entrenchment of existing regimes, as it would certainly mobilize further Western aid and commitments for these regimes, as we have seen in Algeria, Egypt, Saudi Arabia, and Bahrain.

A second possible option is an Islamist-oriented state with a democratic and reformist policy. This may seem an irreconcilable incongruity; it should not. In the midst of current rampant misinformation, moderate and progressive Islamist views generally are not acknowledged. Still, "it is always possible to argue on behalf of Islam by portraying it as the paramount democracy thanks to three concepts: *shura* (consultation), *ijtihad* (independent reasoning), and *ijma* (consensus)" (Leca 1994, 60). Rashid el-Ghanoushi, for example, is a leading Islamist who professes "acceptance of the rules of democracy and multi-party politics."[15] In a survey by the *Economist*, Ghanoushi, the leader of Tunisia's Islamic movement, is specific about his commitment to democracy.[16] He promises that when his party comes to power, as he expects it will, it will submit itself to multi-party elections within five years of taking office. Whoever wins the election will be allowed to become the government, even if the winner wants to overturn what the Islamists have done in five years. Hasan A. Turabi, secretary general of the Popular Arab-Islamic Conference (PAIC) and a leader of Sudan's Islamic movement, expresses views in his public positions similar to those of Ghanoushi. In a recent interview with a Lebanese Arabic newspaper, Turabi emphasizes the need to open a new page in Arab-West relations.[17] He points out that Arab intellectuals, trained in both Arab and Western institutions, constitute the leadership of Islamic movements. He also calls for *hiwar* (dialogue), rejection of violence, and commitment to evolutionary rather than revolutionary change.

The trouble is in the enforcement of these equations and pronouncements by Ghanoushi, Turabi, and others, given the history and pretext of religion where "truth" is revealed to and interpreted only by chosen people. Also, it is not easy for Westerners to distinguish between responsible and irresponsible conduct of various Islamist movements when the mass media consistently misconstrue or misrepresent events, particularly violent acts against innocent people (as in Egypt and Algeria).

A third possibility is a secular, reformist, liberal, and democratic state that also embodies moderate Islamist principles. The power base of this type of government has to come from the new middle class, intellectuals, reformists, nationalists, socialists, and developmental business interests. The strength of this strategy derives from its appeal to the total population and its commitment to addressing glaring discrepancies in wealth and social services. This reformist strategy is premised on the ability to develop efficient and effective public institutions, to create an environment of free and competitive business relations, to develop legitimacy through democratic means, and to build trust through effective and just policies. This is not a prescription for utopia but is perhaps the most practical and realistic alternative. Only such perspectives will prevent a dangerous polarization of Arab society on the inside and improve competitiveness globally. Preliminary foundations for such perspectives are already in place in several Arab states.

It is important to recognize that the experience of Islamists in the Arab political systems has been mixed and uneven. Although Islamists have been an effective force for protest and challenge, to date they have been unable to translate their ideology and promise into a coherent political program that responds to people's practical needs. Islamism "remains vague about the precise political, economic and social programs it would institute, and has no real, proven national successes. Its strength as a movement that seeks a change, goodness and justice has not been matched by its success as an ideology of statehood or an incumbent regime."[18]

Thus, it is reasonable—although speculative—to suppose that the success of Islamists in seizing power will bring about the end of their growth momentum and perhaps permanently shatter their ambition of governing. It is too soon to say this with certainty when so many factors influence outcomes. At the present, Islamism is expanding despite the challenges and counterreactions from the state and from secular groups. Actually, where Islamists are accepted as part of the political system and are allowed to compete for representation—as in Jordan, Yemen, Kuwait—they tend to recognize pluralism and to credibly participate in the political process.

ISLAMISM BETWEEN PERSECUTORS AND ADVOCATES

It is increasingly difficult to identify or define Islamist political movements as they are rather than as they are perceived by either detractors, advocates, or hostile governments. This is a real challenge for analysis as well as for making policy in the West or within Arab societies. As Lowrie (1995, 215) states, "the ferocity and pervasiveness of anti-Islam campaigns are taking a toll on the U.S. government's ability to pursue a flexible and constructive policy toward Islamic movements." Recognizing that there are distortions in mass media coverage or in the literature is not sufficient to guard against hidden agendas and preconceived notions about Islamists and Islam. More and more, a thorough discussion of the Islamist doctrine is complicated by the absence of historical and political argumentation. Uninformed discourse may be blind to exchanges that are arranged so as to highlight content of sacred texts and Islamic law or to project effects on Western societies. Thus, the results of analysis often are flawed, as conclusions are transformed into prosecutorial pronouncements.

Many difficulties emanate from the tendencies of Western policymakers to foil independent political movements in the Arab world that resist foreign dictates or insist on equality in international exchanges. National forces that mobilize opposition to Western designs or to their loyal leaders are viewed with suspicion and hostility. This situation is as true today with Islamist political movements as it was with nationalist governments in the past (such as Abdul Nasser's regime in Egypt).

Foreign disapproval of Islamism has served its advocates as evidence of their credibility and force. At the same time, citizens of the region do not take seriously exaggerations such as this: "[F]rom North Africa to the Persian Gulf, impoverished and disaffected Muslims have embraced the fiery appeal of fundamentalism" (Bordewich 1995, 77). Scholars from the area have a different view of the matter. Islamic conformity, notes Galal Amin, an Egyptian economist and social theorist, "seems an easy way to achieve emotional satisfaction" in dreary times. His conclusion is that it would be "wrong to mistake this for the fundamentalism that encourages bomb-throwing and murder in the name of Islam."[19]

Western critics (particularly those in the United States) have hindered fruitful discourse on policies and programs. Rational analysis is jeopardized when the initial thesis is: "Islam is a terrorist idealogy."[20] Daniel Pipes has many colleagues and substantial resources dedicated to advocating that there are no "good" Islamic fundamentalists, only bad ones who take "different paths." Islamic fundamentalists, from Pipes's angle, are either "terrorists," a "threat to oil supplies," or "extremists." Given such a predisposition, tied to the notion that Islam and the West are on an inevitable collision course as a result of assumed irreconcilable disagreements, reasoning is made futile. A U.S. Foreign Service officer explains how traditional Western attitudes toward Islam have been recently aroused:[21] Communism is defunct. U.S. diplomats, soldiers and intelligence officers must now seek out new missions and new foreign threats. . . . Analysts need jobs, agencies need budgets and governments find external challenges helpful to internal solidarity. . . . This function, in today's world, is perhaps best filled by political Islam." (Horan 1995, 24).

The Islamic threat is made to seem disproportionately fearsome in order to lend support to the thesis that there is a worldwide conspiracy behind every explosion (Said 1996, 28). Samuel Huntington advanced and popularized the controversial notion that envisions a "clash of civilizations" between Islam and the West,[22] a thesis that has been rejected by many scholars (Said 1993; Fuller and Lesser 1995) on several grounds. First, the "clash" thesis does not acknowledge diversity and "assumes that the West and Islam are watertight categories, identities to which every Westerner and every Muslim must choose allegiance" (Said 1993, 62). Second, not only does such a thesis ignore diversity on both sides of the line of demarcation but also it assumes that Islam is inherently anti-West when in reality most of these countries are within the "U.S. orbit."

Also dubious is the suggestion that Islamists are indeed in command of all Muslim forces, which intend to ultimately undermine or destroy the Western civilization. Evidence gathered by Dekmejian (1995) identifies 175 Islamist societies founded during the last twenty-five years (out of an estimated total of about three hundred). Among these societies the author distinguishes four ideologies: the gradualist pragmatic, the revolutionary Shi'ite, the revolutionary Sunni, and the messianic-puritanical.

In 1995, to "assess policy challenge," the U.S. Department of State–affiliated Institute for Peace initiated a series of workshops on U.S. policy and the Islamic world. The workshops "were attended by government officials, academics, journalists, and policy specialists." The conclusion of these discussions: Islamic activism, including its more militant forms, stands for different things in different countries and regions.[23]

Although Islamist political movements cannot be exempted from evaluation and analysis, these should not be based on preconceived notions. Nor should they be dominated by analysts and "experts" in the employ of institutions of advocacy and foreign intelligence organizations. Prejudicial perceptions of Arabs and Muslims are regularly conveyed in mass media coverage,[24] but never more crudely and recklessly than in the aftermath of the Oklahoma City tragedy in March 1995. With uncommon journalistic sensitivity to civil rights of Arabs and Muslims, a commentary in *The Progressive* (June 1995, p. 8) magazine underscores the torridness of the situation:

> In some of the most irresponsible media coverage in recent memory, the networks ran with stories implicating Arabs or Islamic fundamentalists or Middle Eastern terrorists. There was absolutely no factual basis for these reports; it was just vicious, bigoted rumor-mongering. And the same old "terrorist experts" were trotted out to offer their authoritative theories as to why the bombers were probably Middle Eastern.

DEMAND FOR INDEPENDENT APPRAISAL

A primary concern of this study is not to question the provisions of any sacred text but to examine policies and programs proposed by humans, even if rationalized in terms of texts. No promises to remedy political, economic, and social ills of the society can escape the canons of expert evaluation or the judgment of citizens. This is why the tensions caused by the dichotomy between the foreordained and the rationally chosen are both absorbing and complex. In fact, the separation between the text—the central precepts of Islamic doctrine—and the development of temporal systems of government is not always feasible.

Islamic precepts reject the principle of separation between the realm of God and that of Caesar, or the province of ethics from that of law, for Islam is both a religion (*deen*) and a state (*daouleh*). Thus, all methods of evaluation are essentially restricted to human interpretations, amplifications, extensions, and confined reasoning of preexisting precepts. A possible way around such a condition is to effect a method of analysis based on examination of actual contemporary experiences of functioning Islamic states. By comparing performance and results of an Islamist rule, I hope to contribute some insights into the efficacy of the overall system and the proficiency of its managerial and organizational processes in practice. To this end, I submit four dimensions.

Political Leadership

From the earliest times of Islamic rule, conflicting loyalties, geographical isolation, and various environmental factors prevented smooth transition of command as well as a systematic approach to succession of leadership. In fact, of the four caliphs who succeeded the Prophet Muhammad, only the first died a natural death. In the more recent experience of almost six hundred years of Ottoman rule, "a single family supplied the sultans for the Ottoman Empire, the largest and most enduring Islamic state" (Halpern 1963, 8). The message here is loud and clear. Should we have an authoritarian secular government (such as that of the shah of Iran) replaced by another form of authoritarian politics that keep at bay any notion of democratic or popular government? The lesson to Arab states from the legacy of Islamic movements is obvious but also troubling.

As Paul Salem (1994, 144) points out, "the Islamists have articulated opposition to the authoritarian secular Arab nationalist regimes in such a way as to perpetuate many of the authoritarian elements of these dominant regimes." The argument here centers on supplanting one authoritarianism with another and replacing ruling nationalists with ruling Islamists while fundamental features of "statism," individual freedoms, representation, and similar political issues remain virtually unaltered.

Secular critics simply declare that Islamism no longer offers a model for a different society or a brighter future. The French political philosopher Olivier Roy (1994) presents an entirely different verdict, concluding that even if Islamists take power in countries like Algeria, they will be unable to reshape economics and politics. The justification is based on pragmatic rather than dogmatic considerations. He explains:

> Islamism has been transformed into a type of neofundamentalism concerned solely with reestablishing Muslim law, the *sharia*, without inventing new political forms, which means that it is condemned to serving as

a mere cover for a political logic that eludes it–a logic in which we ultimately find the traditional ethnic, tribal, or communal divisions, ever ready to change their discourse of legitimization, hidden beneath the new social categories and regimes. (Roy 1994, ix)

The conclusion: Islamists have not succeeded in establishing a new society even in countries where they have achieved power, such as Iran, Pakistan, Afghanistan, and Sudan. Nor have they solved the problem of succession of leadership to suit the flexible needs of modern rule.

Faith Versus Reason

The design of structures and institutional processes of the promised Islamic state must contend with a perennial problem, namely that "the dominant corpus in Sunni Islamic culture, that of the ulamas, as well as those of the Salafist reformists and contemporary Islamists, conceive of Islam as timeless, ahistorical, and beyond criticism" (Roy (1994, 11). Accepting this characterization means a permanent subordination of reason to faith. "Divine and therefore perfect, perfect and therefore complete, complete and therefore final, final and therefore unalterable—such was the constitution . . . for the Muslim community from God in the midst of the seventh century" (Halpern 1963, 5). How can an Islamist then relate faith and reason without being trapped in one hopelessly stifling contradiction after another?

Mohammed Arkoun suggests a particular perspective on the question. He says: "The contemporary resurgence of Islam—whether on the West Bank or in Iran or Algeria—follows not from the reformist premise of the compatibility of Islam with Western reason but from the initial rejection of reason in the name of faith and the subsequent embrace of reason as a tool for the confirmation, clarification, and administration of that faith" (Arkoun 1994, x). I accept the relevance of Arkoun's argument but question its generalizational connotation. In an interview, Ghanoushi provides a particularly flexible viewpoint on the question of reason in Islamist evidence. He uses the Arabic term *aqlanah* as equivalent to realism, which means "the Muslim should be in a perpetual dynamism with his reality and should give the reality a real value in his planning lest his work would be a futile task governed purely by the text."[25] This is clearly an unorthodox view of the role of experimentation and innovation in the Islamist program.

Defining the Geographical Unit

Islam's ability to survive for so long as a political system and as a rich civilization is a testimony to its capacity to confront challenges and to renew its vigor. But the Islamic experience has not resolved certain fundamental issues of statehood that remain problematic and even at variance with clear historical evidence. One such issue centers on defining the geographical unit of the Islamist state in territorial terms rather than limiting the definition to people of the Muslim faith. The nation-state has been the critical unit throughout modern political history. It has survived, so far, all efforts to dilute it, from Marxist revolutions to European unification projects to recent trends of globalization and multinational corporations. Even in the Arab-Islamic world, the state with fixed geographic boundaries has proved to be more stable and more resilient than many believed possible only a few years ago.

Nevertheless, the Islamists tie their state not to a territory but to a community of the faithful—*al-ummah*—(Roy 1994, 13). Borders and nationalities are considered to be provisional and contingent. Muslims, whether Arabs, Indonesians, Iranians, or Malaysians, are joined in a sort of unity—*a-ummah al-islamiah*—that supersedes all other political, cultural, or economic differences. Islamists' low concern for such earthly national matters of geography, economics, and politics is conveyed by Shaikh Rashid el-Ghanoushi when he says that Islam "is a transcendental truth that is too great for one human to comprehend and too vast for political or civilizational geography to contain and as the Quran explains, its tree is neither eastern nor western."[26]

This element alone marks the Islamic doctrine as ahistorical and its political program as untenable, ignoring realities of modern politics and context. The national political system has not been rendered obsolete even within a global economy. State behavior, whether East or West, provides ample evidence that the nation-state remains the most viable political force. And, yes, the Islamic revolution in Iran, despite all pretence, has not been able to conceal its Persian, nationalistic proclivity in dealing with its Muslim neighbors or with other countries.

Managing the Economy

Managing economic policy is central to the Islamist doctrine of statehood. Islamists consistently denounce Western economic systems for being premised on exploitation of their own citizens and domination of other nations. Marxist and socialist orders are not favored or accepted either; among the objections to Marxism are its materialistic and antireligion assumptions. This explains why after the Islamic revolution in Iran, Ayatollah Khomeini urged his followers to cleanse the universities of all elements connected either to the West or the East (Milani 1994, 201). From the start, the Islamic revolution launched an Islamization of Iran campaign that included changes in law, politics, economics, and cultural patterns to make them consistent with Islamic precepts.

A DISTINCT ISLAMIC ECONOMIC ORDER?

Is there an *Islamic* economic order that is distinct from other schools of economics? If so, what sets it apart and how is it managed? One may pursue two tracks of evidence in delineating the basic features and institutions of this Islamist economic alternative. The first is based on explicit Islamic precepts that define, regulate, encumber, or aid economic activities. The second is derived from observing the management of Islamic economic orders in action, as in Iran, Saudi Arabia, Pakistan, Sudan, or Afghanistan.

A noticeable aspect of Islamic economic teachings or precepts is that they are basically scattered propositions and cases that are used to provide legitimizing evidence of certain activities or prohibition of others. Another striking characteristic is the absence of an integrated economic order that relates various elements into a coherent and logically connected model grounded in Islamic teachings. Any claim to the existence of such a model within the current global economy is an exaggeration. The ultimate test of such an economic order, however, is empirical—related to the workability of a state's economy under real conditions of Islamic authority.

At any rate, an assessment of economic principles has to consider the accomplishment of economic objectives, such as improving general standards of living, creating jobs, narrowing the gap between rich and poor, and achieving overall improvements in education, health care, income security, and so forth. Islamic economic teachings cannot be exempted from measurement and comparison of results, at least of declared values and policies.

Currently, a few states claim to apply Islamic economic systems. Operational evidence from these countries is that the systems are unsuccessful. The five explicitly Islamic states (Iran, Saudi Arabia, Afghanistan, Sudan, and Pakistan) are hardly a collective paradigm of sustainable economic development, effective management, or protected personal freedoms. None of these states have been able to deliver on their promises of improving quality of life for citizens.

The Islamist State of Iran

The Iranian economic experience is perhaps the most authentic application, or attempted application, of Islamic economics in contemporary history. The Islamic revolution of 1978 brought a different ruling class to Iran, dominated by a core of fundamentalists led by Ayatollah Khomeini and his religious elites and their supporters. At an early phase of the revolutionary takeover, factions competed for power and domination in the new system.

As Milani (1994, 198) makes clear, there was no consensus within the Islamic leadership of Iran on the overall features of the new state or its operational economic principles. Nor is it possible to identify many fundamental organizational and institutional changes that differentiate management of the new state. Perhaps the most significant change made was in the area of staffing. Large numbers of functionaries of the shah's regime left their positions or were terminated. Islamists and activists in the revolution, with little operational experience, took over responsibilities beyond their individual skills. Hence, what resulted was a period of confusion, inaction, and procedural inequity.

In terms of economic policy, Milani (1994, 198–199) describes three major political-economic groupings. First is the conservative faction, supported by the rich merchants, landowners, and the high-ranking *ulama*, which championed a free enterprise system and urged creation of a prosperous and expanding economic system. This faction opposed state ownership and management of major industries, limits on private ownership, and land reform and instead favored free trade and conciliatory approaches in dealings with other nations.

Members of the second grouping, the crusader faction—the lower middle class, the low-income people, shopkeepers, the middle-rank *ulama*, and many of the revolutionary organizations—were avid proponents of egalitarianism and self-sufficiency. For this camp, the economy was only a means to achieving "the pristine ideal of Islamic justice." They advocated state ownership and management of the major industries and banks, nationalization of foreign trade, imposition of limits on private property, comprehensive land reform, and formation of state cooperatives. "In some ways, they espoused a crude form of economic socialism within the parameters of Islam."

The pragmatists, who oscillated between the conservatives and the crusaders, were the third and weakest group. The middle class and the technocrats provided the core support. They recognized their limitations in changing their environment, accepted the world as it was, and worked with compromise and caution. This group dominated the system in post-Khomeini Iran.

Certainly, the Islamization of Iran has been an extensive and involved process. Islamic laws were introduced to regulate commerce, trade, usury-free banking, and education. The educational system was revamped to give prominence to Islamic teachings and to ensure ideological commitment to the Islamic revolution. But the promise of a comprehensive transformation from a secular, Western-imitating system to a religiously regulated political order has not been totally fulfilled. A significant part of the problem is the lack of a preexisting definition of what an Islamic economy looks like. Disagreements seem to center on the role of the state in managing socioeconomic development. The diversity of economic viewpoints on the eve of the Islamic revolution in Iran appears not much different from economic groupings found in many developing countries during the 1970s or before. The ideological patterns match those of conservatives, liberal-idealistics (or even the likes of social democrats), and pragmatists (sometimes pejoratively referred to as opportunists or admiringly as professionals or entrepreneurs).

Almost two decades since the successful Islamic revolution, it is unsettling to discover the huge gap between the reality and the promise. As Banuaziz (1994, 2) points out, "[M]any devout Muslims have come to fear that the main threat in Iran today to Islam as a faith is the experience of people under the Islamic government." In managing the economy, Iran faced specific difficulties: First, the revolution had led to capital flight and a serious brain drain (Ehsani 1994, 16). Second, there was the shattering experience of the eight-year war with Iraq. By the end of the Islamic Republic's first decade, government expenditures increased severalfold, diverting funds away from development to military and other purposes. The fact that policymakers repeatedly changed strategies to control the economy is an indication that no definite or fixed Islamic economic approach exists. Even with the Second Republic, Iran remained without a coherent vision of a distinctly Islamic political economy. As Ehsani (1994, 17) explains: "The ruling clerical elite was too heterogeneous and inexperienced to reach consensus on fundamental economic issues."

A recent report from inside Iran describes how the revolutionary rhetoric is slowly being drowned by the winds of change, bringing in fresh demands for political freedoms, pluralism, and modernity.[27] Claims of religious and revolutionary legitimacy have been reduced to shallow slogans and eroded by deteriorating economic and living conditions. "Tehran is buzzing with debate over the urgent need to open up the political system, limit the power of the clerical establishment and change laws biased against women."[28]

Some Western evaluations have been almost dismissive of Islamic economic experiences; Roy states, for instance: "As for the Islamic economy, it is mere rhetoric, masking either a form of Third World state socialism (Iran in the era of Khomeini) or an economic liberalism geared more toward speculation than toward production." Such absolute statements may not reveal the full spectrum of economic and social policies and accomplishments of the Islamic systems. Often objectives are not well defined, reliable economic data are unavailable, and the processes of application are incomplete. Consequently, comparisons are sketchy at best.

Be that as it may, in terms of internationally used indexes such as the UN HDI for 1995, out of a total of 174 countries covered, the Islamic Republic of Iran ranked 70, Pakistan ranked 128, and Saudi Arabia 76.[29] Statistics of the World Bank on Iran, Pakistan, Saudi Arabia, and Sudan are typical for any average or below-average performing economy in the Third World.[30] One plausible, perhaps too optimistic, explanation is that the current

Islamic economic order is in transition from a collection of teachings to a holistic and integrated bona fide system.

Islamic Banking

An area in which Islamic states have made some strides is Islamic banking. The Quran prohibits receiving or paying interest. A growing wave of Islamic consciousness among Muslim depositors is fostering greater acceptance of Islamic banking in both the Arab banking world and the global financial markets. According to *Financial Times* (December 1994), Islamic banking is attracting newcomers and is now seen as the fastest-growing segment of Arab banking. Even Citibank in the United States jumped on the bandwagon and opened a full-fledged Islamic banking subsidiary in Bahrain in 1995.

Although banking statistics are hard to come by, estimates put total funds invested in an Islamic way in the region of $50 billion. In a study of eleven Islamic banks in the Gulf states, Egypt, and Jordan, economist Farah Fadil, formerly with the Central Bank of Kuwait, says Islamic demand deposits account for nearly 17 percent of total demand deposits and almost 15 percent of savings and investment deposits. He estimates that these funds have grown at 8 to 9 percent annually in the last ten years.[31]

Is the growth of Islamic banking the result of the economic program of Islamists? It is not. The progress made so far has not been directly linked to policies of declared Islamic systems. In fact, Saudi Arabia continues to resist granting Islamic banking licenses, lest it draws attention to the fact that all banks deal in interest. But Al-Rajhi Banking and Investment Company, which has a banking license on the condition that it does not officially call itself Islamic, remains the largest Islamic deposit taker, with 1993 assets of $7.6 billion.[32] Also, Western banks are positioned to lead in providing this service to customers for reasons of competition and attracting newcomers. The inherent contradiction in Islamic banking has not been resolved. The faith prohibits interest, but the banks know that when depositors, religious or otherwise, place their money in a bank, they expect not to lose it or reduce it. To meet this challenge, Islamic banks have chosen to imitate conventional banking under different labels and financial subterfuge, helped by Western banks that are all too happy to oblige Islamic banks. The problem is that Western regulatory processes remain unable to establish "a clear and unified definition" of what constitutes "Islamic banking," according to the governor of the Bank of England.[33]

In one application of Islamic banking, as Beaty and Gwyne (1993) point out, the defunct Bank of Credit and Commerce International invented a system called a *murabaha* transaction that would allow depositors to believe that the money they earned came not from interest but from profits of an enterprise. This was made possible by buying commodities—real, tangible goods as opposed to the abstractions of banking—and then selling them for a profit. "In fact, it was nothing more than a trick, simultaneous, offsetting purchase of commodities, creating artificial 'proceeds' of that sale that were remitted to depositors" (Beaty and Gwyne 1993, 111–112). Such masquerading of interest on investment as profit clearly is an accounting deception that sidesteps religious prohibition rather than a fundamental solution to the Quranic interdiction of usury.

Answering the Question

A full-scale Islamic economic order may be emerging, but it certainly is not fully defined or distinct at this stage. Developing a set of principles and concepts with a model to connect them and data to evidence their working is the future challenge to students of the field. Khurshid Ahmad has been a powerful influence on the development of theory and application of the Islamic economic order. He emphasizes in particular these four attributes of the Islamic economy (1983, 5–6):

> (1) It is an integral part of an Islamic society and state and cannot be studied or managed in isolation. (2) The material and the physical forces have to be studied in their inalienable relationship with the moral and the spiritual factors. (3) The Islamic economy is wedded neither to the idea of absolute right of private ownership and enterprise nor to total nationalization of all means of production and consumption. (4) The real objective of an Islamic economy is the establishment of a just social order.

WHICH ISLAMIC MANAGEMENT?

Most Arab universities with public administration curricula offer a course on Islamic management. Typically, such a course ends up including a mixture of historical events that exhibit some distinct leadership style in previous Islamic periods and interpretations of religious principles that underline certain values relevant to Islamic management. Often such a seminar turns into an instructor's oratory on lofty goals and high-sounding policies that an Islamic state would bestow. Materials used in the course on Islamic management typically include leadership styles and performance of the Prophet Muhammad and his pious caliphates during the Al-Rashedeen period.

   Attempts to define Islamic management in a formal teaching setting have not produced information on organization and management processes that go beyond historical episodes or preordained principles. Grappling with the complexity of organizing and managing in a modern state seems to be deferred to the safety of beliefs and sacred precepts.

There have been few attempts to develop new administrative thinking or to offer new managerial approaches in the context of the Islamic state. Any such attempt is usually linked to a religious principle or derived from it. The issue of how to face unprecedented problems or how to deal with failure of an Islamic notion of organization and management remains unsolved, so it is impossible to know whether a manager would experiment and innovate to solve a problem or would resort to a religious authority to provide an answer or a ruling through *ijtihad.*

An interesting study by Basheer el-Khadra (1982) on the subject of Arab leadership examines styles of leadership from the period of the early caliphates to the contemporary Ba'th Party regimes. He identifies four elements that characterize the traditional leadership style: individualism, paramountcy of the self, noninstitutional orientation, and the "great leader" syndrome.

Individualism is the tendency of a leader to rely on himself,[34] not to be mindful of the wishes and preferences of the followers. The self is a derivative dimension of individualism based on the individual leader's seeing himself as the center of reality and the interpreter of the truth. This leader views the position as his personal property. Noninstitutional orientation is a natural continuation of the individual and the self orientations. It indicates behavior unrestricted by procedures and process. Problemsolving is not a methodical or consistent mechanism because of the dominance of the person of the leader. Consequently, deciding succession is generally a personal designation without regard to a specific predetermined method of selection.

The importance of the "great man" or "great leader" theory is that a system that does not abide by institutional frameworks is essentially deepening its reliance on the individual and increasingly glorifying this person as the great leader. Followers develop loyalties and strong beliefs in the magical powers of the leader. With this they become more and more willing to grant him more powers leading to autocracy and absolutism.

If this conceptualization by el-Khadra has any historical validity, it is mostly found in certain features of ancient Islamic regimes. Today, with the modern focus on team-building techniques, motivational factors, and participatory management, autocratic leadership would be out of tune. Modern management is concerned with efficient and effective achievement of results rather than compliance with the wishes of a despotic power.

CONCLUSIONS

Islamist resurgence is a major political development in contemporary Arab societies. Yet, Islamists have not articulated sufficiently the administrative, economic, or political features of the state they propose for the Arab world. In part, Islamists themselves either are not certain or are not in agreement on what their state ought to be. This is more reason that scholarship has to proceed with the examination and analysis of Islamism dispassionately and professionally rather than using the approach of those who see only evil or those who see only virtue and salvation.

NOTES

1. Edward W. Said, "The Phony Islamic Threat," *New York Times Magazine*, November 21, 1993, p. 65.

2. "The Islamic Threat," *Economist* (March 13, 1995), p. 25.

3. Rami G. Khouri, *Jordan Times*, November 15, 1994.

4. Quoted by Said, "The Phony Islamic Threat," p. 64.

5. "How to Stop Militant Islam," July 3, 1995, *New York Times*, op-ed page.

6. World Bank, *Social Indicators of Development 1995*, p. xi.

7. Statement made in a lecture delivered at Tufts University, April 20, 1995. Quoted in "Middle East Realities" on the Internet, July 1995.

8. Oussama Ramdhani, quoted by Andrew Borowiec, in *Washington Times*, March 16, 1994.

9. *Al-Hayat*, May 5, 1995.

10. Mary Ann Weaver, *The New Yorker* (June 12, 1995). The article details how the Central Intelligency Agency (CIA) helped create a militant Islamic network and supplied it with billions of dollars, training, and sophisticated weapons.

11. *Washington Post*, June 3, 1995, p. A14.

12. Ibid.

13. *Economist* (April 13, 1996), p. 33.

14. *Washington Report on Middle East Affairs* 14, no. 2 (July/August 1995), p. 24.

15. Youssef M. Ibrahim, "Conversations: Sheik Rachid el-Ghanoushi . . . , " *New York Times*, Sunday, January 9, 1994.

16. "A Survey of Islam," *Economist* (August 6, 1994), p. 16.

17. "The Islamists Speak," *Ash-Shiraa*, special issue, October 1995, pp. 26–27.

18. Khouri, *Jordan Times*, November 15, 1994.

19. Quoted in Said (1993, 64).

20. Daniel Pipes regularly expresses these views. This statement was in his presentation at the United States Central Command Symposium, Tampa, Florida, May 16, 1995.

21. Hume Horan served as the U.S. ambassador in several countries, including Sudan and Saudi Arabia in the 1980s.

22. Samuel P. Huntington, *Foreign Affairs* vol. 72, no. 3 (1993), pp. 22–49.

23. U.S. Institute for Peace, *Peace Watch* vol. 1, no. 3 (April 1995), p. 1.

24. According to a poll in the *Los Angeles Times* on May 6, 1995, 45 percent of Americans agreed that "Muslims tend to be fanatic."

25. Interview by Zainab Farran, in "The Islamists Speak," *Ash-Shiraa*, October 1994.

26. Lecture at the Royal Institute of International Affairs, London, May 9, 1995.

27. Lamis Adoni, "Winds of Change in Iran," *Middle East International*, no. 500 (May 12, 1995), p. 20.

28. Ibid.

29. As discussed in Chapter 3, the HDI is a combination of three indicators: life expectancy, adult literacy, and real GDP per capita. The rankings are from the United Nations Development Program, *Human Development Report 1995* (New York: Oxford University Press), pp. 156–157.

30. See Tables 1 through 32 in World Bank, *World Development Report 1994* (New York: Oxford University Press).

31. Quoted in Roula Khalaf, "Survey of Arab Banking," *Financial Times*, December 15, 1994, p. 42.

32. Ibid.

33. *Asharq Al-Awsat,* September 29, 1995, p. 1.

34. The text in Arabic uses all male gender expressions.

9

A Strategic Resource: Oil

When our vital interests are threatened, we have to be prepared to use and to threaten to use military force. . . . Now, nowhere—nowhere in the world—does the United States more clearly have vital interests at stake than in the Persian Gulf.

William J. Perry, U.S. Secretary of Defense[1]

At the end of the twentieth century, oil was still central to security, prosperity, and the very nature of civilization.

Daniel Yergin (1991, p. 13)

Oil is the main natural resource for the Arab world; revenues from oil are the largest capital inflow of the region, and the overall impact of oil on socioeconomic development is acute. As oil has been a principal motivator of great powers' relations with the region, so it has a defining role in Arab foreign relations. In recent decades, oil revenues have profoundly influenced Arab social systems and shaped inter-Arab politics.

The end of the Cold War, market demands for oil, and U.S. military superiority prompted redefinition of U.S. objectives in the Middle East. It is no longer sufficient to state these objectives merely in terms of the familiar notions of preventing "hostile forces" from dominating the important Gulf region.[2] Now the United States specifies among its main objectives in the Middle East the free flow of Gulf oil, regarded as a globally vital commodity; and as the superpower, the United States assigned to itself the responsibility of using military force to ensure the flow of that oil. Confirming the "administration's priorities in the region," Robert H. Pelletreau, assistant secretary of state, outlines U.S. objectives to include two major elements:[3]

- "Maintaining our steadfast commitment to Israel's security and well-being" and
- "Enhancing security arrangements that assure stability and unimpeded commercial access to the vast petroleum reserves of the Arabian Peninsula and Persian Gulf"

Secretary of Defense William Perry affirms that "nowhere in the world" does the United States more clearly have vital interests at stake than in the Gulf region. In a report to Congress by the U.S. Central Command, titled "Posture Statement," the military command echoes Perry:

> The global interdependency of the late 20th Century is exemplified by the role Gulf oil plays in the world economy. Our post–Cold War National Security Strategy recognizes that stability in Southwest Asia is important enough to warrant the commitment of military forces to assure the uninterrupted flow of oil. The U.S. central command has the responsibility for the planning and execution of military operations to support that strategy in its region. (United States Central Command 1994, vii)

The concurrence among U.S. officials on the importance of oil is primarily driven by economics. Despite occasional minimizing and prejudicial statements such as "there is abundance of cheap oil" or "Arabs cannot drink their oil," it is hard to exaggerate an industrial society's dependence on oil. More than ever before, the United States recognizes the strategic significance of cheap Arab oil to its economic growth and prosperity.[4] Americans are increasingly dependent on imported oil. This dependency reaches about 55 percent of their needs in 1994[5] and is expected to exceed 65 percent by the beginning of the twenty-first century. A growing part of this imported oil will originate from Arab lands, particularly the Gulf region where two-thirds of the world reserves are located. The "oil factor" was the most important reason, I believe, for the Gulf War of 1991 and for many U.S. foreign policy decisions before and after that war.

To appreciate the importance of oil as a critical strategic asset to the Arab state, consider the following five factors.

1. Oil is an exhaustible, finite natural resource. Demands for oil, the major source of world energy, are continuous and growing because of population growth and a general per capita increase in consumption; supplies are limited. New discoveries are infrequent, so it is likely that shortages will begin to appear within three decades. Any significant lid on supply will bring soaring prices and incalculable economic consequences. True, there may be new discoveries of oil and/or dramatic new technologies that can substitute alternative sources of energy. But in the short run, neither of these possibilities is apt to change the status quo.

2. Because of oil's special qualities, it has become not only the most important source of energy throughout the world but also an indispensable raw material for manufacturing a large number of products. "To appreciate the importance of oil, one only needs to look at the vast assortment of petrochemical-based products, from textiles to medicines and from fertilizers to precision instruments" (Alnasrawi 1982, 3). As Yergin (1991, 14)

notes, "oil provides the plastics and chemicals that are the brick and mortar of contemporary civilization, a civilization that would collapse if the world's oil wells suddenly went dry." Yergin concludes that ours has become a hydrocarbon society and we, in the language of anthropologists, hydrocarbon man.

3. Over the past few decades, the United States, Western Europe, and Japan have had enormous increases in their consumption of oil. Because the 1970s brought about fundamental changes in producers policies (because of the emergence of the Organization of Petroleum Exporting Countries [OPEC], nationalization of oil companies, and sharp price increases), it is informative to examine consumption patterns in prior years. Between 1950 and 1960, for example, oil consumption increased at staggering rates, as Table 9.1 illustrates.

In the decade 1950 to 1960, the United States increased its oil consumption by 51 percent, Western Europe by 241 percent, and Japan by 500 percent. For the same period, total world oil consumption almost doubled (a 97 percent increase), whereas the growth of world energy consumption from all sources of energy was only 67 percent. Between 1950 and 1979 (after the energy crisis in the early 1970s), the world's consumption of oil increased from 10.9 to 64.1 million barrels a day.

During the 1980s and 1990s, as a result of conservation measures, move efficient machinery, and high prices of oil, growth of consumption rates slowed down considerably. In 1992, the world's demand for crude oil was still about 64 million barrels per day (Hepburn 1994, 285). Although this is a 487 percent increase since 1950 and a 200 percent increase since

Table 9.1   Energy Consumption of Industrial Countries, 1950, 1960, 1965, and 1979

	1950		1960		1965		1979	
	Oil[a]	Total[b]	Oil[a]	Total[b]	Oil[a]	Total[b]	Oil[a]	Total[b]
United States	6.4	16.2	9.7	21.8	11.3	26.9	17.9	38.1
Western Europe	1.2	7.2	4.1	11.1	7.8	17.1	14.9	26.6
Japan	.1	.7	.6	1.7	1.8	3.1	5.5	7.7
World total	10.9	35.7	21.5	59.7	31.1	80.1	64.1	141.3

Source: OECD, "Energy Policy: Problems and Objectives," quoted in Alnasrawi (1982, 5, 9, 21, 24).
Notes: a. Oil consumption in millions of barrels per day.
b. Consumption of all sources of energy in millions of barrels per day of oil equivalents.

1960, it is about the same as that in 1979. If increase in demand resumes because of population growth and industrial expansion, even if at a slower rate than in the 1950s and 1960s, the level of consumption could double by the end of the second decade of the twenty-first century. Where would this increase come from?

4. Like that of other natural resources, the distribution of oil is not equal among regions or nations of the world. At present, the Arab world has more than two-thirds of known world reserves.[6] Of the top ten countries in the world in oil reserves (Table 9.2), which together have 86 percent of the world's total (867 billion barrels), the first four are Arab states that together have over 64 percent of the collective reserves.

For how long are proven oil reserves sufficient to meet the world's demands? Accepting the figure of 1 trillion barrels of known oil reserves in the world today and dividing it by the current level of consumption of 64 million barrels a day, the result is about forty-three years before the world completely runs out of oil. If consumption increases as presently estimated, reaching 100 million barrels a day by the first few years of the twenty-first century, the time frame becomes shorter. New discoveries of reserves or future technological breakthroughs, on the other hand, might alter current energy utilization patterns.[7] In fact, technological advancement in the methods of extraction—the ability to dig deeper wells and to explore in deeper waters—have already resulted in raising reserve estimates and increasing amounts of recoverable oil from the ground.

Oil companies resist publicizing information on depletion because it may force conservation and restrictions on consumption, which would cut

Table 9.2   Top Ten Countries in Oil Reserves
(billions of barrels)

Country	Proven Reserve
Saudi Arabia	261
Iraq	100
UAE	98
Kuwait	97
Iran	93
Venezuela	63
Mexico	51
Russia	48
U.S.A	32
China	24

Source: Hepburn (U.S. Central Command: 1994, 282).

into their sales and profits. To illustrate, a 1995 advertisement by Mobil Oil Corporation utilized an interesting twist for inducing consumption, claiming that the objective of the "doomsayers" (presumably conservationists) is to "force consumers to give up an American lifestyle built on ample supplies of market-priced transportation fuels."[8] In effect, Mobil Oil and other multinational oil companies are telling consumers to buy and use more oil despite common concerns for resource depletion or considerations of energy security, let alone issues of environmental pollution.

The fact that the United States imports most of its oil[9] and that its reserves are sufficient only for six to eight years of consumption[10] did not prevent Mobil Oil from advertising that "decades from now, alternative fuels may replace oil for transportation needs." Thus, Mobil concluded that forcing the market "to make the transition prematurely" would harm the economy and the consumers. This transition, Mobil asserted, should evolve only by market forces. Clearly, such reasoning by oil companies is motivated by self-serving objectives. It also flies in the face of strategic interests of the United States and the global economy while it contradicts a mathematical certainty, which indicates a world shortage of oil in the twenty-first century.

Actually, predictions by geologists and scientists about U.S. production have come true in several respects. Despite President Richard Nixon's declaration during the energy crisis of 1973 that the United States would achieve energy independence by 1980, during the past few years oil production in the United States has tumbled, imports have surged, and oil reserves are close to being depleted. This situation did not happen without warnings from several informed sources. M. King Hubert of the U.S. Geological Survey first sounded a warning in 1956 when he drew a curve showing oil production rising to a peak around 1970 and then falling back down sharply. "What the oil industry forgot, Hubert explained in an interview in 1974, was that a sharp rise in oil production in the United States was bound to be followed by a sharp decline since there was only so much oil to draw on. Every time a new well was dug, he said, oil was used up faster—like putting several straws in a glass of milk and drawing on them all at the same time.[12] Today we know that his prediction materialized with alarming accuracy.

5. Nature's endowment of Arab lands with an abundance of oil supplies is not without compelling problems and challenges. One problem for the Arab oil-producing states is their total dependence on oil revenues. The top four states—Saudi Arabia, Iraq, UAE, and Kuwait—derive from 95 to 99 percent of their revenue from oil, which classifies them as rentier states. The term *rentier state* has been popularized in literature to mean states that are dependent on external sources of income rather than relying on indigenous productive capacities. Thus, oil-producing states with

rent (oil revenue) exceeding 90 percent of state budgets are in this category (Luciani 1994, 130; Beblawi and Luciani 1987, 12; Chatelus and Schmeil 1984).

A second problem is that, despite the increasing importance of oil to the global economy, the effects on the Arab society (whether producer or nonproducer of oil) have not always been positive. Foreign ambitions have been stimulated by the strategic importance of oil, and domestic pathologies of materialism and corruption have been induced by the abundance of available cash following the price explosion of the early 1970s. Easy cash and meddling in Arab affairs by multinational oil companies and the big powers behind them have collectively had a negative impact on an orderly and balanced development as well as on building productive capacities of the Arab economic systems.

Complete reliance on oil revenues is a third problem, a contributing factor to the absence of democracy in the Gulf states. Giacomo Luciani (1994, 132) argues that "the roots of democratic institutions are in the state's need to tax in order to support activities." Countries that are dependent on oil revenues do not face the need to tax their citizens. Taxation, Luciani suggests, especially modern direct taxation of the individual, requires compliance and is unlikely to develop under authoritarian rule. Consequently, authoritarian governments are poor managers of their fiscal conditions.

THE PAST SHAPES THE PRESENT

During the nineteenth century, Britain and other powers competing for domination considered the Gulf region of superior strategic importance.[13] Its geographic position as the route to South and Southeast Asia was crucial for trade, communication, and imperial influence. The massive intrusion of Western powers into the region did not cease even when the imperialist system was formally discredited and defeated by forces of self-determination and national liberation. The exigencies of the Cold War and the dependence of Western powers on Middle East oil kept those powers focused on the Gulf region. The Gulf War of 1991 was the most resounding contemporary confirmation of those objectives.

The British presence in the Gulf region materially altered conditions and affected developments. For instance, the British inflamed parochial conflicts in order to keep the natives preoccupied and save the occupier the cost of putting down any resistance to the British presence. In the Gulf, the British perpetuated a system of fragmented authority, ripped by tribal feuds and conflicts. "By obstructing the resolution of conflict through the emergence of a new powerful local state, Britain contrived to assist in the development of a situation in which a number of small powers coexisted under the British umbrella" (Yapp 1980, 50).

The political divisions among the Gulf countries and the arbitrary boundaries created with the active support of the British colonial administration were, and remain, among the most scheming political acts used by a colonial force to preserve its influence. The shape of local powers "had been formed in the eighteenth century, but its survival owed much to the protective umbrella supplied by Britain and its final form to the interaction of the regional and international systems" (Yapp 1980, 68). To a considerable degree, even the configuration of the larger political entities in the region—Iran, Iraq, and Saudi Arabia—has been the consequence of actions by international powers, which defined their boundaries (Yapp 1980, 68).

A significant outcome of the arbitrary demarcation of boundaries of Gulf states to fit colonial ambitions has been the creation of local conflicts and the deepening of existing ones. Saudi Arabia has been in disputes with Oman over Buraimi and with Yemen over borders; Iraq's demands in Kuwait are common knowledge. A three-decades-long conflict between Bahrain and Qatar over a strip of islands, offshore boundaries, and fishing rights became international when the World Court declared jurisdiction (February 15, 1995). Finally, there is the Iran-UAE feud over the islands of Tunb and Abu Musa in the Gulf, now under Iran's military occupation. This one has the potential of escalating into a larger strife involving forces beyond the boundaries of these two states.

Almost every Gulf state is a party to some unresolved conflict or is involved in some claim against its neighbors. Consequently, the politics of these states over the past fifty years or more have had a weighty measure of suspicion, conniving, and search for protection and support from outside powers. Although the British and other foreign powers may have enjoyed greater influence over the Gulf states as a result of the turmoil, the political and economic strategic interests of the region certainly have not been well served nor the legitimacy of local leaders secured.

Between world wars, the Gulf countries were targets of an intensive search for oil. With discovery of significant quantities of oil in Iran in 1908 and 1911, operations were taken over by the Anglo-Persian Oil Company, which was renamed Anglo-Iranian Company in 1935 (McLachlan 1980, 199). The next major discovery was in Iraq at Kirkuk in 1927 (Al-Farsy 1986, 44). Both discoveries were by British companies that were intent on exclusivity that would keep out U.S. competition. But the U.S. companies too were embarking on a campaign to develop new oil supplies worldwide, which would inevitably thrust them into the Middle East. "A fear of imminent depletion of oil resources—indeed, a virtual obsession—gripped the American oil industry and many in government at the end of World War I and well into the early 1920s" (Yergin 1991, 194).

The opportunity for the United States came in Saudi Arabia when a sixty-year agreement was signed in 1933 with Standard Oil of California (Al-Farsy 1986, 45). The discovery of the Dammam field in Saudi Arabia in 1938 was followed by discoveries in Kuwait the same year, Qatar in 1940, Algeria in 1948, Syria in 1956, Abu Dhabi in 1958, Libya in 1959, and Tunisia and Oman in 1965 (Al-Farsy 1986, 44–45). Extensive production and exports of oil from Saudi Arabia began in 1939 but did not expand until 1944. By the 1950s, production was proceeding and growing in most of the Gulf states. Improvements in communication (radio and telephone) were only exceeded by improvements in transportation (roads, railways, and airlines), which linked the region closely with the rest of the world. Subsequent social change and economic consequences were even more dramatic.

The development that had the most profound effect on the future of the Gulf region—the invention and the popularity of the combustion engine—occurred far away from the Arab world. By 1905, the gasoline-powered motorcar was gaining popularity and ultimately changing modern societies everywhere. The growing use of fuel oil in manufacturing and all forms of transportation (trains, ships, and automobiles) dramatically increased the need for oil supplies.

Thus, a new world was unfolding, nourished by petroleum power and driven by economic competition and threats of military clashes. As to the Arab producers of oil, they remained politically divided, militarily insecure, and without prospects of developing viable economic systems. They continue to rely on oil revenues for their public spending and on foreign military powers for protection and survival of their regimes. This affliction permeates the whole Arab world despite nominal divesture from colonial control. Michael Field (1994, 25) sums up the situation, confirming that understanding the contemporary Arab world is contingent on history. He says: "The political failure of the modern Arab world has its origins in the time it was created at the end of the First World War. Nationalists . . . had been hoping for independence from Turkish rule and for unity, but what they got instead was division, colonial rule and imposition of kings they did not want. They also had the beginnings of the Jewish state established on their soil. The whole post-war settlement made for instability."

OIL REVENUES AND ARAB DEVELOPMENT

Since 1970, the magnitude of capital inflow from oil revenues into the treasuries of Arab oil-producing states is unprecedented. For illustration, I calculated income in selected years to reflect variations in price and production for Saudi Arabia (Table 9.3):

Table 9.3   Oil Production and Revenues of Saudi Arabia

Year	million barrels/day	$/barrel	total revenue $ billion
1971	4.72	1.49	2.6
1975	6.97	10.68	26.9
1977	9.04	12.21	40.3
1980	9.49	26.86	93.0
1984	3.43	27.29	34.2
1988	4.40	12.54	20.2
1990	5.69	19.25	40.0
1993	7.38	15.14	41.0

Sources: Middle East Oil, Exxon Background Series, September 1980, p. 26; CDLR, Country Report 1995.
Notes: a. Production in million barrels per day.
b. Revenues in dollars per barrel.
c. Total revenue in billions of dollars annually. As price per barrel varies from month to month, the lower end of the price range has been used in these figures.

Despite fluctuations, the overall huge increases in revenues in the 1970s and early 1980s cemented tribal and religious alliances within the Gulf states, and almost everyone benefited. Saudi Arabia and the other Arab Gulf states are similar in having conservative monarchical systems of government and broadly similar economic policies. They created "extremely generous welfare states providing free education and health services, free medical trips abroad . . . , free telephone calls, enormously subsidized water, electricity and fuel, and moderately subsidized basic foodstuffs" (Field 1994, 23). Citizens received all this as well as paying virtually no taxes and receiving cheap loans for the asking, for a variety of purposes such as buying a home, developing a farm, or building a factory.

What these oil-producing countries (and most external analysts) did not anticipate, however, were the global economic developments that altered the financial thrust downward: periods of international economic recession, a drop in the value of the U.S. dollar (on which oil prices are primarily based), and conservation methods adopted by the consumer countries. The optimistic economic prospects of the Gulf states during the 1970s changed dramatically after the sharp drop in oil revenues. Three major producers—Saudi Arabia, Kuwait, and UAE—earned $186 billion in 1982, $57.6 billion in 1985, and only $27 billion in 1986 (Lawson 1991, 43), before a modest rebound in prices during the 1990s. A parallel negative impact came from the Iraq-Iran war of 1980 to 1988, followed in 1991 by the Gulf War. Moreover, the economic and political troubles of the regimes were immeasurably complicated by the resurgence of a form of Islamic revivalism, giving impetus to other drives for reform and accountability of ruling families.

During the first phase of the sudden wealth (1973–1982), Saudi Arabia and the other Arab Gulf states concentrated on distributing national income, developing a vast infrastructure, and bolstering monetary reserves. The priorities of public spending did not reflect immense endeavors to build the productive capacity of the economy. The unexpected decline in income, internal rivalries, and external pressures induced serious socioeconomic problems and put hitherto unknown stress on the political leadership. But it was Iraq's invasion of Kuwait in August 1990 that caused the Saudi leadership its gravest internal and external policy crisis since the state's creation. It also exposed the weaknesses of the political systems of the Gulf states in general, as it underscored the precariousness of their economies.

To different degrees, oil revenues have huge impacts on the whole Arab world, even those without oil extraction. With respect to oil, Arab countries may be classified into three groups: (1) major producers with annual income from oil exceeding $5 billion, such as Saudi Arabia, Iraq (before 1990), Kuwait, UAE, Libya, and Algeria; (2) minor producers with annual income of less than $5 billion, such as Oman, Qatar, Egypt, Syria, Tunisia, Yemen, and Bahrain; and (3) nonproducer countries without any oil extraction, such as Jordan, Lebanon, Morocco, Palestine, and Sudan.

The most noticeable manifestations of oil revenues have been within countries with high oil exports, such as Saudi Arabia, Kuwait, UAE, and Qatar. Ostentatious spending on huge infrastructure projects comforts and pleases users but does not always add significantly to the productive capacity of the society. Several examples may be cited: airports that can transport the whole population of a country in a day or two, expensive roads that lead only to one or a few fancy mansions of influential families, and costly military installations and weapon systems beyond the absorptive capacity of the state, now or in the foreseeable future. In the absence of accountability, corruption runs deep in the system, generating dislike and disillusionment by citizens of all political leanings.[14]

Benefits from oil revenues trickled down to most citizens, but for a limited number of fortunate individuals—often connected to the centers of political powers—the trickle was a flood. Divorced from any notable means of production, a superclass of wealthy Arabs emerged that included emirs, merchants, developers, contractors, consultants, and military officers. Not only have the methods of wealth accumulation not always been legitimate and the amounts been enormous, but also these funds have mostly been invested outside the Arab economies. George Corm (1995, 2) estimates the amount of Arab capital invested in Organization of Economic Cooperation and Development (OECD) countries in Europe at between

$400 and $600 billion, or more than the GDP of the whole Arab world combined, at the same time that Arab states are facing shortages of investment capital and forced into expensive external borrowing. It is important to realize that these huge fortunes by the new group of Arab entrepreneurs have been accumulated in a few years, in a totally tax-free environment, and in a patrimonial style of economic management in which personal relationships with high officials are more important than professional and technical skills.

A striking characteristic of a segment of the new group of the very rich, who migrated temporarily to the Gulf countries and accumulated substantial savings, is that their ideology and aspirations have been shaped by an emerging neoliberalism (Reaganism) combined with conservative Islamic economic thinking (Corm 1995, 2). This means they are antagonistic to the idea of an active economic role by the state. They have encouraged the opening of Arab centrally planned economies to allow for substantially high short-term investments in real estate, trade, and light industries.

Finally, certain aspects of the oil boom of the 1973–1982 period have had a grim side that usually escaped examination. It is irresponsible for a state that is totally dependent on oil revenue to overproduce and to deplete a valuable resource. Oil producers demonstrated shortsightedness in market expectations and in managing the inflow of easy money in such huge quantities. Other negative consequences include the separation between effort and reward that seriously damaged the work ethic; gross misspending, both in consumption and investment by the private and the public sectors; and national development policies and programs that were opportunistic, mismanaged, uncoordinated, and sustainable only during the inflow of substantial oil revenues (Sayigh 1991, xi).

Perhaps nothing illustrates the situation of the Arab states better than the quick transformation from a condition of capital surplus to one of debt and financial shortages. In 1982, the Organization of Arab Petroleum Exporting Countries (OAPEC) discussed "joint Arab action," saying that "the relative abundance of oil in the Arab world provides a unique opportunity which must be exploited in transforming the Arab economy from dependence on a depletable resource for national income to a more diversified productive base."[15] The purpose was to "guarantee" continual growth of national income by creating productive industries and training the workforce required for the functioning of "the Arab economy."

Today, Arab oil-producing countries are operating with deficit budgets and enormous public debts. National development has not only come to a halt in several countries but what had been accomplished over decades is in ruin in the mid-1990s, as in Iraq and Kuwait. In the budgets of 1994, 1995, and 1996, the government of Saudi Arabia had to cut its expenditures by almost 19 percent each year to control the deficit. The UAE also has been enduring significant deficits in its budget, reaching 9.7 percent in 1990, 9.5 percent in 1991, 4.6 percent in 1992, 12.3 percent in 1993, and 11.8 percent in 1994.[16] The Industrial Bank of the UAE with reluctance acknowledges that an even lower tier of Third World economies cannot survive a deficit above 6.5 percent and maintain good financial and commercial standing internationally.[17]

Although budget deficits, external debts, inequitable tax systems, and mismanagement of national development are all common problems in the Arab states, the severity of each of these varies from one country to another. Also, the most-affected economies—those that rely heavily on oil revenues—have adopted sharply divergent policies in facing the economic crisis. As Fred H. Lawson (1991, 43) points out, Bahrain reacted by reducing state intervention in the economy, whereas the opposite took place in Kuwait, where the government imposed a greater degree of state supervision over domestic economic affairs and expanded central planning. Still, virtually all governments of the GCC countries have dramatically reduced the level of spending on infrastructure and other development projects. They have curtailed the number of immigrant workers making their living in the area and substantially delayed payments to outside contractors. Also, the political leaders in each country have pressured their subordinates to improve efficiency of public administration at all levels of government (Lawson 1991, 44).

In terms of strategic economic policy, the monumental damage to Arab economies has been in missed opportunities. The failures of political leaders to utilize oil revenues for achieving strategic developmental objectives and for integrating Arab markets into a viable (productive and competitive) global economy remain the gravest shortcomings. As Eric Davis (1991, 2) states, from the vantage point of either the global political economy or domestic sociopolitical considerations, the authority and legitimacy of Arab oil-producing states seem to be much more precarious than implied by writings of Western social scientists.

FOCUS ON SAUDI ARABIA

Saudi Arabia is the largest oil producer in the world (8 to 9 million barrels a day) and the major supplier of the U.S. market; it has the biggest oil reserve. Saudi Arabia has the capacity to extract more oil than all other Middle Eastern producers together. Therefore, the country has an enormous economic influence on the oil markets and a powerful political leverage over countries of the GCC as well as the whole Arab world.

What do we know about this twentieth-century creation of a state? What political, economic, and institutional processes govern its policies and decisions? Before investigating these questions, I must offer two caveats. First, attempts to research any aspect of the Saudi society run into a protective stone wall of secrecy. An outsider quickly discovers that this is virtually a closed country. Information is difficult to obtain. Hence, Western observers and journalists tend to either exaggerate or underestimate Saudi Arabia's policies and actions. Reliable economic data, if available, tend to be out of date. Essentially, Saudi Arabia remains compulsively secretive, occasionally vilified, and often inaccessible and incomprehensible, particularly to Western observers and analysts. An American journalist who faced this reality reports:

> It is hard to get data to gauge the health of the Saudi economy. International Monetary Fund officials declined to be interviewed for this story, citing objections from government officials in Riyadh. . . . Western diplomats, bankers and corporate executives stationed in Saudi Arabia balk when asked to discuss the economy over the telephone; in private meetings, they fret about wiretapping and beg to not be quoted saying anything negative about the kingdom's finances.[18]

Second, I rely here on published information, personal experience,[19] and insights from informed Saudi citizens. To be sure, many of these citizens are dissidents, but they are also individuals with the highest level of professionalism. One specific source, "A Country Report About Saudi Arabia's Political and Economic Situation," has been circulated by the Committee for the Defense of Legitimate Rights (CDLR; further references to this report will be cited as CDLR).[20] The CDLR indicates that it commissioned this report and that it has been independently researched and produced by consultants. The sources are "informed individuals and institutions," and the authors are described as "internationally recognized experts on Middle East affairs who have written extensively on the subject."

Historical events, particularly the British colonial rule of the Arab Peninsula, are relevant to an understanding of Saudi Arabia. The British government entered into an agreement with Ibn Saud in 1927, recognizing his sovereignty over most of the current borders in return for his acknowledgment of the British rule of Bahrain and the rest of the Gulf region (Al-Farsy 1986, 37). Until that time, Saudi Arabia had been rent by civil wars as it was subjected to external intervention and great power intrigues. With British support, Ibn Saud managed to oust other local leaders in Hijaz and in Nejd.

In 1933, Ibn Saud granted Standard Oil a concession for oil exploration, and in 1944 the company was renamed the Arabian American Oil

Company (ARAMCO), with additional American companies joining in the ownership—currently these are known as Texaco, California Standard, Exxon, and Mobil Oil (Al-Farsy 1986, 47). The formation of ARAMCO created an important entity, almost of equal power to that of the state. ARAMCO controlled the development of the petroleum industry, its related finances, economic and educational development, foreign affairs, and defense matters. For all intents and purposes, ARAMCO constituted a state within a state. It ensured the survival of the political state and attained the wealth it needed. Although ARAMCO is now controlled by the Saudi government, the company still acts as a lobbyist in foreign capitals, as an intermediary between the king and Western leaders, and as an intelligence service (CDLR). Until 1972, ARAMCO also had a decisive influence on the price of oil on the international market.

One may view the Saudi system of government as a triangle of power, consisting of ARAMCO, the royal family, and the religious establishment. The religious element goes back to the mid-eighteenth century when an alliance was formed between a tribal chief, Ibn Saud, and a religious reformer, Muhammad Abdul-Wahhab. To this day, the country ostensibly operates according to this alliance with the Wahhabi sect, a conservative and purist Islamic faction that provides the Saudi ruling family with political and religious legitimacy.[21] This distinctive system of government seems to have survived so far by successfully balancing these three centers of power while maintaining various security arrangements with foreign countries—mainly Britain and the United States.

The Wahhabi doctrine is more influential in the Nejd (the central region, around Riyadh) than on the east and west coasts. The current leader of the sect is a blind sheikh, Abdul-Aziz bin Baz, the enforcer of the Wahhabi religious codes and strictures. The influence of the Wahhabis on government policy is extensive. As an illustration, after Iraq's invasion of Kuwait, King Fahd solicited Sheikh bin Baz's opinion before the public could be informed. According to Saudi citizens, it was five days before the Saudi public was informed of the invasion, even though the rest of the world was receiving hourly reports (CDLR). Sheikh bin Baz, in some instances, is even consulted on oil prices, economic development plans, and educational policies.

Buttressed by oil wealth and influence, the Saudis struggle to convey cultural, ethical, and moral superiority. The problem is that contemporary Saudi society no longer lives by the Wahabi doctrine. Violations are rampant and excesses are all too familiar, particularly when the Saudis are outside their country. In fact, the negative Arab image abroad has been largely a caricature of that of the Saudi rich or the members of the royal family. Too many reports tell of large-scale corruption and financial shenanigans.[22] A study by Aburish (1995) claims that the Saudi regime for nearly thirty years used its vast riches to pit one Arab state against another and to undermine Arab unity. The Committee for the Defense of Legitimate Rights also supplies a regular menu of information on the broad misuse of state funds and abuse of authority by the house of al-Saud. To be sure, some of this information may be exaggerated, anecdotal, or even fabricated, but it is the compulsive secrecy of government and the lack of the most basic freedoms in the society that prevent independent verification of facts.

Today, the Wahhabi establishment must contend with militant Islamic movements in Algeria, Egypt, Sudan, and Iran that have a profound impact on the public. The Saudi radicals are calling for Islamization of all areas of public life. They demand that all political, economic, administrative, and educational activities be based on Islamic principles. The Islamic radicals also insist that social justice and equality be universal and based on the precepts of Islamic law (*shari'a*). The new radical Islamists have been championing some popular causes: elimination of corruption among officials, cancellation of all military pacts with non-Muslim powers, and establishment of a genuine legislative authority derived through citizens' representation.

On the surface, these reformist demands appear redundant. The Wahhabi/Saudi rule has in theory always followed Islamic practices, and its government is supposed to be based on consensus derived from consultation with tribal and religious leaders. However, the militants' arguments are far more earnest and profound. They strongly reject Western, especially U.S., influence and command in their country. They consider Westernization a proxy for economic and military dependencies, and they decry the rapid erosion of Islamic principles. They accuse the Wahhabi leadership of not steering the country back to its true sources of law and power. In other words, they accuse the *ulama* of collusion with the al-Saud family, even of heresy and corruption. Particularly important is the reformers' charge that about one-third of national oil revenues land in the royal purse (that is about the same figure used by Ayatollah Khomeni when he campaigned against the shah in Iran).

The government is fighting the radicals and the reformers from both religious and liberal camps with arrests, censorship, and banishment. But the movement seems to have gained considerable sympathy among the unemployed, dispossessed, alienated, and those who feel a strong affinity with similar movements abroad, such as those in Egypt, Algeria, and Iran. The need to balance temporal and spiritual leadership is increasingly troubling the Saudi leadership. The king and his brothers are caught in a political impasse: If they accommodate the liberal elite, they will alienate the powerful *ulama;* if they cater to the zealots (either traditional or modern), they will estrange the technocrats, Westernized intellectuals, and merchants.

Moreover, elements in the armed forces—many educated in the West—support liberalization along Western standards and could become restless.

The only manifest response to demands for political reform so far is the creation of the Consultative Council, Majlis ash-Shura. A grand structure has been designated to house this council, which has a history that goes back over a quarter-century. As early as the 1960s, under pressure from members of the Saudi elite returning from studies at Western universities, the reigning house of al-Saud began to recognize the limits of absolute rule. In 1980, despite resistance from within his own family and from conservative religious circles, then–Crown Prince Fahd created a study commission for the creation of a consultative assembly. Construction of its headquarters began in 1984, but it was not until spring 1993 that sixty prominent men appointed by the king convened in the first session of the Majlis. The approach to legislation in a Muslim society, according to the president of the council, is determined by the Quran and its interpretation.

Members of the council are appointed for a maximum of two four-year terms. They have at their disposal, in their lavish building, an infrastructure the likes of which parliamentarians in most countries could not imagine. There is no official word on construction costs for what has been popularly referred to as the Saudi Taj Mahal. A domed and arched assembly hall, designed to hold 450 members, is used only once a year for the reading of the crown's government program. Otherwise, working committees meet in separate rooms to deal with specific subjects, such as a new environmental protection law.

This Consultative Council is not regarded as a substantive response to the reformist demands for public participation. As in the past, the king remains the final arbiter. The dilemma he faces, however, is far more complicated than the ones faced by his predecessors. If internal strife continues to escalate, it will have taken a toll on Westernized intellectuals and technocrats as well as on merchants and traders who are powerful and generally loyal to the present ruling elite. The support from this group usually lasts only as long as the system provides a profitable business environment. If the country becomes unstable, the merchant/business class may turn against the regime and align itself with the opposition. The lesson of Iran is not totally absent from the minds of the Saudi regime, as it was the bazaaries (merchants) in Tehran who gave the shah his finishing blow. In brief, if the government fails to restore confidence in the economy and to reduce the budget deficit, the opposition groups are likely to see their camp expanded.

The Saudi military is an integral part of the political establishment, despite some distinctions. All the services (army, navy, and air force) are headed by royal princes or are responsible to a ministry headed by a prince. The regime has secured its interests and survival through a very tight intelligence and security services structure. The services are equipped and trained by external powers (primarily the United States). In recent years, tribal elements have been admitted to the higher echelons of the military, but they seem to settle mainly to desk jobs that do not involve combat conditions.

The Saudi military establishment has not yet attained a sense of "national service" or internalized the concept of "national defense" in its doctrine or practice. In exchange for various privileges (high pay, advanced and expensive weapons, travel and training in the West), the military has offered loyalty to the ruling family so complete that it overrides all other loyalties, even to their tribal elders. It is for that reason that King Fahd in late 1990 introduced the notion of national service, whereby the whole population would have to serve in the armed forces, a program similar to the British national service after World War II.

As one of the most modernized (some would say pampered) elements of Saudi society, the military can also be a threat to the regime. The king is buying loyalty by offering what is probably one of the highest military salary structures in the world. With defense expenditures at present amounting to over 30 percent of the budget, the king knows very well that the armed forces can be a double-edged sword: a friend or a foe.

Appraisal of any aspect of the Saudi government inevitably leads to the U.S-Saudi relationship, a rare chapter in the history of international dealings. The relations are unidimensional, largely economic, and have been consistent since the 1940s. "On the Saudi side, support from Washington has continued to play a central part in the preservation of the royal family's rule" (Halliday 1982, 126). In a discussion I had in 1995 with a former U.S. ambassador to Saudi Arabia and a recognized scholar of Middle East politics, he observed, "I do not recall ever meeting with the king or other high officials when the security issue was not raised." I asked: "What security, that of the country or the ruling family?" His answer: "Definitely the latter." The regime knows that it is powerless to defend itself against any serious internal or external enemy; it therefore relies on foreign powers for survival.

At the same time, this unique situation generates its own internal stresses and potential instability. This dependence is a major contradiction in the politics of the Saudi regime: It may give the al-Saud family a sense of safety, but it also highlights the regime's fundamental weakness and reinforces its crisis of legitimacy. The armed forces, so heavily dependent on Western military equipment, could be used by Western powers to effect political change if the system were under threat or if it adopted a course of action inimical to the interests of the West. The U.S. Congress as far back as 1974 and 1975 studied the feasibility of occupying the oil fields in the Saudi eastern province and the possibility of securing safe trade routes.

Understanding the Saudi passions and needs, Washington has exploited them for financial and commercial benefits. Saudi defense spending has stretched the country's budget. Following the Gulf War, military costs soared and have now reached nearly a third of annual expenditures. Thus, it is not a baseless concern when Saudi citizens express fear that all this spending on U.S. weapons has in fact made the system less secure by saddling it with new financial obligations. Actually, the United States is part of the Saudi predicament. The Saudis buy from the United States to satisfy and to please, and the Americans continually employ hard-sell techniques for more. Even presidents have entered the fray of hard sell, as Bill Clinton did in 1994 when he pushed for the $6 billion Saudi purchase of transport airplanes to help employment in the United States. As *Business Week* reports about the struggle for succession among members of the royal family, "For the U.S., in particular, the stakes are huge. Saudi Arabia is the largest foreign purchaser of U.S. military hardware and a key client for such multinationals as AT&T, Boeing, and Mobil."[23]

In the meantime, the United States has not announced overall policy in the region except that of maintaining the free flow of oil and safeguarding Israel. But acquiring oil is an objective for all consuming nations. Currently, U.S. foreign policy in the Gulf region is either punitive or reactive. Efforts to broaden alliances in the region and to develop mutual interests, beyond punishing or defending one autocratic leader or another, do not seem to bear much fruit.

The Saudi position is not helped by the common knowledge that the royal family and some of their benefactors have seized the lion's share of the huge wealth accumulated from the oil boom. Citizens see the excessive secrecy of the government as an attempt to prevent outside scrutiny of billions of dollars in revenue channeled to members of the royal family. This is particularly troubling when regions such as the southwest coastal area, Asseer, vast areas of the Makkah governorate, and the far north, near the Iraqi and Jordanian borders, have been grossly neglected. The CDLR published what it claims is documentary evidence, a letter from the minister of the interior to the king that describes villagers as close as forty-five miles from Makkah as living in "conditions similar, or comparable to that of African bush dwellers."[24]

Despite such criticisms of the government, loyalty to the regime is based on its Islamic legitimacy, not on the existence or proper distribution of wealth. Swift urbanization of the society has created a broad middle class known for its political apathy. There is no indigenous underclass as there is in Egypt, for example. Poorly paid "dirty work" is uniformly done by foreign labor, mostly from the Indian subcontinent, and the members of the Saudi upper class generally are less concerned with the power structure at home than with the interior decoration of their villas and penthouse apartments in Europe. Violent revolutions can be carried out only by desperate people with nothing to lose, and there are very few of them in Saudi Arabia. Seen from this perspective, recent reports in the Western media comparing Saudi Arabia today with Iran before the fall of the shah would seem premature. The rule of the Saud dynasty, while hardly popular at home, still exudes confidence and uncompromising stands on initiatives by reformers.

The analysis of destabilizing forces versus powers of the status quo cannot underestimate the economic factor. Today, the Saudis are cash poor because of the Gulf War and lavish spending, and they face painful choices. As Chandler reported from Riyadh, "When Iraqi tanks rumbled into position along the Kuwaiti border [October 1994], Saudi Arabian government and business leaders joked darkly that they couldn't decide which posed the greater threat: the return of Saddam Hussein's Republican Guard or paying for all the tanks and troops President Clinton sent to chase the Iraqis back across the sands."[25]

Two of the largest drains on the Saudi budget are massive social subsidies and defense spending. Government subsidies touch every aspect of Saudi life. In addition to free health care and interest-free home loans, the state doles out free college education to all its citizens, monthly living allowances for college students, and interest-free loans to businessmen. Government support holds the price of gasoline to as little as twenty-five cents a gallon. Options such as privatization are endorsed publicly but not pursued diligently by the political leadership. One reason given by insiders is that privatization will take time; few of the government enterprises will be profitable right away without huge price increases, continued state subsidies, or both. More important, genuine privatization would loosen the royal family's hold on power. Until now the Saudi system has been: "I feed you; I can rule you."

In conclusion, unless far-reaching budget reforms are put in place, the financial problems of the country could escalate into a more severe crisis. The world's "most extravagant welfare state" may not be able to continue providing all of the social subsidies just outlined. But even if subsidies are reduced, improved spending patterns will not be attained without transparency of public decisions, better accountability of public spending, and enforcement of a rationalized public budgeting process. The potential for oil wealth to increase social and political instability is one that can be diverted only through reforms at all levels of the political-administrative structures. Again, the development of a reformed financial order that is responsible and accountable will depend on building independent institutions with the capacity to enforce such order. The history of the region indicates that political leaders do not voluntarily curtail their excessive powers or willingly allow honest representation of the common interest.

NOTES

1. Remarks by Secretary of Defense William J. Perry at a conference sponsored by the Middle East Council in the Dirksen Senate Office in Washington, DC, December 7, 1994.

2. *Hostile forces* is a euphemism of diplomacy generally denoting the former Soviet Union and its allies.

3. Statement by Robert H. Pelletreau, assistant secretary of state, Bureau of Near East Affairs, Department of State, before the House Foreign Affairs Committee, Subcommittee on Europe and the Middle East, March 1, 1994, p. 2.

4. Part of the reason for the low cost is that underground rock formations of Arab oil fields permit extremely high production rates for individual wells. Whereas in the United States average production per well is about 17 b/d, in the UK about 6,100 b/d, and in Australia about 1,100 b/d, the average well in Saudi Arabia produces more than 10,000 b/d (Exxon Background Series, *Middle East Oil,* 2d ed. [September 1980]), p. 2.

5. In 1937, the United States produced locally 92 percent of its needs and imported the rest; Venezuela was the biggest supplier of imported oil. In 1972, the United States produced 71 percent locally and imported the rest, Canada being the biggest supplier. In 1994, the United States produced about 45 percent of its oil needs and imported the rest. This time, Saudi Arabia was the biggest foreign supplier of imported oil. (Louis Rukeyser, *Wall Street Week,* September 22, 1995).

6. Hepburn (1994, 281) estimates that the Middle East has 65.3 percent of proven oil reserves—oil that can be recovered with known production technology under existing operating costs and crude prices.

7. Odel (1995) reports forecasts that estimate total global oil supplies at 68.7 million barrels a day (mb/d) in 2000, 73.4 mb/d in 2010, and 77.3 mb/d in 2020.

8. Mobil Oil Corporation advertisement, *Newsweek* (May 8, 1995), p. 15.

9. For example, in November 1995 U.S. petroleum imports were 9.4 million barrels per day, and total U.S. crude production was 6.5 million barrels per day. In January 1996, imports were 9 m/b/d and local production 6.47 mb/d. Between 18 and 20 percent of U.S. petroleum imports are from the Gulf region. (American Petroleum Institute, *Energy Backgounder: Facts at a Glance* [December 1995; January 1996].)

10. Aarts (1994) estimates the U.S. deposits at 3.4 percent of world oil reserve. Figures on U.S. oil reserves and consumption have been largely consistent.

11. Interview with Hubert by Washington Post Service, published in *St. Petersburg Times,* April 7, 1974, p. 6-A.

12. Ibid.

13. Today's Gulf countries are Iran, Iraq, Kuwait, Saudi Arabia, Qatar, Bahrain, UAE, and Oman. The Arab Gulf countries are members of the GCC, which includes all these countries except Iran (a Muslim, non-Arab state) and Iraq.

14. *Economist* (January 6, 1996), p. 14.

15. Editorial in *OAPEC Newsletter* 8, no. 6 (June 1982).

16. These figures from UAE's Industrial Bank were published in *Asharq Al-Awsat,* July 3, 1995, Business and Finance, p. 8.

17. Ibid.

18. Clay Chandler, *Washington Post,* October 28, 1994.

19. I visited Saudi Arabia twice. On the second trip I lived in the country for five months as a consultant to the University of Riyadh (now King Saud University).

20. The report by the Committee for the Defense of Legitimate Rights was issued from London on January 3, 1995. It was signed by two Saudi dissidents: Dr. Muhammad Al-Massari and Dr. Saad Al-Faqih.

21. Estimates of the number of members of the royal family of al-Saud range from 5,000 to 7,000, according to various Saudi sources and CDLR. This number presumably includes extensive additions through intermarriages with members of other principal tribes, such marriages often occurring in order to build political alliances.

22. For examples, see *Newsweek* (November 27, 995), p. 45; *Business Week* (November 27, 1995), p. 54; and *Economist* (January 6, 1996), p. 14.

23. *Business Week* (December 25, 1995), p. 56.

24. The CDLR claims that a secret letter, numbered 29/T 915/2S and dated A.H. 07/04/1412, from the minister of the interior to the king acknowledges and describes poverty in neglected regions of the state.

25. Clay Chandler, *Washington Post,* October 28, 1994.

10

Alternative Development Strategies

Removing the remaining veil of delusion . . . , we derive the guide-lines of world order: the rich men of the rich societies are to rule the world, competing among themselves for a greater share of wealth and power and mercilessly suppressing those who stand in their way, assisted by the rich men of the hungry nations who do their bidding. The others serve and suffer.

Noam Chomsky (1194, 5)

National development is a comprehensive societal transformation that consists of improvement of economic productivity as well as reform of the political, administrative, and technological processes (Jreisat 1992a, 1). To accomplish such developmental aims, effective organizations and institutional management are indispensable.

The analysis so far in this book highlights an alarming deterioration of developmental efforts in the Arab states since 1975. Several indicators confirm this trend: negative economic growth, high unemployment, hyperinflation, low investment in human development, and huge public debts. Reviewing the performance of developing countries during the past decades, a 1995 World Bank study concludes that countries of the Middle East and North Africa "had the slowest rates of export growth, the largest budget deficits, the largest current account deficits, the smallest private capital inflows, and among the highest government consumption and lowest national savings rates" of all developing regions.[1]

Authoritative sources from within the Arab world convey similarly unsettling conclusions. Statistical data from the annual Unified Arab Economic Report, which is published annually by the Arab Monetary Fund, the League of Arab States, the Arab Fund, and OAPEC, describe the most disturbing aspect of Arab socioeconomic development efforts since 1975—the gap between a high rate of population growth and an inadequate rate of economic expansion. "The Arab population in the period 1980–1994 grew by 48 percent, from 165 million to 245 million, while total Arab gross domestic product (in current prices) during that period grew by only 15 percent, from $437 billion to $502 billion. This means that over the last decade-and-a-half the per capita gross domestic product of the entire Arab region declined by 22 percent, from \$2612 to \$2048."[2]

Such a deplorable economic performance is illustrative of fundamental defects in policymaking and policy implementation. What were touted as comprehensive development plans often turned out to be mere collections of badly coordinated infrastructure projects with minor additions to productive capacities. Except for oil extraction, Arab states have been economically marginalized in world trade. In manufacturing, agriculture, application of advanced science and technology, and information communication, the Arab economies remain alarmingly behind most regions of the world. Even the huge cash revenues from oil exports flowing into a few countries have created as many social and political problems as they have solved. Despite the fact that oil revenues have been a primary cause of important processes of social change, Davis (1991, 15) argues that "more often than not oil wealth has served as an 'intrusion' into ongoing processes of that change."

Studies by the World Bank, consultants' reports, and scholarly literature all agree that the Arab world has been a laggard in political and economic development. "The Arab world has not been a happy or successful place in the last fifty years, and the misery and disenchantment of the people has recently become acute" (Field 1994, 3). To illustrate this dreary record, one needs to compare the performances of Arab nations with those of developing countries in Asia and Latin America. Until recently, some of the countries now making momentous progress toward their socioeconomic objectives were socially and economically less developed than the Arab countries. A few decades ago, Egypt, Jordan, Lebanon, and Syria, for example, were ahead of many Southeast Asian countries in economic standards, quality of education, health care, nutrition, and total quality of life. Between 1955 and 1966, Jordan was one of the fastest-growing countries among developing nations, both in GNP and per capita GNP. During the 1970s, Western mass media lamented the possibility of "capital-rich–oil-producing" Arab countries buying American corporations and controlling Western industries.

Present conditions in the Arab world are profoundly different. If the experience of the last decade or so is any guide, even most modest expectations of political and economic changes are not likely to be met. States with enormous potential—Algeria, Iraq, Sudan, and Egypt—have mismanaged their economies, taking them to the brink of collapse. Even those countries that only a few years ago had a huge capital inflow and cash reserves—Saudi Arabia, Kuwait, and the rest of the GCC states—have blundered into financial downfall. In the six countries named, "cash-strapped governments are cutting back social services, while the stream of rich contracts that helped the economy has dwindled to almost nothing."[3] In addition to drained treasuries and huge debts, all Arab states are facing drastic budgetary cutbacks and rescheduling of their public-debt payments. Moreover, they face the common economic ailments of inflation, unemployment, low rates of investment, and widespread corruption of public officials. The picture is indeed bleak.

In addition to mismanagement of the economy, the Arab states suffered protracted conflicts that leaders were unable to resolve peacefully or otherwise. The most destructive interstate wars since the middle of the twentieth century were the Arab-Israeli conflict, the eight-year Iran-Iraq war, the Israeli invasion of Lebanon in 1982, and the Gulf War of 1991. In addition, there have been internal conflicts, such as the Lebanese civil war, conflicts between North and South Yemen and between North and South Sudan, Kurdish uprisings in Iraq, and the Somali civil war (Waterbury 1994, 26; Ibrahim 1995, 34).

The consequences of these wars and internal conflicts, in addition to human and financial losses, are incalculable. Development objectives suffered most, as resources were diverted from investment in productive capacities and human development, particularly education, to spending on military mobilization and armaments. The subversion of national priorities also created fundamental imbalances in the society's economic, political, and institutional power structures that will not be easily restored. As I have already pointed out, the financial loss to Iraq and to the Arab economies from the Iraq-Iran war reached $600 billion and from the Gulf War about $650 billion. The total loss from the Arab-Israeli wars, Iraq-Iran war, and the Gulf War is estimated at 600,000 casualties and $1.3 trillion (Ibramim 1995, 35).

Military conflicts not only consume a disproportionate amount of resources but also deform powers and processes of decisionmaking. Today, according to Saad Eddin Ibrahim (1995, 34), "the Middle East region is the principal buyer and consumer of lethal arms in the Third World." He estimates spending at an average of $100 billion annually over the last two decades. When the total costs of defense are included, the figure is twice as high. All this in a region that faces, among other problems, huge external debts, shortages of drinking water, expanding poverty, environmental pollution, deficient health care, and inadequate educational services.

The critical task ahead of these societies remains that of defining possibilities of corrective actions, policy choices, and appropriate strategies. In this regard, one immediately encounters a realm of state actions that is fragmented and ideologically barren. Unsuccessful interludes of nationalist programs left the scene empty of coherent doctrinal economic commitments. The old practices and the traditional theocratic ideologies that stunted previous reform campaigns (capitalist, socialist, Marxist, and variations) are still ineffectual and inconsequential. The absence of an ideological underpinning of governing is manifested in the lack of image of the future. Contemporary Arab leaders do not show a profound understanding of past influences, knowledge of current capabilities, or preparedness for future contingencies.

The ideological vacuum illustrates both a lack of faith in and appreciation of the powers of citizens in the governing process. Leaders have failed to construct reliable connections with their people in order to bring about needed consistency between leaders' visions and societal values. Usually, these contextual relations act to mitigate acceptance of or resistance to transplanted strategies and structures. In social systems slated for reform, resistance almost always increases the risk of rejection.

All this underscores the importance of articulating a vision of the future that is harmonious with basic values of the society. Such a vision cannot imitate extraneous glitter nor be subservient to fundamentalist decrees and impositions. Perhaps the Egyptian editor quoted by a *New York Times* correspondent correctly simplified the issue: "Money? we have money. Workers? we have workers. Vision? we have no vision?"[4]

The current alternative directions of economic public policy appear to be concentrated in the strategy of *structural adjustment,* or *economic liberalization. Structural adjustment* is the preferred euphemism for less palatable concepts such as *privatization, free market,* or simply *capitalism.* This strategy has been assiduously promoted by the World Bank, the U.S. Treasury Department, and other creditor nations as a response to the fear of debt meltdown after the crisis of the early 1980s (Rich 1994, 110). The World Bank and the IMF also provided massive "quick fixes" of foreign exchange to countries facing a debt crisis.

But the main thrust of any structural adjustment policy continues to be reduction of domestic imports and expenditures and expansion of exports in order to earn the foreign exchange required to continue servicing the debt. The World Bank's designation of structural adjustment as the approach for dealing with current economic adversities of developing countries has, in fact, placed it on the agenda of almost every Arab state. The Arab governments nevertheless accept only reluctantly the impetus for change coming from the arm-twisting of the World Bank, Western creditor governments, and the sheer logical necessity of reform (Field 1994, 208).

ECONOMIC LIBERALIZATION: PRIVATIZATION

The operating assumption of economic liberalization policies is that government is inefficient as a producer of commodities and products because of the absence of market competition. "Public choice economists liken the provision of services by government to monopoly of production" (Jreisat 1992b, 91). According to this economic perspective, government has no incentive to search for lower cost, to eliminate inefficiencies, or to be too concerned about customers' preferences. It is not surprising then that advocates of economic liberalization seek to use privatization to reintroduce competition to public enterprises that had enjoyed government protection and subsidies while growing careless, inefficient, and mismanaged.

Other claims made for privatization are that it reveals true costs of production, limits growth of the public budget, reduces public personnel costs, and achieves greater flexibility in managing people and materials (Jreisat 1992b, 91). Perhaps the most popular defense of privatization is the expectation that it induces greater innovative and entrepreneurial drives in management and production.

Proponents of economic liberalization and privatization in the Arab world argue that improved economic performance is attainable only by reducing the role of government as an owner and manager of business enterprises. The World Bank conditions its lending decisions to Egypt on provision of an "appropriate" policy environment—that is, "a more liberal policy climate, one which encourages private sector investment and which diminishes the capacity of the state to control (read to inhibit) economic activity" (Sullivan 1992, 30). The U.S. AID policy is equally determined to encourage free-market policies and to promote private investment. The end result of these external pressures is to get government out of production and to induce it to denationalize industries it owns.

At the global level, the end of the Cold War and the destruction of the Soviet empire secured U.S. economic and military hegemony. U.S. power came to be the stabilizer of the global economy, and the American dollar provided the essential liquidity for growth and development. Until only a few years ago, notes Kuttner (1991, 15), "the United States ran the IMF, the World Bank, the GATT, the Coordinating Committees on Multilateral Exports Controls, and other nominally international agencies of hegemony, usually through foreign surrogates." These institutions were understood to be proxies for the United States. In fact, as Bruce Rich (1994) indicates, both the World Bank and IMF were created in 1944 to be at the apex of the "economic world order" of the postwar era, in accordance with prescriptions originating in the U.S. Treasury Department. The United States continues to be the largest contributor of funds to the Bank, and by tradition the post of president has been filled by an American since the birth of the institution, located in Washington, D.C. As Kuttner (1991, 17) argues, "conservative Americans accepted nominally supranational institutions only because they were surrogates for American power."

Other sources also promote economic liberalization and convincingly endorse privatization policies through mechanisms that aim at curtailing and downsizing all economic activities of the state. A headline in *Business Week* read "Europe for Sale: A Privatization Drive Could Raise $150 Billion."[5] This report indicated that "at least 100 major deals" were seeking the attention of the world's capital markets. "Squeezed by budget deficits and eager to taste the fruits of free-market competition, Western Europe's governments are about to begin a massive sell-off of state companies," according to *Business Week*. A round of sales in the 1990s is a follow-up to an earlier phase in the 1980s. As Iliya Harik (1992, 1) points out, we have witnessed this process of privatization "unfold recently in free-market economies such as Britain and Western Europe, in the centrally controlled markets of China and Eastern Europe, and in the interventionist regimes of many of the Less Developed Countries (LDCs)."

Experiences of developing countries from Latin America, Eastern Europe, and Southeast Asia (in addition to fanfares of the World Bank and U.S. AID) evidence a momentum toward privatization. "As governments across Latin America turn to private-sector concessions to satisfy their people's hunger for infrastructure projects, investment opportunities loom large for companies from the United States."[6] With the World Bank increasingly restricting long-term, below-market financing to poorer nations, many countries are turning to private business in order to build up their facilities and services.[7]

In the Arab world, policies of Infitah, liberalization, and especially privatization are not accepted without challenges and profound misgivings. Unlike Eastern Europe, the Arab state hegemony in the economy is rooted not just in ideology but also in the nature of the economies of the region (Harik 1992, 3). The role of the state expanded as a result of unmet needs, because the state has many advantages over the private sector, or as a way to enforce policies of equity and social justice. These are some of the rational arguments for the interventionist economic policies of the state over the past four decades. The problem, in addition to poor outcomes, is an accumulation of a variety of negative consequences that have contributed to the economic marginalization indicated earlier.

There are several arguments against privatization in the Arab world.

Risk to Essential Welfare Policies

The outcome of neoliberal economic policies in general and privatization in particular "has been marked decline in the level of job creation in the public sector, a pattern of wage compression for civil service employees, diminishing public resources for the social sectors, and cutbacks in the food ration and subsidy system" (Farsoun 1995, 15). Inherent in this argument is the premise that the assault on the welfare state will benefit a small middle class and ruling elites at the expense of the majority of citizens who live in poverty. "Once the IMF and the World Bank have succeeded in imposing financial discipline on an Arab debtor they set about rooting socialism out of its economy" (Field 1994, 208). Thus, massive unemployment and cutbacks in welfare spending have followed wherever governments have seriously implemented privatization.

It is not surprising, therefore, to detect a widespread distrust of the World Bank's policies throughout the Arab societies. The Bank is fundamentally identified with the new policies of economic restructuring and privatization; it also represents "foreign" pressures on the economies of these countries. Arab intellectuals and economists carefully point out that the Bank is being too friendly with national governments that have plundered natural resources and failed to deliver promised economic payoffs. This is the same institution that, only a few years ago, represented a pioneering optimism about the ability of governments and centralized planning to manage economic forces. Today, the Bank is pressing governments in the Arab world to get out of the business of economic development altogether. A problem is that these Arab governments already have accumulated huge foreign debts on many projects funded by the Bank. The performance record of these projects is abysmal, Bruce Rich (1994, 62) concludes, "if one reads the literature not prepared by the Bank or under its sponsorship."

Actually, Rich (1994) delivers one of the most concentrated and documented critiques anywhere of the Bank and its policies. Rich makes the point that projects funded by the World Bank created environmental havoc and promoted unsuitable developmental schemes. According to Rich (1994), in 1989 the Bank's own review of eighty-two agricultural projects, approved mostly between 1975 and 1982, showed that 45 percent had not met their goals. Moreover, a 1993 internal review of the Bank's $140 billion portfolio (a significant portion of it in Arab countries) found that 37.5 percent of recently evaluated projects did not adhere to social and environmental policies or failed to meet performance goals. Even if the Bank's lending solved temporary problems for some leaders, it has not alleviated the long-range difficulties of managing and sustaining self-reliant development in any of these states.

The Hidden True Motives of Privatizing Governments

Local leaders' push for privatization and restructuring is not driven primarily by needs of economic development but by shortage of revenues to balance the budgets, by the need to service public debts, and by the accelerating costs of bad decisions and corrupt politics. "Privatization programs in the Middle East," Ayubi (1992, 39) points out, "do not follow from empirical evaluations of the performance of the public sector, nor do they result from pressures exerted by native entrepreneurs." Instead, Ayubi argues, they mainly represent public policy carried out in response to the "fiscal crisis of the State" and "under pressure/temptation from globalized capitalism and from its international institutions."

If the commitment to liberal economic policies is authentic, then why have such policies that seem so readily accepted by certain Arab leaders not been bolstered by a simultaneous movement toward liberal politics? On the contrary, privatization and neoliberal economics, despite all claims, have not propagated liberal politics in the Arab state. Although evidence from China, for example, indicates possible separation of economic policies from political factors, the Arab state illustrates inconsistency and confusion among alternatives. The liberalization pursued or aspired for is not necessarily the equivalent of total democratization but is only a modest and constrained variation of it.

Foreign Pressures and Incompatible Values

The United States and the international institutional network it controls have pushed for economic liberalization and free-market economies in other countries—this while the United States was pursuing economic policies at home that contradicted policies of free market or laissez-faire. In fact, the U.S. domestic economic stance applied a powerful mix of governmental interventionist policies to produce desirable outcomes of economic growth, employment, and stabilization of wages and prices. These deliberate public policy objectives are pursued through various interventionist means such as public expenditures, taxes, subsidies, regulations, and even outright prohibitions.

Moreover, outside the United States, successful and dynamic economies of the late twentieth century have never subscribed to the conservative economic theory of free market espoused by many Americans. Japan, Korea, China, and other successful Asian economies have been explicitly utilizing a developmental approach. Their instruments invariably safeguarded government social responsibilities, but certainly they do not have free markets (Kuttner 1991, 7). Actually, as *Business Week* editorialized on April 15, 1996, "[T]he real challenge to American national interests in Asia is mercantilism," that is, state-directed capitalism and protectionism. Still, the Arab states seem to be squeezed between two unappealing choices: accepting a doubtful medicine or suffering a debilitating disease. This situation is primarily caused by inept leaders who do not rely on native institutional capacity to master the conditions essential for adoption and implementation of appropriate solutions.

Condition for Acceptance of Privatization

According to this view, the potential of privatization will be realized only if proper preconditions are established. One precondition is reforming the private sector itself. The private sector in the Arab economies has not contributed significantly to productive capacity nor has it paid its fair share of taxes to society (Corm 1995). Thus, structural adjustment and reform efforts cannot exclude the private sector and be limited to government.

A second precondition is the improvement of the regulatory capacity of the state in order to be able to set standards of conduct and monitor the implementation of such standards. Economist George Corm (1995, 3), who has extensive knowledge of the Arab economies, warns that "we are heading towards a new extremist position by allowing the private sector to become uncontrollably hegemonic without any assurance that it can deliver welfare and productivity to Arab societies." This precondition is crucial if the states are to maintain socially responsible economic growth, protect the environment, and foster policies of fairness and justice in the society.

Finally, a crucial element in the success of privatization is having the necessary managerial capacity. Under restructuring programs, public enterprises need to serve totally new functions by people trained to do the work. Even in Egypt, for example, with relatively more advanced utilization of administrative knowledge and skills than most Arab states, some of the most basic functions of any company competing in a free market hardly exist (Field 1994, 212). Employees have generally spent their working lives in a centralized-command economy that experienced little uncertainty. With privatization, the tasks of managing research, quality control, accounting, and marketing end up in the hands of the same people who are running the holding companies and who have no idea about how a market economy operates (Field 1994, 212). Actually, all Arab industries and businesslike services have operated in systems of fixed prices, import controls, and protection by the state and often received direct subsidies. Arab managers of public enterprises have had no experience in controlling quality, attending to consumers' preferences, or coping with global market competition. Therefore, to privatize without developing such necessary capacities and skills is risky. Arab leaders must learn the lessons of the economic restructuring in Russia and Eastern Europe after the collapse of the socialist order.

The movement toward privatization in the Arab world has also been hampered by noneconomic considerations. The political system is not readily willing to give up important economic powers derived from ownership of large numbers of public enterprises. Nor are these regimes interested in losing a major source of employment and political patronage. Moreover, in countries such as Jordan and Saudi Arabia, a form of mixed economy has been taking hold, where the state owns part of the capital in partnership with the private sector. In Jordan the cement industry, oil refinery, phosphate extraction, and a few other small industries are all built on the basis of public-private ownership. The Saudi Arabian Basic Industries Corporation (SABIC) is also a conglomerate of public and private capital in the non–oil producing sectors (industries, construction, and petro-chemicals).

FUTURE STRATEGIES: SOME CHOICES

The search continues for strategies that might solve the current crisis of the Arab economies. Failure often creates an opportunity to rethink policies and make hard choices. Just as a bankrupt corporation is forced to rethink everything—strategy, leadership, training, organizational culture, quality of products, and so forth—so did a failing government. Genuine reform requires tough decisions, and nothing should be kept from review. Arab economic policies need comprehensive strategic analysis and evaluation before the design of future policies. In contemporary fashionable terminology, the Arab world must reinvent itself, unlock itself from its shackles, have a vision, and create institutional leadership that can change the tide. No small change can do the job.

Redefined Economic Policy and a Restructured State

Certainly, the state remains the principal vehicle for accomplishing developmental objectives. To meet its redefined, restructured responsibilities, the state will need to ensure a measure of shared ideology and a great deal of institutional capacity, sustained by professional management down through the ranks of organizational hierarchies. Unquestionably, the state will always have a far-reaching impact, and improving its effectiveness will make a major difference. However, it is premature to assume that political change—whether liberalization or democratization—is predicated on economic realities of regional and global significance. Alan Richards (1993, 1) argues that "the glimmerings of civil society undeniably glow rather more brightly in the region." But this optimism is not based on evidence on the ground as much as on expectations from what Richards perceives as "economic imperatives." He expects economic pressures to dictate heightened political change in the region. These pressures emanate from global conditions of the economy in which information technology, competition, and consumers' choices allow only economies that are less centralized than those of the Arab world to stand a chance of survival (Richards 1993, 1).

The proposition that restructuring of the Arab state will force acceptance of citizens' participation in order to achieve higher economic returns is tenuous. The nature and history of and the factors contributing to autocratic rule do not support the conclusion that economic considerations by themselves will produce democratization. As we have seen, most of the significant changes in systems of Arab governing since World War I have resulted from external, dominant power that dictated such change or from internal military action, often sanctioned by the external powers. Only infrequently have insider reformists or even massive citizens' uprisings resulted in mild alterations of public policy.

Currently, the external pressures for economic reform, restructuring, or liberalizing are irresistible. They come from different directions and through diverse channels—international lenders and donors of capital, global investors, and powerful political-economic trends promoted by alliances among large industrial nations. Nevertheless, Arab leaders continue to vacillate between gradualist approaches or radical changes; they are fully aware of formidable domestic opposition to policies of privatization.

No doubt a new economic policy will fall somewhere between the extremes of pure socialism and laissez-faire. A global process has already separated many worthy from unworthy policies, and a practical middle-ground policy seems to be evolving in which economies can operate dynamically within a system supportive of the emergence of a civil society. Necessity appears to foster pragmatism, and the debate is increasingly over policies that work and those that do not rather than over ideological homogeneity. In the coming decades, Arab leaders will be judged on their progress in such a direction. Policy manifests understanding of current realities, selecting the most appropriate concepts and fitting these concepts to a larger strategy. This is where leadership counts most. Leaders define the mission and set the goals, then bring the various parts together in a coordinated whole, including citizens' demands. Leaders also motivate people and mobilize the necessary human and material resources in the service of the defined mission. In summary, fundamental change is needed in the areas of policy, leadership, and management according to a defined action plan. Although each area is distinct, all are interrelated and mutually reinforcing. Because I deal with issues of leadership and management in Chapter 11, here I shall limit the discussion to economic policy.

Regardless of the arguments for or against privatization, economic change requires an environment suitable for expansion of economic activities and capital investments. The core element of such a favorable environment is a redefined Arab state. This new state must manifest political accountability and professional managerial competence. Accountability encompasses many changes that are instrumental to development: binding mechanisms, rule of law, meaningful constitutionalism, and internal willpower to kick the national habit of spending on things that do not matter.

In this regard, economic public policies also need to be free from past benign neglect and to seriously reconsider production and distribution of the wealth. Confirmation of existing inequities shows in individual income tax proceeds, which represent a very low proportion of total tax receipts (between 0.5 percent and 10 percent in 1990), as revealed by IMF government finance statistics. More than 85 percent of this low rate is being paid by workers and employees and is deducted from their salaries by employers. In capitalist countries, individual income tax proceeds range between 20 percent and 40 percent of total tax receipts (40 percent in the United States, 34 percent in Turkey, 24 percent in Israel) in addition to very heavy payments for social security (another 20 to 40 percent). In the Arab countries, social security payments in the highest case, that of Tunisia, do not exceed 12 percent of total tax receipts (Corm 1995, 4).

To be sure, the income tax rate could be quite high in certain Arab countries, but tax loopholes and evasion are so large that the Arab world is almost a tax-free zone. Even the older traditional class of entrepreneurs has been able through various investment codes to accumulate wealth (as in the textile sectors) without having to pay income tax. Most of the time, wealth accumulated in one type of activity has not been reinvested in the same activity as a means of upgrading management and technological capacity. Instead, wealth has either been transferred abroad or reinvested domestically in real estate transactions with a very high rate of untaxed profit.

Whatever economic restructuring will ultimately evolve, future actions must strive to achieve certain objectives within a rational economic policy that governments and citizens can rally behind. Economic restructuring, market forces, Infitah, privatization, and the like have been mere slogans imported wholesale from different contextual conditions and values. Solutions have to evolve after problems have been empirically defined and community understanding and support has been secured.

The choices listed here are not a complete agenda but are possibilities with potentially superb outcomes.

1. Act decisively and convincingly to attract and bring home Arab capital deposited abroad, estimated at $400 to $600 billion. To achieve this goal, the state has to provide incentives and guarantee fair treatment and protection under the law. It is imperative that the state rebuild its credibility and trust through greater accountability, transparency of decisions, and more professional institutional management of public policies.

2. Restructure priorities of the public budget by reducing spending on the military and increasing it on science, research, technology, and human development. To do so will require identifying education as an investment in people and expanding learning opportunities in areas that improve the expertise and technical know-how essential for development.

3. Build the productive capacity of the economy in all sectors, particularly in industries with high return and the potential of competing in foreign markets.

4. Protect the environment from degradation and further deterioration through effective regulatory processes responsive to public policy needs. Emphasize prevention today for enormous savings in the future.

5. Develop the state's institutional capacity to monitor and to regulate implementation of public policy. Include in this evaluative processes of program outcomes enforced by competent and reliable public institutions.

6. Improve productivity of public organizations by setting standards of performance and enhancing the overall economic efficiency of the system to be able to operate and compete effectively in the global market. Even small countries can have advantages in the competition for global markets. According to Gary S. Becker, economic efficiency requires small states to concentrate on only a few products and services, so they often specialize in niches that are too small for large nations to fill. Consequently, their goods and services tend to be less exposed to trade quotas and other restrictions.[8]

A focus on economic liberalism and restructuring reveals many of the ills of bureaucracy. Based on actual performance and practice in Egypt and the rest of the Arab states, there is ample negative evidence to cast doubt on the whole administrative process, but this does not have to be true. In many countries, the ideas of reform have actually emanated from offices of the bureaucracy that manage well and with integrity. International experiences inform us that when state policymakers are genuinely committed to reform, bureaucratic resistance can be overcome and positive response can be induced.

There is evidence from large developing states such as India and China (Feinberg, Echeverri-Gent, and Muller 1990) and small states such as New Zealand (Mascarenhas 1993), Singapore (Quah 1991), and Jamaica (Kitchen 1989) that commitment to reform by political and administrative leaders has consistently and dramatically improved government performance. In the United States, where criticisms of bureaucracy are widespread, various reform initiatives at national and state levels have emphasized the importance of empowering employees to get results by stressing human resources development, decentralization, and executive leadership (Sherwood 1994, 10).

Thus, criticisms based on distrust of the inherent qualities of public organizations—considering them fatally flawed tools of socioeconomic development—are overstated. Such criticisms deny the potential contributions of a professionalized administrative system that applies ethical standards of conduct and seeks to achieve public service in its most idealized sense. The contention here is that defects of bureaucratic action are not inevitable consequences of some sort of mutant institutional "genetics."

Rather, they are learned behaviors that are constantly influenced and even shaped by political, economic, legal, and cultural contexts.

Investing in People

Empowering individuals and communities and investing in peoples' development are fundamental departures from traditional Arab socioeconomic politics. Global experiences indicate that countries that invest in people achieve higher development. Evidence from the so-called Asian Tigers, such as Korea, Hong Kong, Singapore, and Taiwan, is instructive. They invested heavily in educating their citizens and in improving the skills and managerial competency of their labor force at an initial phase of their development.

"There is a particular connection," Richards and Waterbury (1990, 13) conclude, "between economic development and the development of skills, or 'human capital formation.'" Relying on earlier work by T. W. Schultz (1981), Richards and Waterbury point out that the entire growth process is inconceivable without the improvement of human skills. In this view, education and other types of skill formation are the core of the development process as well as the core of technological change that is essential for economic growth. Specifically, Schultz's original hypothesis, supported by Richards and Waterbury (1990, 13), is that the more educated and trained the population, the more rapidly it can respond to imbalances created by economic growth and structural transformation.

Comparing Western and Southeast Asian experiences with those of the Arab world, Fergany (1995, 2) explains the relative "backwardness" of the Arab society in terms of low investment in education. It seems that Richards and Waterbury (1990, 13) also agree that educational standards in many Middle Eastern countries have "lagged behind what is expected, given the rates of growth in incomes." Thus, Fergany (1995, 3) is convinced that one of the fundamental lessons of history is the decisive importance of investment in human capital; consequently, removing the "blockage" to development requires investing in education.

On the basis of data from the UNDP *Human Development Report* for 1994, Fergany (1995, 2) compares Arab and east Asian countries and reaches disturbing conclusions. Relative to a percentage of industrialized countries (100), the average number of years of education per person in the Arab countries between 1960 and 1992 increased from 21 to 33 percent; the percentage for east Asian countries in the same period increased from 70 to 79. The cumulative impact of past investment in education is measured by this indicator of mean years of schooling just as per capita GNP is used for measuring economic development. Another way to measure investment in education is by current expenditures on education per individual of education age (six through twenty-one). Expenditure figures disclose an unsettling story of Arab achievement in education. In 1990, the expenditure on education per individuals aged six through twenty-one for the entire Arab world was $339, for OECD countries $6,510, and for all countries $1,256 (Fergany 1995, 2; all of these figures as well as the ones that follow are in U.S. dollars).

Of course, these numbers vary dramatically among countries. In Egypt, for example, the expenditure per individual is $117 whereas in Saudi Arabia it is $1,324, in Israel $2,471, and in Switzerland $10,837 (Fergany 1995, 5). Both indicators—mean year of schooling and expenditure per individual—place the Arab world at a lower level of investment in human development than the majority of countries of the world. A multitude of other available data consistently depicts a similar pattern of low investment in human development throughout the Arab world. This is not to suggest that all problems of development and meager reform achievements are caused by low educational investment, because too many other obstacles exist, ranging from political resistance to lack of managerial competence.

Perhaps nowhere is the deficiency of Arab policies and practices in terms of human development more apparent than in regard to women. The rate of adult female literacy in the Arab world is about 40 percent, compared to 71 percent for East Asia and 84 percent for Latin America and the Caribbean. Numbers on health care disclose significant failings: The maternal mortality rate per 100,000 live births between 1980 and 1992 for the Arab states was 294, compared to 92 for East Asia, 189 for Latin America and the Caribbean, 7 for European Union countries, and 5 for Nordic countries. Finally, the number of Arab women in positions of power—positions such as national parliamentarian, municipal councilor, and cabinet member—is the lowest among developed and developing countries alike.[9]

The inequality of women, who represent more than half of the population in the Arab states, "hinders economic growth and lowers production levels," according to a World Bank publication.[10] The World Bank's manager for gender analysis and policy finds "compelling reasons for the World Bank to consider investing in women as the key to a strategy for promoting economic growth and reducing poverty."[11] Discussion of the rights of Arab women cannot be separated from those of their counterparts in Western countries or narrowly viewed as merely a Muslim phenomenon. Writing mainly about Algerian women, Marnia Lazreg (1995) argues that many determinants are responsible for the current gender inequality. She describes the unique history of Algerian women from the French colonial period to postcolonial times and relates how gender inequalities have been the consequence of colonial domination, the war of liberation, economic conditions, and social and cultural norms.

Women undoubtedly have been the casualties of the struggle between tradition and modernity; they have been caught in the uncertainty of changing definitions and roles in a rapidly changing social system. Nevertheless, perhaps no other factor has affected gender equality as much as the economic marginalization of women in the society. The momentous shortcomings of public policies inescapably resulted in denial of the necessary vehicles of economic independence (education, training, jobs, ownership). It is particularly important, therefore, that future development avoid the past flaws of policies that impaired gender equality and hobbled women in an inferior legal status.

Education has the greatest potential for diluting existing norms, habits, and cultural taboos that inhibit improvements in women's conditions. Thus, investment in women's education is universally recognized as an absolute for the new, modern societies that the people aspire to have. The impact of education is as far reaching as it is varied. Education increases productivity, enhances civic communities, and empowers citizens to express themselves and take charge of their own affairs. In a fundamental way, education provides effective means for women to attain equal rights and equal opportunities. Such equality cannot be limited to the job market or the right of ownership, for example, but must also include the struggle to institutionalize those rights.

Economic Empowerment and External Links

The overall development of the Arab countries is profoundly affected by external considerations. The two connections that are particularly significant are inter-Arab relations and global competition.

Inter-Arab relations. The twenty-one Arab countries have more in common than most existing regional political and economic alliances. Despite many military defeats and political and economic setbacks, the Arab people continue to sustain deep emotional ties and a sense of mutuality. The study of inter-Arab economic relations, however, indicates a pattern of conflicts and contradictions rather than congruence. Stated objectives of regional cooperation, or the more ambitious aspirations of Arab unity, have never evolved into an effective economic or political alliance of significance. Each state continues to guard its sovereignty and freedom of action, largely motivated by immediate political gains or short-range tactics of power games among insecure political leaders. The economic rationality of the state appears to have been too often sacrificed for reasons of political expediency.

The most egregious economic defeat of contemporary Arab public policy is that of missing the opportunity of economic integration among these states. For decades, the concept has been recognized, endorsed, formalized, and ratified in agreements that were supposed to lead to an Arab common market. In reality, very little has been done to implement such agreements, despite numerous meetings under the auspices of the League of Arab States.

Regional integration, Mahasneh (1991, 6) points out, was first used to denote objectives of some economic programs directed to the reconstruction of Europe after World War II. U.S. economic assistance to Western Europe in 1947 was conditional on the cooperation of the European countries for their economic development and recovery. In 1948, the European response included establishment of the OECD, which included fourteen countries. The sequence of events in cooperation and economic integration illustrates the continuing blending of security and economic objectives.

Another example of regional cooperation is the Association of Southeast Asian Nations (ASEAN), which is comparable to the League of Arab States. Actually, the league has decisive institutional, cultural, and language advantages over ASEAN. Yet ASEAN, unlike the league, has rendered valuable services to its members in its brief history, particularly in promoting issues of free trade and regional security among its members. The ASEAN summit meeting in Bangkok (December 14–15, 1995) was described as "a success."[12] The group celebrated the informal camaraderie among its members, worked by consensus, and always reached agreement on the issues.[13]

In contrast, the League of Arab States consists of twenty-one countries that have much more in common than the European or the Asian groups but many fewer accomplishments, whether in political cooperation or economic integration. Over the years, the league brought itself to the verge of nonexistence in the daily lives of the Arab people, becoming a forum for empty rhetoric rather than a council for collective policy actions. It has fostered intergroup conflicts and has been used as an instrument of domination by ineffectual leaders and policies.

The mutual economic benefits of cooperation among the states are so apparent that one does not need to make the case in these days of global interdependence. Economic integration of the Arab countries would be the short way to expand trade, encourage establishment of new industries, limit dependency on foreign industries, and improve utilization of both human and capital resources. The expanded market would offer new dynamism and accelerate economic development on a regional basis above and beyond the capability of any single state. It would rationalize the use of foreign exchange by directing it to importation of essentials for productivity and economic growth. Ministates with huge capital would have a chance to achieve economies of scale in production and even compete globally.

But the leaders of the Arab states have gauged the security and economic concerns of their states mainly in terms of power gain or loss for their own persons and dynasties. The continuation of these current policies and attitudes of the leaders—going it alone or creating superficial, weak alliances that form or crumble at the will of a single leader—will not solve the present predicament. The usual inter-Arab policies based on individual initiatives by states or autocratic leaders have repeatedly proved to be inadequate. In fact, such an approach has eroded any past integrationist tendencies and exhausted the organic relationship that continues to identify the collection of political entities called the Arab world.

The economic consequences of personal feuds among leaders have been horrendous. Fruits and vegetables produced by Jordanian farmers rot on the ground while neighboring Arab countries import the same from Europe and Latin America at several times the cost. For years, Morocco imported oil from the Soviet Union while next door Algeria searched for markets to which to export its oil. A very small fraction of the textiles and clothing imported by Arab states originate in Syria, Egypt, or Tunisia, which all have excellent textile and clothing industries. After the Gulf War, Saudi Arabia and Kuwait summarily dismissed their workers from Jordan, Yemen, and Palestine, causing enormous economic and human suffering. They were replaced by workers from non-Arab countries who do not speak the language, understand the local culture, or demonstrate the same level of skills. Once more, rancorous political reasons supersede rational economic logic.

Global interactions. A monumental global transformation is unfolding, creating new realities in all aspects of life. Increase in global commerce and international investment is only one outcome. The information revolution is another. On various fronts, nations are forging new links or strengthening old ones. The technological transformation is reinventing the job market and increasing competition among nations and within nations for ideas, skills, and capital. As a result of these various changes, world views on liberty, human rights, protection of the environment, freedom of the press, and empowering citizens are converging and becoming increasingly similar. According to Ismail Serageldine (1996, 2) of the World Bank, "Globalization is driven by growing interdependence of the world's economies, and the integration of financial and telecommunications markets. The political boundaries that divide the sovereign nation states have become permeable to the ethereal commerce of ideas as well as funds."

Only through participation in these global integrative forces will Arab economies become serious factors in world trade. Economic integration will inhibit monopolistic tendencies in small economies and introduce genuine competition within the regional market, which will improve efficiency of production and the quality of output in preparation for the still-unfolding fierce global competition. Arab states that are seeking refuge in a variety of relations with outside forces to shore up their economic failures or guard against security threats have no alternative but to begin with their own assets and potentials. Other relations will simply deepen already existing asymmetrical economic conditions.

NOTES

1. Caio Koch-Weser, vice president of the World Bank for the Middle East and North Africa, *World Bank News* 14, no. 24 (June 15, 1995), p. 2.
2. Rami G. Khouri, "The Arab Nation: Trends, Assets, and Directions," *Jordan Times,* April 2, 1996, op-ed page.
3. *Business Week* (November 27, 1995), p. 54.
4. Thomas L. Friedman, *New York Times*, October 25, 1995, op-ed page.
5. *Business Week* (July 19, 1993), p. 38.
6. *New York Times* (November 12, 1994), p. Y17.
7. Ibid.
8. Gary S. Becker, "Why So Many Mice Are Roaring," *Business Week* (November 7, 1994), p. 20.
9. All of these numbers are from United Nations Development Program's, *Human Development Report 1995* (New York: Oxford University Press), pp. 42, 53, 56.
10. *World Bank News* 14, no. 31 (August 31, 1995), p. 2.
11. Ibid.
12. *The Economist* (December 16, 1995), p. 31.
13. Ibid.

11

Politics Without Process, Administration Without Discretion

My belief is that the biggest challenge facing the Middle East in the years to come is the development of better systems of governance. This means governments that are accountable, in some acceptable manner, to their people.

William B. Quandt (1995)

The crisis of leadership today is the mediocrity or irresponsibility of so many men and women in power, but leadership rarely rises to the full need for it.

James MacGregor Burns (1978)

The crisis of modernity and change in the Arab world is severe and relentless, and public estrangement from the ruling elites is intensifying. Few institutions promote public discourse across lines between groups, classes, religions, and political ideologies. The fact that "all substantive changes begin and end at the top of the political pyramid" (Jreisat 1992a, 14) explains why citizens are restless and increasingly cynical as they wait for the inevitable to occur. The dismal performance of the state—its leaders and its policies—has failed to modify or redress the potentially menacing polarization in each country.

Ultimately, if not checked or reversed, such polarization threatens to fragment and disconnect communities. Arab rulers, not proficient in either liberal individualism or in communal attachments and civic engagement, cannot govern except through coercion or maintain the collectivity except through force. Consequently, citizens are so politically alienated from their governments that economic deterioration is certain to bring about dramatic responses that threaten stability. So far, the most organized threat to the status quo, although not the only one, has been that of the Islamists, as in Algeria, Bahrain, Egypt, Sudan, Saudi Arabia, and other communities. Islamists have employed various tactics, including violence, in their dissension with current political orders.[1]

The extraordinarily inept Arab political leaders have accumulated an uncommon record of failures in many aspects of their public responsibilities. From building proficient political and administrative institutions to generating technological or economic vitality in their societies, these leaders can show only lackluster achievements. The consequences have been more than grave losses of resources or missed historical opportunities. Swelling impoverishment, against a background of social dislocation, is slowly undermining the foundations of the states. Moreover, autocratic rule by individuals, dynasties, or clans has marginalized organizational actions and institutional roles. The outside world has taken notice of the feebleness of the Arab political systems, and thus more powerful states both within the region and without have taken advantage of the Arab vulnerabilities and ineffectual leaders on political, economic, and military fronts.

Manifestations of the crisis are radically different among states. Lebanon, for example, is enduring the dire, self-destructive consequences of the bloody internal strife that lasted from 1975 to 1989[2] and was made more onerous by the Israeli invasion in 1982 and bombardment in 1996. Algeria continues to anguish over its future and how to resolve a violent internal conflict between ineffective traditional leaders and radical Islamists. Iraq is in agony, trapped between the erratic actions of its leadership and reckless external powers determined to debase and to control. Under Saddam Hussein, Iraq "is still in the grips of one of the most prolonged and painful traumas it has experienced since its emergence as a national state in 1921" (Hisham 1996, 10). Sudan, which until recently promised to become the breadbasket of the Arab world, now is on the verge of economic disaster. Poverty, hyperinflation, civil war, and ineffectual political leadership combined to take the wind out of the country's sails. Even Egypt, the largest Arab state, although continually aspiring to lead the region, has a government unable to competently manage its own affairs. After a visit to Cairo, a *New York Times* columnist provided a cartoonish portrayal of the political scene:

> [President] Mubarak has failed to provide any blueprint for making Egypt more competitive, democratic, free-market oriented and open to the world, and so stability has hardened into stagnation. Mr. Mubarak's economic ministers are constantly pulling him in different directions, because he provides no clear signals from the top. Except for a couple of young ministers, the Mubarak Cabinet is dominated by aging apparatchiks who think the Internet is something you catch fish with on the Nile.[3]

Clearly, there are no reformers blazing a new pathway into the political future of the contemporary Arab society. Even such shallow administrative and political reform attempts that are made tend, in the absence of an over-all framework that institutes and integrates developmental policies, to focus on segments of the society rather than its totality. Segmental approaches are convenient because they exclude significant processes that could increase the risk of failure. In part, this is why most developmental efforts in the Arab world have been disjointed. A striking example is administrative reform, which has often moved in paths that fail to converge with those of socioeconomic development.

A conspicuous deficiency of Arab national development is the absence of meaningful efforts to forge a civil society. No development plan has incorporated a vision of a more just, egalitarian, and free society, much less implemented policies leading in those directions. Arab leaders appear to tolerate system change only if the consequences are benign. They have actively resisted building competing sources of decisionmaking and prevented the evolution of autonomous channels of influence and communication in the society. Several years ago, in another study, I examined administrative reform programs in seven Arab states and found efforts that produced only "mediocre results based on a poor implementation record attributable to incongruities of methods and objectives of reform" (Jreisat 1988, 85).

Currently, public debates appear limited to justification of decisions or criticism of particular events rather than including a broader delineation of strategies or proposals of bold initiatives to redress formidable problems. The crisis continues to demand answers to exacting questions: what change, what reforms, and how to manage them? Objectives such as cultivating a civil society, attaining a rule of law, and fostering economic vibrancy cannot be accomplished, or even advanced, if the focus of discourse is limited to the recent past or the forthcoming election. In fact, elections are not ipso facto democracy nor a sufficient measure of it.

Thus, intellectual debates on the future of the Arab society continue to mask many limitations. In a recent conference focusing on "Arab renaissance," panelists presented research on "the crisis of governance in the Arab states," "Arab human development," "culture as social activism," and other related subjects.[4] Discussions revealed fragmentation of research efforts and a tendency to disaggregate issues for considerations of feasibility and convenience. One critic vehemently disagreed with a panelist for limiting his discussion to "regime maintenance" instead of concentrating on internal dynamics and their complexities as the key to understanding problems of societal change. Other speakers raised issues of education, women's education, civil society, and Western hegemony. Each speaker seemed to present his or her topic as the foundation of all difficulties or the basis for explaining the current malaise of the Arab society.

Actually, the multiple components of the Arab crisis are best described in a standard war metaphor. Focusing on a single battle or two and forgetting about the full-scale war being waged is inappropriate, to say the least. Authors tend to lose sight of the central fact that profound issues are at stake and their solutions defy quick, partial actions. The range of difficulties includes not only political and economic factors but also social, cultural, and even global. The scope of required change encompasses education, health care, employment, the role of women, foreign policy, and a myriad of other issues. Failing in any of these areas will unavoidably retard progress in others.

In this chapter I focus on fundamental political issues that have a determining influence on building the necessary administrative capacity. The connection of the political and the administrative is so powerful that distinctions often are justifiable only for analytical convenience. Still, my purpose is to serve theoretical and practical knowledge by extending explanatory reasoning, delineating promising solutions, and identifying prospective strategies. I pursue these aims through the examination of three domains deemed crucial for the future of the Arab state: (1) the political domain, which comprises issues of leadership, succession, relationships among Arab states, corruption, and democracy; (2) the domain of administrative and institutional capacity, which involves administrative reform issues and building professional managerial and organizational competence; and (3) the foreign attachments domain, which examines interactions with foreign powers, particularly those displaying a domination predilection, and the effects on the independent actions of the Arab states.

THE POLITICAL DOMAIN

The Arab political state was ineffectual at birth, grew up corrupt, aged with a seemingly incurable authoritarian bent, and has been too often led by recklessly self-serving political autocrats. For too long, regime politics have revolved around the core of survival of the leader or the ruling group. Even relations with outside powers have often been a function of inter-Arab regime feuds or schemes for sustaining or augmenting the powers of a ruler or his dynasty. An important factor in these power contests has always been the perpetual search for allies within the Arab states as well as for protection by a dominant foreign power.

Arab leaders have kept very tight rein on all powers of the state, particularly those related to public funds and military control. Except for Lebanon before 1975, citizens have very few outlets through which to express their political views or to develop their particular community needs and interests. In most Arab states, no competitive political parties, associational groups, or organized political activities are permitted to function without weighty restrictions. In some states, such activities are totally banned. Currently, one cannot find an accountable, legitimate, and participatory political process in the entire Arab world.

The political features of the state also gave the administrative process many of its current attributes: highly centralized, beset by nepotism and political patronage, and burdened by its own weight of swelled ranks of ill-trained public employees. Public employees usually are underpaid, have few incentives, and are deficient in skills relevant for the conduct of their responsibilities. All important personnel and budgetary decisions continue to be made according to the personal wishes and preferences of the chief of the state. In brief, the overall political and administrative practices highlight the key features of the state that have been most resistant to change. Particularly important are the issues of succession, legitimacy of decision-making powers, corruption, and democracy.

Succession

The usual path for reaching the top of the Arab state's political pyramid is through inheritance or military takeover. Family inheritance dictates succession in monarchist regimes, such as in the six Gulf states, Jordan, and Morocco. Former military officers or their surrogates rule in Egypt, Iraq, Syria, Libya, Sudan, and Algeria. Neither method provides any assurance that the most qualified or competent person will ascend to power. Nor does the level of performance in office matter much to a leader's tenure. Arab presidents, like kings, all seem to view their bond with the job as the same: in success and in failure, "in sickness and in health . . . till death do us part."

Monarchies perhaps offer a smoother and more predictable change of regime than the military. Comparatively, military leaders frequently cause uncertainty of succession and even lead to violence and chaos during the transition. Military officers rarely give up power willingly and have to be deposed by force, just as they came to power in the first place. In all situations, citizens have little if anything to do with the change. And when military autocrats permit a popular vote, it is usually a political scheme rather than a valid citizens' choice. In several of these states, a popular vote has been relegated to meaningless exercises: elections that produce almost perfect scores or have no viable political opposition.

Decisionmaking Power

A peculiar aspect of the Arab political process is the method and outcome of exercising political power. Both the military officers and the monarchs tend to concentrate power in their persons and to draw loyalty and support primarily from their families, tribes, cronies, small elite groups, and military ranks. Consequently, these groups also are the main beneficiaries of regimes' policies, accentuating the personalized features of decisionmaking.

Not surprisingly, during the past three to four decades, such exercise of power has engendered a curious dysfunction of governance that highlights the inability of political leaders to transform their power into legitimate authority. Power that is transformed into authority is less resisted; also, it addresses the issue of institutionalizing social control (Pfeffer 1981). Typically, institutionalized powers develop independent norms and expectations, thus making the exercise of influence expected and accepted. Arab political authority systems—whether those of inherited individual authority or of forced military rule—have failed to develop contextual connections or to promote and institutionalize processes of governing. Their power has not evolved into an authority that abides by binding mechanisms of accountability, rule of law, or institutional frameworks, and its holders are unwilling to accept authentic means of competitive politics, including grassroots participation. Power remains personal and egocentric, and public decisions are largely reflections of preferences, self-interest, and the values of the personality in the top position.

Corruption

Autocratic governments, in addition to being oppressive and prone to making flawed decisions, are notoriously corrupt. To be sure, corruption is common to all political systems in various degrees. In recent years Brazil deposed its president, Korea indicted its president, and the United States appears to be perpetually investigating its president—all on corruption charges. From Japan to Mexico and from Russia to Nigeria, public officials at all levels have been accused of bribery, embezzlement, and use of unlawful means to influence the outcomes of government decisions. But the problem in the Arab world, in addition to widespread corruption among public officials, is that there are no effective mechanisms for dealing with it. No Arab president or king has ever been indicted or imprisoned for corruption; no leader has been charged, investigated, or adjudicated by an independent authority. In the meantime, the reputations of members of many ruling families for fast living and their penchant for demanding payoffs on government contracts are legendary. Some of them have amassed wealth of astounding magnitude, sometimes on a global scale, even while their governments face serious budget deficits, capital shortage, and debt burden. (The Western press often provides a regular menu of corruption of Arab governments, such as articles in *Newsweek* on November 27, 1995; *Business Week,* November 27, 1995; and the *Economist,* January 6, 1996.)

True, there is no guaranteed remedy to cure the disease of corruption. There are, however, measures, that offer hope of initially containing and limiting its spread until reform can be accelerated within a strategy of eradication. A helpful beginning in this intricate process of fighting corruption is a careful rethinking of all regulations in order to simplify enforcement. A combination of transparency and proper documentation of public decisions is another potentially useful measure. A freer press is definitely a step in the right direction. A far-reaching behavioral change is possible through integration of the subject of ethics and honest behavior into education curricula and training programs for public employees. Independent investigative agencies, supported by an effective neutral judiciary and armed with enforceable ethics laws, are certain deterrents. Independent and regular financial and performance audits that publish their results are such tools. Undoubtedly, designing better laws and instituting more effective prosecution of violations are imperatives for any progress on this front.

Democracy, Liberalism, or Representation

Deficiencies of political actions and failures of leaders to transform personal power into legitimate authority affect state performance in several important functions. Mancur Olson (1993, 567) points out that "autocracies will rarely have good economic performance for more than a generation" and notes that no society can work satisfactorily if it does not have a peaceful order. But options for the Arab states ought not to be limited to a choice between anarchic violence or stultifying stagnation, as will be the case if absolute power will not permit the emergence of any other independent power of decisionmaking in the society for fear of deciding the selection of the next leader. Because such independent capacity will constrain the existing power or hasten its replacement, Arab political leaders have monopolized absolute power. Particularly, they are not expected to create, permit, or tolerate an independent political opposition in their systems. This is a fatal historical dilemma of the current Arab political systems that paralyzes orderly development and limits their capacities to function effectively.

Do autocrats willingly transform into democrats? More specifically, will democracy find its way into the Arab state with existing political leaders? Evidence from the past four to five decades of Arab political history offers little ground for optimism that democratic governments will emerge out of autocratic systems. In fact, it is difficult to explain the emergence of democracy except in terms of the absence of conditions that foster autocracy. Mancur Olson (1993, 573) predicts that democracy would be most likely to emerge spontaneously when leaders who orchestrated the overthrow of an autocracy could not establish another autocracy, much as they would gain from doing so. Hence, a helpful strategy is to implement a dispersion of forces and resources to make it impossible for any one leader or group to overpower all of the others. Admittedly, there is no assurance that proposed dispersion of power always works toward the ends described. In Lebanon, as commonly known, the outcome of dispersed powers, without effective institutional controls, has not been solidifying democracy but a destructive civil war.

Middle East scholars have increasingly pondered conceptual problems of political development in the Arab-Islamic society. A volume by Brynen, Korany, and Noble (1995) brings together contributions from a select group of Middle East specialists that includes Michael Hudson, Saad Eddin Ibrahim, Lisa Anderson, Giacomo Luciani, and others. The editors aimed at identifying areas of agreement and disagreement among scholars within the broader context of comparative politics. They suggest that four themes—"political culture and discourse, civil society, political economy, and the regional and international context—lie at the core of any theoretically informed study of political liberalization and democratization in the Arab world" (Brynen, Korany, and Noble 1995, 20).

In their introduction, the editors distinguish processes of political liberalization from those of democratization. On the one hand, liberalization "involves the expansion of public space through the recognition and protection of civil and political liberties, particularly those bearing upon the ability of citizens to engage in free political discourse and to freely organize in pursuit of common interest." Democratization, on the other hand, "entails an expansion of political participation in such a way as to provide citizens with a degree of real and meaningful collective control over policy" (3). Such a distinction is useful in recognizing variations in political development as well as in identifying the limits of autocratic regimes that may be willing to "reform" in the liberalization sense but very reluctant to comply with requirements of democratization that involve power sharing.

Another valuable volume addressing the same theme of democratization is edited by Ghassan Saleme (1994), with contributions from such prominent scholars of Middle East studies as John Waterbury, Aziz Al-Azmeh, and Roger Owen. In the introduction, Salame (1) specifies exceptionalism as the orientation of the book: "Contemporary events in the Arab-Islamic region" have "reinforced a contrary but widespread idea according to which that part of the world has been too slow in adjusting" to the general trend of democratization. This presumed exceptionalism, Salame (2) points out, is what he decided to examine. The contributors' most frequently suggested explanatory reasons for the so-called exceptionalism are found to be in religion, in culture, in a specific combination of sociohistorical factors, or in the permanence of intractable conflicts (2). Cautiously, Waterbury (1994, 32) argues "that there is something exceptional about the degree of authoritarianism that prevails in the Middle East today.

It does not derive from any single factor but rather from a combination of factors." Among those he considers are the ambivalence of the bourgeoisie, the taxation issue, and Islam.

The issue of political culture is prominent in these discussions, presumably for its explanatory power of political development in the Arab world. Although Michael Hudson seems to recognize potential and real misapplication of cultural notions in reference to the Arab society, he attempts to argue, nevertheless, in favor of rehabilitation of the cultural variable. The title of his chapter in the Brynan, Korany, and Noble volume sums up Hudson's (1995) thesis: "The Political Culture Approach to Arab Democratization: The Case for Bringing It Back In, Carefully."

Despite a lack of consensus on what it means, culture is a profound source of values and attitudes that shape behavior. As I argued elsewhere (1992, 13), a serious analysis of cultural dimensions can be beneficial. But I also recognize that to achieve balanced and practical conclusions, we must understand the limitations of the cultural perspectives and "guard against the tendency to slide into stereotypes or to seek methodological feasibility in reductionism" (Jreisat 1992a, 13). Without equivocation, Lisa Anderson (1995, 78) also debunks the argument and recognizes the heavy baggage attached to it: "Much of the social science literature treats the Arab world as congenitally defective, 'democratically challenged' as it were, and seeks to find biological, cultural, and/or religious causes for this disability."

In brief, there is nothing exceptional about the Arab people or their culture when the opportunity to participate is provided. The flood of media witnesses that monitored the Palestinian election in 1996 certified that, in the words of former U.S. President Jimmy Carter, "The Palestinian people had an historic opportunity to choose their leaders yesterday, and they did so with enthusiasm and a high degree of professionalism."[5] In a moving eyewitness account, President Carter provides this note: "An old man came in with his son, his grandson, and his great-grandson, all with tears in their eyes as they cast their votes. The first voter in one Jericho site had been in line all night. He came in, showed his credentials, marked his ballots, then knelt and kissed both ballot boxes before inserting his envelopes. The participation and enthusiasm of women was heartening . . . they jammed the polling sites."[6]

To be sure, the Palestinians' enthusiasm for voting is affected by their experience under an oppressive occupation, but people's attitudes in practicing such a right are indicative of other important factors. The examples above challenge arguments that there is "a deep confusion in the Arab public mind" about the meaning of democracy. "The confusion, however, is understandable since the idea of democracy is quite alien to the mind-set of Islam," according to Kedouri (1994, 1).

The anomaly referred to as exceptionalism is much more than a cultural characteristic; it is primarily an outcome of certain political and economic factors.

1. There is a lack of effective organizations that are able to function with a measure of professionalism and detachment at the managerial as well as the political levels. This is true of the state and its institutions, ranging from municipal councils to national parliaments and from public service organizations to universities. Political powers are highly concentrated in the hands of ruling families and elites who jealously guard the status quo. Consequently, effective democratization is unacceptable for the risk it creates to existing powers and privileges.

2. During the Cold War and its aftermath, the approach by Western powers (particularly the United States) to the Arab world has been a major source of support to autocratic rule. Preoccupied with Israel's security and absorbed with containing Soviet Russia, the United States was unwilling to take chances with political change that might produce assertive, independent, or effective Arab governments that could be a source of threat to the twin objectives of its policies in the region. Hence, U.S. policies opposed, frustrated, or toppled governments according to those two criteria. Today, the United States stands out as sustaining and protecting the status quo in most Arab countries, particularly in the Gulf states. Adding the objective of protecting the flow of oil to Western markets, U.S. foreign policy in the region has formalized what has been common knowledge for a long time: The United States will continue to provide protection to the ruling dynasties from internal or external threats as long as they follow policies that are desirable, from Washington's perspective. Agreements with the Gulf states commit the United States to aiding these states in case of attack, and in turn the agreements help preserve U.S. hegemony in the region (Hadar 1996, 4). It is precisely this relationship that inspired a magazine headline after the bombing in Riyadh (November 13, 1995): "Attack on the House of Saud: America Protects the Kingdom—and at the Same Time Makes It Vulnerable."[7]

3. Inter-Arab state politics during the second half of the twentieth century produced regular political and military stalemates. Arab states precipitously form alliances among themselves for the sole purpose of aborting any attempt to dramatically change the status quo even while Egypt aspires to lead the Arab world. The Hashemite family in Jordan (and in Iraq before 1958) attempts to formulate its own alliances to balance other suspicious affiliations. The most determined players with the most cash to sway positions are the Saudis. The Saudi government has often used its huge oil revenues to buy influence, bribe politicians, subsidize local news media,

and corrupt the political process throughout the Arab world, for its own security reasons (Aburish 1995).[8]

Of course, there are other reasons why autocratic processes are thoroughly entrenched in addition to foreign hegemony, ruling dynasties, the military, and inter-Arab alliances. A lack of viable and institutionalized political opposition, a subservient press, low educational standards, and poverty—all have created deadly combinations that have converged against organized and effective public response. Politicians, sensing the public mood, have become more punitive and more willing to ruthlessly crush popular resistance. Leaders habitually violate the human rights of citizens. Opposition to corrupt and oppressive political leaders has literally had no legitimate means to manifest itself or effect change, so that civil strife, violence, and intermittent popular outbursts have been the tools of discontent and opposition.

Nevertheless, it is indeed amazing that popular resistance has so often been localized and made ineffective in the campaign for fundamental change in Arab political systems. A considerable part of the explanation is linked to the absence of political alternatives championed by prominent oppositional leaders serving as catalysts for change. A proficient leader can inspire trust, rally support, and skillfully articulate desired objectives for a popular uprising. Lack of organization also has been a formidable obstacle to mass mobilization. Leadership and organization are the imperatives for effective application of techniques of responsible and sustained civil disobedience. Arab popular uprisings have never been a match for the far-reaching networks of the secret police and the military. Even fairly well-organized and well-funded Islamist opposition groups proved to be no match to the state security and military machine, as the Islamists in Algeria, Bahrain, Saudi Arabia, and Egypt learned belatedly. The potency of the status quo is made formidable when combined with a government-sponsored press and habits of citizen distrust and fear. Hence, these popular uprisings have not been able to realize the major parts of their demands.

All of this explains why a strategic point of departure is to ensure widespread citizen input in the establishment of the accurate diagnosis and description of the problems. Much of what goes on in political offices, bureaucratic organizations, newspapers, and even educational institutions is conducted in utter ignorance of the public's sentiments and preferences. At the same time, reform has raised great expectations among citizens, including businesspeople who were once opposed to change. It would be difficult for any Arab government, whoever is in power, to go back to the old ways of governing. Despite increased public enlightenment, however, the vision of the future is no clearer and the path to it is even less defined.

This vagueness is the burden of the coming generations of Arab people and rulers who will be in charge early in the twenty-first century.

Some objectives of political change can be quite specific and demonstrable. Expanding the rule of law, redefining and reducing the power of the state, and attaining greater protection of individual and property rights are among such objectives. Above all, however, the crucial need is to create a basic commitment to values of equity and liberty as the foundation for the emerging Arab civil society. Certainly, such political changes would result in significant economic consequences, not the least of which would be the increase of capital inflow and the encouragement of a favorable environment for private investment. Moreover, citizens would finally have real opportunities for meaningful participation in decisions affecting their lives.

I must emphasize here that political change is critical not only for its instrumental values but also for what it represents for society beyond job creation, capital investment, or food production. At the same time that political repression discourages development it erodes the quality of life for the whole society. There is little hope, however, that economic imperatives alone will cause the required political change. In part, I agree with Anderson's (1995, 78) conclusion that "the nature of the political regimes in the Arab world, like those elsewhere in the world, can best be understood as reflections of the political economy of the countries in question." But also Arab regimes are subjected to other historical constraints and external intrusions that counteract normal processes of change and profoundly limit real alternatives for action.

ADMINISTRATIVE AND INSTITUTIONAL CAPACITY

During the past several years, management reform has been a constant objective, included in the public agenda of every Arab state. Implementation, however, is a different matter altogether. As I have discussed in earlier chapters, the problems of administrative systems range from excessive centralization of decisionmaking to low pay, low skills, and overstaffing, and the dilemma of rampant corruption is compounded by inadequate funding and poorly conceived and implemented reform programs (Jreisat 1988, 94). Political leaders do not issue clear policy directions or set implementable plans, and they tolerate change only when modest in coverage and benign in political effect.

Conventional political attitudes such as these have two major consequences. First, central control by a political leader is not aimed at developing broad and creative policies (which the existing bureaucracy might not be able to implement anyway) or at developing the necessary support for ensuring implementation of strategic goals of government. Instead, central control is primarily geared to maintaining loyalty to the person of the head of state. When loyalty is the highest value, then considerations of merit, particularly expertise and neutral competence, often are sacrificed.

Second, when recruitment to top administrative posts is primarily based on loyalty, higher bureaucrats and political leaders develop close identification and mutuality of views and interests. This tendency toward fusion of higher civil servants and ruling leaders deprives decision processes of independent, professional input. Thus, administrative discretion is reduced to administrative subservience. Whether in presidential systems, such as those of Algeria, Egypt, Iraq, Syria, and Tunisia, or in monarchical ones, such as those in Jordan, Morocco, and Saudi Arabia, the political and the bureaucratic elites are integral parts of the same power structure.

Distinctions between different types of bureaucratic systems are central, from a theoretical perspective, in the public administration literature. One of the most widely acknowledged distinctions is Max Weber's (1947) traditional and legal-rational authority systems. Administrative patterns within the first are determined by family connections and wealth, not merit or achievement. Within a legal-rational system, however, administration is through a bureaucracy that is rationally structured in order to maximize efficiency. Responsibility and authority are hierarchically arrayed and balanced throughout. Rules are specific in content and universal in application. Employees are recruited and promoted exclusively on the basis of objective standards of merit and achievement.

Earlier, I outlined programs of administrative reform in several Arab states (see Chapter 4) and noted their chronic bids to rationalize public service, despite a sparse record of implementation. Rationalizing the organizational capacity of the state has often been drowned by claims of procedural tinkering and other routine personnel matters. Another aspect of these attempts is that agencies acquire costly gadgetry without assessing needs or ensuring availability of skilled operators. Almost always reform ideas are dictated from the top; discussions with employees or citizens are infrequent. Moreover, governments do not measure outcomes of reform programs, nor do they systematically collect data on performance of administrative units.

Definitions of feasible alternatives of institutional reform strategies, particularly those related to building administrative and organizational capacities, can be unwieldy and multifaceted. To establish some comparative framework, this analysis is arranged according to three interrelated aspects: internal organizational relationships, leadership functions, and administrative relationships with the external environment.

Internal Organizational Relationships

The administrative capacity needed cannot be transient or temporary but must be sustainable over time. Such a capacity includes a dynamic quality that ensures flexibility and adaptability in order to guard against the chronic rigidities that tend to accumulate slowly within the managerial process. To develop institutional effectiveness, the people working in the system must be targeted in a planned change that involves the whole organization and its culture. A sustained effort of applying knowledge, particularly behavioral science knowledge, is essential in order for employees to learn, grow, and be professional.

Perhaps a starting point is to empower public employees: Give them a "mission" and let them figure out how to achieve it. Encourage them to experiment and to try different managerial processes. Link rewards, incentives, and disciplinary actions to performance gauged by some objective measure. Try to control methods through the power of persuasion and analysis rather than order and command. Strengthen feedback, performance tracking, and focus on trust and honesty in public service. Avoid the addictive feeling of managerial denial, self-centeredness, and illusion of power and control even when the methods are unethical.

Arab public employees and institutions rarely justify their existence or mode of operation because they have no say in any of them. They do not take risks, nor do they think innovatively. All sorts of attitudes, habits, and practices need to be altered and brought into the modern age. The bureaucratic culture has to change to a culture that values efficiency, effectiveness, accountability, and empowerment of citizens. Archaic systems of hiring, assigning responsibility, evaluation of performance, and promotion and training of staff are all detrimental to the developmental policies that Arab states profess. Officials have to experiment with and to adapt their approaches to social and economic policy and not to accept a prescient perspective. They must recognize that there are no perfect policies, just ones that work and others that do not.

Many of these ideas are in the category of limited neutral competencies, amplifiable through available means. The purpose is to suggest a managerially based approach to personnel development that offers opportunities from within the organization but also scans the immediate environment for learning opportunities. In this latter situation, administrative units may seek help from potential catalysts for change such as academic institutions, institutes of public administration, consultants, and skilled personnel within these institutions. To put it differently, organizations cannot be effective if they are passive and habitually dependent on directions from outside their boundaries for every step they take. Effective organizations exercise a great deal of initiative even within autocratic political systems.

They are able to vitalize motivational factors, decentralize decisionmaking, and institute a host of improvements in the methods of operation, such as improving goal setting, communication, evaluation, and monitoring as well as measuring output. Finally, to ensure accountability, public organizations cannot evade their responsibilities in instituting basic honesty and conformity to law as well as preventing conflict of interests in conducting official duties.

Administrative Leadership

An emerging trend within the new global economic reality indicates that highly trained professional groups are leading modern organizations in all the fast-growing economies. These professionals, as managers of complex organizations, are a part of international professional associations as much as of their own countries. They are modern organization managers, communication experts, and technological whizzes. These professionals understand the role of motivation in modern organizations and how to maximize results and achieve goals. Such organization men and women also play central roles in national development. "As career officials in the service of their state and society, and as politicians come and go, development managers are the more permanent stewards or custodians of a public interest that extends beyond the satisfaction of immediate individual or program interests" (Esman 1991, 42).

Actual experiences from Latin America and eastern Asia indicate that institutional leaders provide the main energy that brings about desired changes. In managing the contemporary Arab state, the most urgent need is for organizational leaders who strive to soar above the mundane and the self-serving battles and focus on results and their congruity with the common interests. These leaders must be able to bypass contentious and fractionalizing organizational cultures by activating a visionary role that integrates national culture with effective tools of governing and mobilizes human and material resources in the service of developmental needs. Certainly, success propels the legitimacy of leaders' powers to a higher level of credibility in enforcing the laws.

Breaking away from the habits of micromanagement and preoccupation with procedures and reaching new grounds of original thinking with a focus on results remains a hope in the Arab world rather than a reality. Originality is a result of independence, of dissent from the customary. As Serageldine (1996, 8) points out, originality "requires the challenge of the established order, the right to be heard however outlandish the assertion, subject only to the test of rigorous method." If originality and dissent are marks of freedom and independence of mind, Arab managers are indeed denied and deprived. Currently, perhaps the main hope is that the political leadership is sufficiently besieged by public resentment and distrust that leaders may encourage some reforms to diffuse the pressures. They may also favor controlled reforms rather than explosions of unpredictable consequences.

The leadership needs of the contemporary Arab state can also be explained by using Burke and Litwin's conceptual model of transactional change and transformational change (see French and Bell 1995, 85). As I discussed in the concluding section of Chapter 4, Arab reform efforts do not seem to have gone beyond the transactional, or first-order, level. Even at this level, which focuses on personnel matters, Arab managers have not done well. It should actually be possible for effective and committed public managers to generate significant progress at the first-order level, but it takes transformational leaders to move on to the second-order level of performance.

Transformational leadership is more than holding power—it ultimately helps "release human potentials now locked in ungratified needs and crushed expectations" (Burns 1978, 5). This is easier said than done in a system in which "patronage appointments allow political elites to consolidate their position of forging networks of dependent loyalists whose jobs and living standards depend on the continuing power of their patrons" (Esman 1991, 44). When political loyalty is the price for having a job, the abilities of transformational public managers are restricted. If given political support, transformational leaders could rise above existing standards and motivate followers. But the absence of professional management and the dominance of an autocratic political order in the Arab world seriously constrain such transformational change. Again, the issue becomes one of dilution or modification of political control to accommodate economic and technological changes sweeping across borders and regions and to elevate reliance on professional accountability and performance standards in evaluation.

Administration and the Larger Context

I suggest that the political context of the Arab state is hobbling administrative institutions and causing them to bungle significant developmental tasks. Because of this situation, the contemporary Arab state appears to be living in a self-perpetuating disorder that is generating its own vicious cycle. Still, economic imperatives, domestic needs, and global pressures may force the action it takes to build needed administrative capacities. Improving managerial competence is feasible if the fixation of regimes with self-perpetuation is divorced from the exercise of administrative discretion. Unfortunately, until radical political change is realized, alternatives permitting bureaucratic adaptation to needs of the new age of economic restructuring and political liberalism are quite limited.

The continuing emphasis within the political context on command and control and on political loyalty narrows the choices for reform even further. Even though the overall power of the state is being redefined and public participation in public policy is more frequently debated, the basic characteristics of the system and the individuals ruling it have not changed much. Establishing links with citizens has been a central exercise for public organizations that are seeking greater relevance to their communities and environments, particularly when those organizations are engaged in developmental activities. Arab institutions, traditionally isolated from their publics, are totally unprepared to face public participation in government decisions. *Participation* here is defined as "a process through which stakeholders influence and share control over development initiatives and decisions and resources which affect them."[9] Participation gives the poor and disadvantaged groups a voice in the development process and provides a mechanism for empowering those who have a stake in the sustainability of projects. The ethics of democratic responsibility are not restricted to the policy level, either; within an agency or institution in the United States, for example, "citizen participation is encouraged, even required, in governmental programs" (Wilbern 1988, 16).

Thus, I distinguish two methods of participation that the Arab administrative settings have not effectively utilized to improve their information and support bases. One is employee participation in decisionmaking to induce cooperation and commitment while benefiting from employees' varied experiences and know-how. Second is citizen participation that opens new linkages between public programs and affected citizens. In these two types of linkages, public organizations can lead the way in seeking involvement of their employees and of the citizens they serve. Such organizational participation is not necessarily contingent on total success of societal democratization, even if the values and motives of both are comparable.

In practical terms, every time I suggest an idea of reform, I discover that a formidable obstacle to action exists in the political arena. Therefore, making organizational improvements a high priority on the reform agenda without facing up to problems of political decline will only repeat familiar lessons about the limits of organizational reform. Even agreeing on a strategic vision of administrative reform and adapting political forms are insufficient measures to ensure the accomplishment of such objectives, as we have learned from two decades of experience in central planning. Without political support, the institutional capacity is impaired in accomplishing its diverse responsibilities. A flexible and accountable political process is imperative for the effective application of institutional capacities to carry out the public mandate.

In conclusion, at this historic juncture, building the institutional capacity of government is crucial for reasons that exceed traditional functions of management. The idea of organizational capacity is gaining added urgency because of new issues and problems related to privatization, structural adjustments, and global dependencies. Organizational and institutional competence, manifested through effective, efficient, and sustained functioning (United Nations Development Program 1994, 2), is the key for assuming such new obligations. Indeed, the required capacity is more than setting or simplifying operating procedures—it is shaping an innate competence in the organization to diagnose, design, implement, monitor, and adapt actions in order to meet needs and demands, independently and cooperatively with other institutions. Only then is accountability for results possible.

FOREIGN CONNECTIONS

Independence from colonial rule has been a watershed for nations that struggled for emancipation from political and economic subservience. In many ways, the Arab experience in resurgent nationalism, self-reliance, and ambitions for indigenous rule is comparable to that of other developing countries. The difference, however, is that Arab countries faced new, more deleterious conditions in the period after their nominal independence. First, the emerging Arab states were forged as political entities not for reasons of coherence and economic viability or because of historical actuality or antecedent but to accommodate imperial interests and to prevent the emergence of a credible Arab power in the region. The new states, as Quataert (1991, xi) points out, "were created, more or less willy-nilly, by European diplomats when World War I ended in 1918."

Second, until the present, old colonial systems continued overtly and covertly to meddle in Arab affairs, obstructing any of their policies and plans that might be inconsistent with Western designs in the region. For various reasons, the West never really left the Middle East to its travails. Instead, British, French, and, subsequently, U.S. powers continued their deep-seated interest and close involvement in the area.

By 1947, the United States promulgated the Truman Doctrine and began to replace Britain as the major Western power in the Middle East. The United States became directly involved and militarily intervened in the civil war in Lebanon in 1958 (American Enterprise Institute 1968, 6). Not surprisingly, "by now most people are familiar with the CIA-led overthrow of the Mossadegh government in Iran after it replaced the Shah in 1951 and then dared to nationalize the oil industry" (Tanzer 1991, 263). Also well known is the 1958 British-French-Israeli invasion of Egypt after it nationalized the Suez Canal and exercised its sovereignty over its waterway. A significant event with a far-reaching impact on the modern history of the region was the overthrow of the monarchy in Iraq in July 1958. That fomented political ferment in the entire region, incited U.S. intervention, and brough U.S. troops into Lebanon and British paratroopers to Jordan. That Iraq was the real target at that time was more than an idle talk; the New York *Herald Tribune* reported that initially the U.S. government gave "strong consideration" to "military intervention to undo the coup in Iraq."[10] The intervention was called off when the new Iraqi government offered assurances of respecting Western oil interests. The new government of Colonel Qasim was overthrown in 1963 by another coup, "which followed the formation of a state oil company to exploit oil lands seized from the companies in 1961; the Paris weekly *L'Express* stated flatly that the coup was inspired by the CIA" (Tanzer 1991, 263).

The purpose here is not to chronicle all the events and interventions by foreign interests or to write the modern diplomatic history of the region. Instead, I merely want to underline a pattern of ceaseless superpower meddling in the region. Several years after the Gulf War of 1991, Leon T. Hadar (1996, 1) states, "the result has been the establishment of a Pax Americana in the Middle East . . . that finds the United States in the same position that Great Britain occupied after World War I."

U.S. policy in dealing with the Arab world has, however, served more than security factors. In addition to complete freedom of access to Arab oil, the U.S. policy also has projected the Israeli position on fundamental military, economic, and political issues. The permeation of Israel's assumptions and preferences within the U.S. decisionmaking process is so deep that it is rarely questioned. This includes continuing direct military and economic aid of more than $3 billion annually and increasing technology transfer and intelligence sharing (Hadar 1996, 4).

Certainly, the main U.S. objectives in the Middle East are not mutually exclusive nor do they always require separate plans of action. U.S. hegemony in the region has served most objectives simultaneously. Keeping the Soviets out of the region, for example, helped safeguard the flow of oil and strengthen the hands of regimes serving as proxies for U.S. policy. The Gulf War sealed U.S. dominance and allowed specific measures for its continuance, such as agreements with the GCC states that commit the United States to come to their aid in case of attack (Hadar 1996, 4). Consequently, the United States has managed to obtain concessions from leaders of these countries to place its military in the region on a continuous basis.

Critics question the motives, instruments, and outcomes of U.S. policy in the Middle East and elsewhere. Noam Chomsky depicts U.S. policy as solely formulated to attend to the interests of capitalism and to maintain access to world markets. "In the operative sense of the term," Chomsky (1993, 3) points out, *stability* means security for "the upper classes and large foreign enterprises." He argues that from the successful CIA operation that overturned the democratic capitalist government of Guatemala in

1954 to the attack on Iraq in 1992, the purpose is the same—maintaining imperial control and ensuring subordination of countries of the South.

Robert Kuttner (1991) notes that if the Cold War ended on November 9, 1989, the day the Berlin Wall came down, the post–Cold War era began on August 2, 1990, the day Iraq invaded Kuwait. The Middle East crisis that ensued, Kuttner concludes, signaled the outlines of a new geopolitical order in several ways. "It suggested a concert of great powers, essentially status quo nations that believe in liberal capitalist democracy, upholding world order against a small group of nations with radical, system-threatening aims" (22). Also, it suggested that President George Bush's vision of a new world order that he enunciated in his State of the Union Address in 1991 was a confirmation of a more determined U.S. imperial presence in the Middle East.

"Having reduced southern Iraq to rubble, and having inflicted six-figure casualties on a people with whom he said 'we' had no quarrel, George Bush felt uniquely qualified to lecture the American people on the values of democracy . . . " (Bennis and Moushabeck 1993, xv). Whatever explanation is employed for the Gulf War, the fact is that the United States fought to restore autocracy in Kuwait.

Nor was the Russians' sudden conversion to a status quo power any less ironic or contradictory. It was startling to hear spokesmen for the Soviet Union—which had after all annexed Estonia, Germany, Romania, and Czechoslovakia in the 1940s and which had invaded sovereign Eastern European nations as recently as the early 1980s—railing against Iraq's invasion and defending the sanctity of national borders (Kuttner 1991, 22). Also remarkably, the United Nations, so recently attacked by U.S. administrations, was used to the U.S. advantage as an instrument of "collective security." As the most recent imperial encroachment on the sovereignty of the Arab world, the Gulf War of 1991 and the subsequent stationing of U.S. troops in the region finally achieved a long-standing U.S. policy objective: obtaining a military presence in Saudi Arabia and the Gulf region.

CONCLUSIONS

Today, the Arab region is attempting to make up for the dearth of political heroes with extravagant peculiarities. Isolated from their citizens, political leaders seem addicted to obstinacy and intrigue in dealing with each other, but lax and even subservient when negotiating with the imperial systems that preserve many of them in power. By any standards, the political process has become a sordid tale of incompetence and corruption.

Change is therefore essential at both the internal and external levels in order to prevent dangerous deterioration. Internally, reforms outlined in this chapter are paramount. Eminent among those suggested reforms are the political ones, such as accountability of the system, linkages with the community, building institutional capacity, and professionalizing management. Although administrative notions often overlap or combine with political concepts, a promising opportunity exists in easing excessive centralization of public institutions and in creating greater opportunities for citizens to participate in public policy. Public participation achieves its promise when citizens' involvement is supported by the necessary means: a free press, overall openness of public decisionmaking, and transparency of government actions—the absolute minimum rudiments for the evolution of a civil society.

In the economic arena, existing modes of operation cannot generate sustainable development that mobilizes the rich human and capital resources of the Arab people. Without these assets, self-reliant economic development is an illusion. Also, to be viable such an economic system has to seek dramatic improvements of the standards of living for all citizens and to initiate effective methods for protecting the environment from existing neglect and defilement. Official imprudence and private avarice are no substitutes for adept political leadership and effective institutional settings. "On balance," as Quandt (1995, 2) states, "one must conclude that the twentieth century has not been kind to most peoples of the Middle East. Far too many have died in wars; far too many have lived in poverty and ill health; far too many have been deprived of basic human rights; and far too many still live under repressive, unaccountable political regimes."

Returning to the external domain for a final note is an indication of its equally decisive bearing on future policies. Contemporary inter-Arab relations verge on being a form of self-flagellation and self-infliction of wounds. Even the ineffective political framework for inter-Arab relations, provided during the past fifty years by the League of Arab States, has finally faltered. The league has become an empty shell with a history of failures and virtually no profound accomplishment. A creation of the British imperial order, it offered an illusion of unity when there was none and gave hope of collaboration when there were only machinations. In the words of a former ambassador of the league, marking the league's fiftieth anniversary, "the time has come for the institution to shape up or make a dignified exit."[11]

In fact, most Arab states are too small to cope with global economic interdependence, generate effective environmental policies, or manage destructive military technology. Thus, change must start with a basic but far-reaching step in which the states collectively reach a competent definition of their strategic political and economic interests. I must emphasize that a perfect union is not attainable at present, despite its rationality and benefits. But to achieve an integrated economic system and harmonized political relations among these states is within reach. And with more political harmony and better economic integration, the Arab states will be equipped to achieve more than a large market, huge resources, and interrelated economic activities of their own. They will also be better equipped to shape more effectual relationships with the rest of the world, including developing regions in Southeast Asia, Latin America, and Africa.

Continuation of the status quo—directionless drift—may buy time but will not bring about solutions to complex problems. Moreover, a policy of drift is short lived and frequently ends with explosions and violence, even chaos. Examples abound in the region and the lessons learned in the past few years are all too numerous. With no consensus ideology to generate a coherent vision of the future, and without administrative institutional capacity and effective leadership, the currently fashionable cursory tinkering with the system—called *reform*—is only a continuation of the drift.

NOTES

1. *New York Times,* February 12, 1996, p. A3, reports that a bomb exploded in a luxury hotel in Bahrain and "an Islamic organization claimed responsibility." Also, "two powerful car bombs killed 17 people and wounded 93 others in Algiers today as bloodshed from an Islamic insurgency continued." Both incidents took place February 11.

2. David Lamb, commenting in the *New York Times Book Review* on Robert Fisk's book on events in Lebanon, *Pity the Nation* (1990), appropriately described Lebanon's situation: "war without heroes and once-envied nation that seems hellbent on suicide."

3. Thomas L. Friedman, *New York Times,* October 25, 1995, op-ed page.

4. The twenty-eighth annual convention of the Association of Arab-American University Graduates, Washington DC, October 20–23, 1995.

5. From the Editor, *Middle East Report,* no. 198 (January–March 1996), p. 3.

6. The quote is from a letter from President Jimmy Carter to me and to supporters of the Carter Center, February 28, 1996.

7. *Newsweek* (November 27, 1995), p. 44.

8. Stories of corruption in Saudi Arabia (and the other GCC countries) are regular features in the Western press. See, for examples, *Newsweek* (November 27, 1995), p. 45; *Business Week* (November 27, 1995), p. 54, and December 25, 1995, p. 56.

9. This definition is from a speech by World Bank President James Wolfensohn, "Participation Works," *World Bank News* 15, no. 8 (February 29, 1996), p. 1.

10. Quoted by Tanzer (1991, 263).

11. Clovis Maksoud (who served as ambassador of the league to the United States and the UN), *Al-Hayat,* March 19, 1996, op-ed page.

Bibliography

Aarts, Paul. 1994. The New Oil Order: Built on Sand? *Arab Studies Quarterly* 16, no. 2 (Spring).

Abu-Laban, Baha, and Sharon McIrvin Abu-Laban. 1992. Primary Education and National Development: The Case of Arab Society. *Arab Studies Quarterly* 14, nos. 2 and 3 (Spring/Summer).

Abu-Rabi', Ibrahim, ed. 1994. *Islamic Resurgence: Challenges, Directions and Future Perspectives.* Tampa, FL: World and Islam Studies Enterprise.

Aburish, Said. 1995. *The Rise, Corruption, and the Coming Fall of the House of Saud.* New York: St Martin's Press.

Affendi, Atieh H. 1994. Administrative Reform in the Arab States: A Comparative Approach. Paper (in Arabic) prepared for a symposium on administrative reform, February 5–6, at University of Cairo.

Ahmad, Khurshid. 1983. Introduction. In Imam Ibn Taymiya, *Public Duties in Islam.* Translated from Arabic by M. Holland. London: The Islamic Foundation.

Al-Azmeh, Aziz. 1995. Nationalism and the Arabs. *Arab Studies Quarterly* 17, nos. 1 and 2 (Winter and Spring).

———. 1994. Populism Contra Democracy: Recent Democratic Discourse in the Arab World. In Ghassan Salame, ed., *Democracy Without Democrats?* London: I. B. Tauris Publishers.

Al-Farsy, Fouad. 1986. *Saudi Arabia: A Case in Development.* London: Kegan Paul.

Al-Husary, Sate'. 1955. *Nushou Al-Fikrah Al-khoumiah (Origin of the idea of nationalism).* 2d ed. Cairo: Dar Al-Hana Press.

Al-Madfai, Madiha. 1993. *Jordan, the United States, and the Middle East Peace Process.* New York: Cambridge University.

Alnasrawi, Abbas. 1982. *Arab Oil and United States Energy Requirements.* Belmont, MA: Association of Arab-American University Graduates, Inc.

American Enterprise Institute. 1968. *United States Interests in the Middle East. Special Analysis.* Washington, DC: American Enterprise Institute for Policy Research.

Amin, Samir. 1992. Contribution to a Debate: The World Capitalist System and Previous Systems. In Fawzy Mansour, ed., *The Arab World: Nation, State and Democracy.* London: Zed Books.

Anderson, Lisa. 1995. Democracy in the Arab World: A Critique of the Political Culture Approach. In Rex Brynen, Bangat Korany, and Paul Noble, eds., *Political Liberalization and Democratization in the Arab World.* Boulder, CO: Lynne Rienner Publishers.

Antonius, George. 1946. *The Arab Awakening.* New York: Capricorn Books.

Apter, David E. 1965. *The Politics of Modernization.* Chicago: The University of Chicago Press.

245

Arkoun, Mohammed. 1994. *Rethinking Islam*. Translated and edited by Robert D. Lee. Boulder, CO: Westview Press.

Aruri, Naseer. 1995. The "Peace Process" As a Negotiating Strategy: Reversing the Order. *Mideast Monitor* 10, no. 2 (Spring).

Ayubi, Nazih N. 1992. Political Correlates of Privatization Programs in the Middle East. *Arab Studies Quarterly* 14, nos. 2 and 3 (Spring/Summer).

————. 1989. Bureaucracy and Development in Egypt Today. In J. G. Jabbra, ed., *Bureaucracy and Development in the Arab World*. New York: E. J. Brill.

————. 1980. *Bureaucracy and Politics in Contemporary Egypt*. London: Ithaca Press.

Balfour-Paul, Glen. 1991. *The End of Empire in the Middle East: Britain's Relinquishment of Power in Her Three Arab Dependencies*. New York: Cambridge University Press.

Banuaziz, Ali. 1994. Iran's Revolutionary Impasse: Political Factionalism and Social Resistance. *Middle East Report*, no. 191 (November/December).

Barakat, Halim. 1993. *The Arab World: Society, Culture, and State*. Berkeley: University of California Press.

Bayley, David H. 1970. The Effects of Corruption in a Developing Nation. In A. J. Heidenheimer, ed., *Political Corruption: Readings in Comparative Analysis*. New York: Holt, Rinehart and Winston.

Beaty, Jonathan, and S. C. Gwyne. 1993. *The Outlaw Bank*. New York: Random House.

Beblawi, Hazem, and Giacomo Luciani, eds. 1987. *The Rentier State*. London: Croom Helm.

Bennis, Phyllis, and Michel Moushabeck, eds. 1993. *Altered States*. New York: Olive Branch Press.

Berger, Morroe. 1957. *Bureaucracy and Society in Modern Egypt*. Princeton: Princeton University Press.

Bill, James A., and Robert Springborg. 1990. *Politics in the Middle East*. 3d ed. New York: HarperCollins.

Black, C. E. 1967. *The Dynamic of Modernization: A Study in Comparative History*. New York: Harper and Row.

Boone, Catherine. 1994. States and Ruling Classes in Postcolonial Africa. In Joel S. Migdal, Atul Kohli, and Vivienne Shue, eds., *State Power and Social Forces*. Cambridge: Cambridge University Press.

Bordewich, Fergus M. 1995. A Holy War Heads Our Way. *Reader's Digest* (January).

Brand, Laurie A. 1992. Economic and Political Liberalization in a Rentier Economy: The Case of the Hashemite Kingdom of Jordan. In I. Harik and D. J. Sullivan, eds., *Privatization and Liberalization in the Middle East*. Bloomington: Indiana University Press.

Brynen, Rex, Bahgat Korany, and Paul Noble, eds. 1995. *Political Liberalization and Democratization in the Arab World*. Vol. 1. Boulder, CO: Lynne Rienner Publishers.

Burns, James MacGregor. 1978. *Leadership*. New York: Harper and Row.

Caiden, Gerald E. 1991. Administrative Reform. In A. Farazmand, ed., *Handbook of Comparative and Development Public Administration*. New York: Marcel Dekker.

Caiden, Gerald E., and Naomi J. Caiden. 1977. Administrative Corruption. *Public Administration Review* 37, no. 3 (May/June).

Cardoso, Fernando Henrique, and Enzo Faletto. 1979. *Dependency and Development in Latin America*. Translated by M. M. Urquidi. Berkeley: University of California Press.

Chatelus, Michel, and Y. Schmeil. 1984. Towards a New Political Economy of State Industrialization in the Middle East. *International Journal of Middle East Studies,* no. 2.

Chomsky, Noam. 1994. *World Orders Old and New.* New York: Columbia University Press.

———. 1993. Introduction. In Phyllis Bennis and Michel Moushabek, eds., *Altered States.* New York: Olive Branch Press.

Colman, Davis, and Frederick Nixon. 1986. *Economics of Change in Less Developed Countries.* 2d ed. Totowa, NJ: Barnes and Noble Books.

Corm, George. 1995. Issues in Developing Arab Economies. *Mideast Monitor* 10, no. 3 (Summer).

Cottam, Richard W. 1964. *Nationalism in Iran.* 2d. ed. Pittsburgh: University of Pittsburgh Press.

Cunningham, Robert B., 1988. *The Bureau and the Bank: Organizational Development in the Middle East.* Westport, CT: Praeger.

Cunningham, Robert B., and Yasin K. Sarayrah. 1993. *Wasta: The Hidden Force in Middle Eastern Society.* Westport, CT: Praeger.

Davis, Eric. 1991. Theorizing Statecraft and Social Change in Arab Oil-Producing Countries. In E. Davis and N. Gavrielides, eds., *Statecraft in the Middle East: Oil, Historical Memory, and Popular Culture.* Miami: Florida International University Press.

Dawn, C. Ernest. 1991. The Origins of Arab Nationalism. In Rashid Khalidi, Lisa Anderson, Muhammad Muslih, and Reeva S. Simon, eds., *The Origins of Arab Nationalism.* New York: Columbia University Press.

Dekmejian, R. H. 1995. *Islam in Revolution: Fundamentalism in the Arab World.* 2d ed. Syracuse, NY: Syracuse University Press.

Diamant, Alfred. 1966. The Nature of Political Development. In J. L. Finkle and R. W. Gable, eds., *Political Development and Social Change.* New York: John Wiley.

Diwan, Ishac, and Lyn Squire. 1993. *Middle East and North Africa,* World Bank, Discussion Paper Series, no. 9 (November).

Ehsani, Kaveh. 1994. "Tilt but Don't Spill:" Iran's Development and Reconstruction Dilemma. *Middle East Report* 24, no. 191 (November/December).

El-Khadra, Basheer. 1982. *Al-Namad Al-Nabawi Al-Khalifi—An Arab Theory of Leadership.* Amman, Jordan: University of Jordan.

El-Sherbini, Abdel Aziz. 1993. Changes and Trends in Public Administration in Egypt. Report submitted to the Arab Organization of Development Organization.

Esman, Milton J. 1991. *Management Dimensions of Development: Perspectives and Strategies.* West Hartford, CT: Kumarian Press.

———. 1966. The Politics of Development Administration. In J. D. Montgomery and W. J. Siffin, eds., *Approaches to Development, Politics, Administration, and Change.* New York: McGraw-Hill.

Farsoun, Samih. 1995. Privatization and Democratization in the Arab World. *Mideast Monitor* 10, no. 3 (Fall).

Feinberg, R. E., J. Echeverri-Gent, and F. Muller. 1990. *Economic Reform in Three Giants.* Washington, DC: Overseas Development Council.

Fergany, Nader. 1995. On Arab and Human Development. A paper presented at Annual Conference of Arab-American University Graduates, October 20–23, Washington, DC.

Field, Michael. 1994. *Inside the Arab World.* Cambridge: Harvard University Press.

Fornos, Werner. 1990. *Population Growth and Tensions in the Middle East.* (A statement to a subcommittee of the House Foreign Affairs Committee of the U.S. House of Representatives.) Washington, DC: The Population Institute.

French, Wendell L., and Cecil H. Bell Jr. 1995. *Organization Development.* 5th ed. Englewood Cliffs, NJ: Prentice-Hall.

Fuller, Graham, and Ian Lesser. 1995. *A Sense of Siege: The Geopolitics of Islam and the West.* Boulder, CO: Westview Press.

Gellner, Ernest. 1983. *Nations and Nationalism.* Ithaca: Cornell University Press.

Gerth, H. H., and C. Wright Mills. 1946. *From Max Weber: Essays in Sociology.* Trans. New York: Oxford University Press.

Goldberg, Ellis, Resat Kasaba, and Joel Migdal, eds. 1993. *Rules and Rights in the Middle East: Democracy, Law, and Society.* Seattle: University of Washington Press.

Goodsell, Charles T. 1994. *The Case for Bureaucracy.* 3d. ed. Chatham, NJ: Chatham House.

Gross, Jonathan L., and Steve Rayner. 1985. *Measuring Culture: A Paradigm for the Analysis of Social Organization.* New York: Columbia University Press.

Hadar, Leon T. 1996. America's Moment in the Middle East. *Current History.* (January).

Haim, Sylvia G., ed. 1962. *Arab Nationalism: An Anthology.* Berkeley: University of California Press.

Halliday, Fred. 1982. A Curious and Close Liaison: Saudi Arabia's Relations with the U.S. In Tim Niblock, ed., *State, Society and Economy in Saudi Arabia.* New York: St. Martin's Press.

Halpern, Manfred. 1963. *The Politics of Social Change in the Middle East and North Africa.* Princeton: Princeton University Press.

Harik, Iliya. 1992. Privatization: The Issue, the Prospects, and the Fears. In Iliya Harik and Dennis J. Sullivan, eds., *Privatization and Liberalization in the Middle East.* Bloomington: Indiana University Press.

Hawatmeh, George. 1994. *The Middle East International* (September 9).

Heady, Ferrel. 1996. *Public Administration: A Comparative Perspective.* 5th ed. New York: Marcel Dekker.

Hepburn, Donald. 1994. Observations from an Oil Vantage Point: Focus—The Persian Gulf. *Forces for Change in Southwest Asia. Proceedings of a U.S. Central Command symposium,* May 16, Tampa, Florida.

Herman, Barry. 1989. The Outlook of Development. In *Debt Disaster? Banks, Governments, and Multinationals Confront the Crisis.* New York: New York University Press.

Hinnebusch, Raymond A. 1989. Bureaucracy and Development in Syria: The Case of Agriculture. In J. G. Jabbra, ed., *Bureaucracy and Development in the Arab World.* New York: E. J. Brill.

Hisham, Ahmed. 1996. Iraq: Fin de Regime? *Current History* 95, no. 597 (January).

Hofstede, Geert. 1980. *Culture's Consequences: International Differences in Work-Related Values.* Beverly Hills, CA: Sage.

Horan, Hume. 1995. The Dilemma of Islam. *Foreign Service Journal* (July).

Hourani, Albert. 1991. *A History of the Arab Peoples.* Cambridge: The Belknap Press of Harvard University Press.

Hourani, Hani. 1994. Jordanian Elections of 1993: Readings in Its Backgrounds, Conditions, and Results. *Qira'at Siyasiyyah* (Arabic quarterly) 4, no. 2 (Spring).

Hudson, Michael C. 1995. The Political Culture Approach to Arab Democratization: The Case for Bringing It Back In, Carefully. In Rex Brynen, Bahgat

Korany, and Paul Noble, eds., *Political Liberalization and Democratization in the Arab World*. Vol. 1. Boulder, CO: Lynne Rienner Publishers.

————. 1988. State, Society, and Legitimacy. In Hisham Sharabi, ed., *The Next Arab Decade: Alternative Futures*. Boulder, CO: Westview Press.

Huntington, Samuel P. 1987. The Goals of Development. In Myron Weiner and Samuel P. Huntington, eds., *Understanding Political Development*. New York: HarperCollins.

Ibrahim, Saad Eddin. 1995. Liberalization and Democratization in the Arab World. In Rex Brynen, Bahgat Korany, and Paul Noble, eds., *Political Liberalization and Democratization in the Arab World*. Vol. 1. Boulder, CO: Lynne Rienner Publishers.

Jabbra, Joseph G. 1989. Bureaucracy and Development in the Arab World. *Journal of Asian and African Studies* 24, nos. 1, 2 (January/April).

Janowitz, Morris. 1964. *The Military in the Development of New Nations*. Chicago: University of Chicago Press.

Jreisat, Jamil E. 1995. Faltering Bureaucratic Reforms: The Case of Egypt. *Journal of Developing Societies* 11, no. 2.

————. 1992a. Managing National Development in the Arab States. *Arab Studies Quarterly* 14, nos. 1 and 2 (Spring/Summer).

————. 1992b. *Managing Public Organizations: A Developmental Perspective on Theory and Practice*. New York: Paragon House.

————. 1991. Bureaucratization of the Arab World: Incompatible Influences. In A. Farazmand, ed., *Handbook of Comparative and Development Public Administration*. New York: Marcel Dekker.

————. 1990. Administrative Change and the Arab Manager. *Public Administration and Development*, 10.

————. 1989. Bureaucracy and Development in Jordan. In J. G. Jabbra, ed., *Bureaucracy and Development in the Arab World*. New York: E. J. Brill.

————. 1988. Administrative Reform in Developing Countries: A Comparative Perspective. *Public Administration and Development* 8, no. 1 (January/March).

Kazziha, Walid W. 1975. *Revolution Transformation in the Arab World*. New York: St. Martin's Press.

Kedouri, Elie. 1994. *Democracy and Arab Political Culture*. London: F. Cass.

Kennedy, Paul. 1987. *The Rise and Fall of the Great Powers*. New York: Random House.

Keynes, John Maynard. 1936, 1949. *The General Theory of Employment, Interest and Money*. London: Macmillan.

Khalidi, Rashid. 1994. Ottoman Notables in Jerusalem: Nationalism and Other Options. *The Muslim World* 84, no. 1–2, (January–April).

Khalidi, Rashid, Lisa Anderson, Muhammad Muslih, and Reeva S. Simon, eds., 1991. *The Origins of Arab Nationalism*. New York: Columbia University Press.

Kitchen, Richard. 1989. Administrative Reform in Jamaica: A Component of Structural Adjustment. *Public Administration and Development* 9.

Klaren, Peter F. 1986. Lost Promise: Explaining Latin American Underdevelopment. In *Promise of Development: Theories of Change in Latin America*. Boulder, CO: Westview Press.

Kohl, Atul, and Vivienne Shue. 1994. State Power and Social Forces. In Joel S. Migdal, Atul Kohl, and Vivienne Shue, eds., *State Power and Social Forces*. London: Cambridge University Press.

Kramer, Martin. 1993. *Daedalus* (June 22).

Kuttner, Robert. 1991. *The End of Laissez-Faire: National Purpose and the Global Economy After the Cold War*. New York: Alfred A. Knopf.

Laqueur, Walter Z. 1956. *Communism and Nationalism in the Middle East.* London: Routledge and Kegan.

Lawson, Fred H. 1991. Managing Economic Crises: The Role of the State in Bahrain and Kuwait. *Studies in Comparative International Development* 26, no. 1 (Spring).

Lazreg, Marnia. 1995. *The Eloquence of Silence: Algerian Women in Question.* London: Routledge.

Leca, Jean. 1994. Democratization in the Arab World. In Ghasan Salame, ed., *Democracy Without Democrats?* London: I. B. Tauris Publishers.

Lenczouski, George. 1962. *The Middle East in World Affairs.* New York: Cornell University Press.

Lewis, W. Arthur. 1966. *Development Planning.* New York: Harper and Row.

Lowrie, Arthur. 1995. The Campaign Against Islam and American Foreign Policy. *Middle East Policy* 4, nos. 1 and 2 (September).

Lowrie, Arthur, ed., 1992. *Islam, Democracy, the State and the West: A Round Table with Dr. Hasan Turabi.* Tampa, FL: World and Islam Studies Enterprise.

Luciani, Giacomo. 1994. The Oil Rent, the Fiscal Crisis of the State and Democratization. In Ghassan Salame, ed., *Democracy Without Democrats?* London: I. B. Tauris Publishers.

Luke, Timothy W. 1990. *Social Theory and Modernity: Critique, Dissent, and Revolution.* Newbury Park, CA: Sage.

Mahasneh, Abdelkarim M. 1991. The Arab Cooperation Council: Prospects for Intra-Regional Trade Promotion and Industrial Development. Ph.D. diss., Graduate School of Public and International Affairs, University of Pittsburgh.

Mansfield, Peter. 1995. Against Received Wisdom. *Middle East International* (March 3).

Mansour, Fawzy, ed. 1992. *The Arab World: Nation, State and Democracy.* London: Zed Books.

Mascarenhas, R. C. 1993. Building an Enterprise Culture in the Public Sector: Reform of the Public Sector in Australia, Britain, and New Zealand. *Public Administration Review* (July/August).

McLachlan, Keith. 1980. Oil in the Persian Gulf Area. In A. J. Cottrell, ed., *The Persian Gulf States: A General Survey.* Baltimore: The Johns Hopkins University Press.

MEIRC, 1989. The Making of Gulf Successful Managers (unpublished study).

Mendez, Ruben P. 1992. *International Public Finance: A New Perspective on Global Relations.* New York: Oxford University Press.

Meyer, John W., and Brian Rowan. 1992. Institutionalized Organizations: Formal Structure as Myth and Ceremony. In J. W. Meyer and W. R. Scott, eds., *Organizational Environments: Ritual and Rationality.* Newbury Park, CA: Sage.

Migdal, Joel. 1993. In Ellis Goldberg, Resat Kasaba, and Joel Migdal, eds., *Rules and Rights in the Middle East: Democracy, Law, and Society.* Seattle: University of Washington Press.

Migdal, Joel S., Atul Kohli, and Vivienne Shue, eds., 1994. *State Power and Social Forces.* Cambridge: Cambridge University Press.

Milani, Mohsen M. 1994. *The Making of Iran's Islamic Revolution.* 2d ed., Boulder, CO: Westview Press.

Murphy, Caryle. 1994. Egypt: An Uneasy Portent of Change. *Current History* 93, no. 580 (February).

Murphy, Richard W. 1988. *Protecting U.S. Interests in the Gulf.* Washington, DC: National Council on US-Arab Relations.

Myrdal, Gunnar. 1970. Corruption as a Hindrance to Modernization in South Asia. In A. J. Heidenheimer, ed., *Political Corruption: Readings in Comparative Analysis*. New York: Holt, Rinehart and Winston.

———. 1968. *Asian Drama: An Inquiry into the Poverty of Nations*. New York: Pantheon.

Nelson, Joan M. 1987. Political Participation. In M. Weiner and S. P. Huntington, eds., *Understanding Political Development*. New York: HarperCollins.

Nyrop, Richard, ed., 1980. *Jordan: A Country Study*. Foreign Area Studies. Washington, DC: The American University.

Odel, Peter R. 1995. Toward the Regionalization of Oil Markets. In K. Gillespie and C. M. Henry, eds., *Oil in the New World Order*. Gainesville: University Press of Florida.

Olson, Mancur. 1993. Dictatorship, Democracy, and Development. *American Political Science Review* 87, no. 3 (September).

———. 1993. The Practice of Electoral Democracy in the Arab East and North Africa. In Ellis Goldberg, Resat Kasaba, and Joel Migdal, eds., *Rules and Rights in the Middle East: Democracy, Law, and Society*. Seattle: University of Washington Press.

Osman, Osama A. 1978. Formalism vs. Realism: The Saudi Arabian Experience with Position Classification. *Public Personnel Management* 7, no. 3.

Owen, Roger. 1994. Socio-Economic Change and Political Mobilization: The Case of Egypt. In Ghassan Salame, ed., *Democracy Without Democrats?* London: I. B.Tauris Publishers.

Palmer, Monte et al. 1989. Bureaucratic Innovation and Economic Development in the Middle East: A Study of Egypt, Saudi Arabia, and the Sudan. In J. G. Jabbra, ed., *Bureaucracy and Development in the Arab World*. New York: E. J. Brill.

Palmer, Monte, Ali Leila, and El Sayed Yassin. 1988. *The Egyptian Bureaucracy*. Syracuse, NY: Syracuse University Press; Cairo: The American University in Cairo Press.

———. 1973. *Dilemmas of Political Development*. Itasca, IL: F. E. Peacock.

Parsons, Anthony. 1991. Foreword. In Glen Balfour-Paul, *The End of Empire in the Middle East: Britain's Relinquishment of Power in Her Three Arab Dependencies*. New York: Cambridge University Press.

Pfeffer, Jeffrey. 1981. *Power in Organizations*. Mansfield, MA: Pitman Publishing.

Pryce-Jones, David. 1991. *The Closed Circle: An Interpretation of the Arabs*. New York: HarperCollins.

Pye, Lucian W. 1962. *Politics, Personality, and Nation Building: Burma's Search for Identity*. New Haven: Yale University Press.

Quandt, William B. 1995. The Middle East on the Brink: Prospects for Change in the 21st Century. Keynote address at Middle East Institute Annual Conference, September 29, Washington, DC.

Quah, Jon S.T. 1991. Administrative Reform: Singapore Style. *International Review of Administrative Sciences* 57.

Quataert, Donald. 1991. Foreword. In E. Davis and N. Gavrielides, eds., *Statecraft in the Middle East: Oil, Historical Memory, and Popular Culture*. Miami: Florida International University Press.

Rich, Bruce. 1994. *Mortgaging the Earth: The World Bank, Environmental Improvement, and the Crisis of Development*. Boston, MA: Beacon Press.

Richards, Alan. 1993. *Economic Imperatives and Political Systems in the Middle East and North Africa*. Santa Monica, CA: RAND.

————. 1991. The Political Economy of Dilatory Reform: Egypt in the 1980s. *World Development* 19, no. 12.

Richards, Alan, and John Waterbury. 1990. *A Political Economy of the Middle East: Class, State, and Economic Development.* Cairo: The American University in Cairo Press.

Riggs, Fred W. 1991. Bureaucratic Links Between Administration and Politics. In A. Farazmand, ed., *Handbook of Comparative and Development Public Administration.* New York: Marcel Dekker.

Robbins, Stephen P. 1989. *Organizational Behavior.* 4th ed., Englewood Cliffs, NJ: Prentice-Hall.

Robins, Philip. 1990. Democracy Gathers Strength in Jordan. *The Christian Science Monitor* (January 22).

Rouleau, Eric. 1995. America's Unyielding Policy Toward Iraq. *Foreign Affairs* 74, no. 1 (January/February).

Roy, Olivier. 1994. *The Failure of Political Islam.* Translated by Carol Volk. Cambridge: Harvard University Press.

Sadowski, Yahya. 1991. *Economic Crisis in the Arab World: Catalyst for Conflict.* Washington, DC: Overseas Development Council.

Said, Edward W. 1996. A Devil Theory of Islam. *The Nation* (August 12–19).

————. 1993. *Culture and Imperialism.* New York: Alfred A. Knopf.

Salame, Ghassan, ed., 1994. *Democracy Without Democrats?* London: I. B. Tauris Publishers.

Salem, Paul. 1994. *Bitter Legacy: Ideology and Politics in the Arab World.* Syracuse, NY: Syracuse University Press.

Satloff, Robert. 1986. *Troubles on the East Bank: Challenges to Domestic Stability in Jordan.* New York: Praeger.

Sayigh, Yusif A. 1991. *Elusive Development: From Dependence to Self-Reliance in the Arab Region.* London: Routledge.

Schultz, T. W. 1981. *Investing in People: The Economics of Population Quality.* Berkeley: University of California Press.

Serageldine, Ismail. 1996. Liberating the Arab Mind: Essential Tasks for the Arab Renaissance. *Mideast Monitor* 11, no. 1 (Winter).

Sharabi, Hisham. 1988. *Neopatriarchy: A Theory of Distorted Change in Arab Society.* Oxford: Oxford University Press.

Sharabi, Hisham, ed., 1988. Introduction. In *The Next Arab Decade: Alternative Futures.* Boulder, CO: Westview Press.

Sherwood, Frank P. 1994. Comparing the Florida Reinvention with the Prescriptions of the Gore and Winter Commission Reports. In J. E. Jreisat and F. P. Sherwood, eds., *Reinventing Government in Florida.* Tallahassee: Florida Center for Public Management, Florida State University.

————. 1992. Really Comprehensive Administrative Reform: The Case of New Zealand. In *Thinking Differently About Government Reform in Florida.* Tallahassee: Florida Center for Public Management, Florida State University.

Smith, Tony. 1985. The Dependency Approach. In H. J. Howard, ed., *New Directions in Comparative Politics.* Boulder, CO: Westview Press.

Sonn, Tamara. 1990. *Between Qur'an and Crown: The Challenge of Political Legitimacy in the Arab World.* Boulder, CO: Westview Press.

Steel, B., S. Davenport, and R. L. Warner. 1993. Are Civil Servants Really Public Servants? A Study of Bureaucraic Attitudes in the U.S., Brazil, and Korea. *International Journal of Public Administration* 6, no. 3.

Sullivan, Denis J. 1992. Extra-State Actors and Privatization in Egypt. In Iliya Harik and Dennis J. Sullivan, eds., *Privatization and Liberalization in the Middle East.* Bloomington: Indiana University Press.

Tanzer, Michael. 1991. Oil and the Gulf Crisis. In Phyllis Bennis and Michel Moushabeck, eds., *Beyond the Storm.* New York: Olive Branch Press.

Tetreault, Mary Ann. 1996. Gulf Winds: Inclement Political Weather in the Arabian Peninsula. *Current History* 95, no. 597 (January).

Thomas, Jim. 1993. *Doing Critical Ethnography.* Qualitative Research Methods Series, no. 26. Newbury Park, CA: Sage.

Thompson, Fred., 1993. Matching Responsibilities with Tactics: Administrative Controls and Modern Government. *Public Administration Review* 53, no. 4 (July/August).

Thompson, Victor. 1964. Objectives of Development Administration. *Administrative Science Quarterly* 9.

Tibi, Bassam. 1990. *Arab Nationalism: A Critical Enquiry.* 2d ed., New York: St. Martin's Press.

Todaro, Michael P. 1989. *Economic Development in the Third World.* 4th ed., New York: Longman.

United States Central Command. 1994. *Posture Statement. Report Presented to the 103rd Congress by General Joseph P. Hoar, Commander in Chief, United States Central Command.*

United Nations Development Program. 1994. *Capacity Development.* New York.

Viorst, Milton. 1994. *Sandcastles: The Arabs in Search of the Modern World.* New York: Alfred A. Knopf.

Vitalis, Robert. 1994. The Democratization Industry and the Limits of the New Interventionism. *Middle East Report* 24, no. 187/188 (March/April and May/June).

Waterbury, John. 1994. Democracy Without Democrats? The Potential for Political Liberalization in the Middle East. In G. Salame, ed., *Democracy Without Democrats?* London: I. B. Tauris Publishers.

Weber, Max. 1947. *The Theory of Social and Economic Organization.* New York: Oxford University Press.

Weiner, Myron. 1987. Introduction. In Myron Weiner and Samuel P. Huntington, eds., *Understanding Political Development.* New York: HarperCollins.

Wiarda, Howard J. 1985. *Toward a Nonethnocentric Theory of Development: Alternative Conceptions from the Third World.* Boulder, CO: Westview Press.

Wilbern, York. 1988. Types and Levels of Public Policy. In *Ethical Insight, Ethical Action.* Washington, DC: ICMA.

Wilson, Mary C. 1994. Jordan: Bread, Freedom, or Both? *Current History* 95, no. 580 (February).

Wilson, Rodney, ed., 1991. *Politics and the Economy in Jordan,* London: Routledge.

Yapp, Malcolm. 1980. The Nineteenth and Twentieth Centuries. In A. J. Cottrell, ed., *The Persian Gulf States: A General Survey.* Baltimore: The Johns Hopkins University Press.

Yergin, Daniel. 1991. *The Prize: The Epic Quest for Oil, Money and Power.* New York: Simon and Schuster.

Index

Abu-Laban, Baha, 53
Abu-Laban, Sharon McIrvin, 53
Abu-Lughod, Ibrahim, 26
Abu Rabi', Ibrahim, 160, 161
Aburish, Said, 194, 233
Administrative structures, 4, 5, 17, 41, 76, 228, 234–238
Affendi, Atieh H., 19, 71, 80
Africa, 3, 50, 57, 60, 244
Agriculture, 14, 119
Ahmad, Khurshid, 176
Ajamy, Fouad, 37
Al-Ahram, 147
Al-Azmeh, Aziz, 26, 37, 230
Al-Dustour, 138
Al-Farsy, Fouad, 187, 188, 193
Algeria, 18, 50, 64–67, 165, 169, 170, 190, 204, 220; Islamic movement, 163, 164, 223, 224, 233
Al-Hayat, 159
Al-Husary, S. 29, 35
Ali, Sherif Hussein Ben, 27, 28
Alnasrawi, Abbas, 182
Al-Turabi, Hassan, 38, 156, 162, 165
Amin, Mustafa, 149
Amin, Samir, 7, 8, 17, 45, 160
Anderson, Lisa, 38, 230, 231, 234
Antonius, George, 25, 26
Al-Madfai, Madiha, 121
Al-Magreb, 39
Almond, Gabriel A., 11
Apter, David E., 6, 7
Arab administrative change/reform, 20, 56–61, 71, 72, 89, 226, 235, 239; bureaucracy, 4, 65, 234, 235; democratic trends, 16, 37, 89, 117, 118, 228–232, 239; developing administrative capacity, 89, 224, 226, 234, 235; education, 27, 41, 51, 53, 54, 216, 217, 233; foreign investment, 48; Organization of Administrative Development, 71, 72; Nationalist Movement, 30, 34–35; Revolt, 27; ruling oligarchy, 57, 58, 65; Socialist Union, 24; women, 50–52, 217, 218
Arabian American Oil Company (ARAMCO), 193, 194
Arkoun, Mohammed, 170
Aruri, Naseer, 159
Asia, 3, 50, 204, 210, 237, 244
Asian countries, 9
Association of Southeast Asian Nations (ASEAN), 219
Ayubi, Nazih N., 57, 58, 61, 75, 106, 108, 209

Bahrain, 46, 47, 50, 60, 64, 165, 175, 187, 190, 223; civil service reform, 84
Balfour-Paul, Glen, 28
Banuaziz, Ali, 174
Barakat, Halim, 19
Ba'th Party, 24, 32–34
Bayley, David H., 60
Beaty, Jonathan, 175, 176
Beblawi, Hazem, 186
Becker, Gary S., 54, 215
Bell, Cecil H., Jr., 61, 90, 248
Bennis, Phyllis, 242
Berger, Morroe, 106
Bill, James A., 35, 36
Black, C. E., 6, 7
Boone, Catherine, 20
Bordewich, Fergus M., 167
Brand, Laurie A., 122
British colonial rule, 8, 18, 19, 28, 46, 186, 187, 240, 241
Brynen, Rex, 230, 231
Bureaucracy, 4, 11, 17, 19, 56, 58, 235
Burns, James MacGregor, 223, 238

Business Week, 198, 208, 210, 228

Caiden, Gerald E., 13, 56
Caiden, Naomi J., 13
Cardoso, Fernando Henrique, 9
Carter, Jimmy, 231
Chandler, Clay, 199n
Chatelus, Michel, 186
Chomsky, Noam, 7, 18, 203, 241
Christian Arabs, 27
Classic management theories, 4, 148
Cold War, 7, 8, 19, 53, 160, 181, 207, 232, 242
Coleman, J. S., 11
Colman, Davis, 12, 15
Committee for the Defense of Legitimate Rights, 193–195, 198
Comparative administration, 86, 88, 136
Comparative method, 12, 18, 40
Corm, George, 15, 190, 191, 211, 214
Corruption, 60, 61, 65, 88, 108, 149, 158, 205, 226–229
Cottam, Richard W., 39
Cultural domination, 9–11, 160
Culture: attributes, 37, 68, 231; definition, 10
Cunningham, Robert B., 57, 130, 132

Davis, Eric, 192, 204
Dawn, C. Ernest, 26, 27
Dekmejian, R. H., 168
Dependency theory, 8, 9, 14
Deutsch, Karl W., 3
Development ideology, 23, 36
Diamant, Alfred, 16
Diwan el-Mazalem, 144–146

Eastern Europe, 13
Economic Development Institute, 7
Economist, 34, 165, 228
Egypt, 18, 31, 46, 48, 50, 54–55, 64–66, 89, 147–150, 158, 160–165, 204, 207, 220, 232; administrative reform, 19, 72–76, 86, 88; bureaucracy, 58, 59, 71, 72, 98, 106, 108, 149; corruption, 110, 148, 149, 158; institutional performance, 20, 36, 72, 101, 107; political opposition, 223, 233
Ehsani, Kaveh, 174
Energy consumption, 182–184
Esman, Milton J., 4, 7, 12, 14, 15, 237, 238

Fadil, Farah, 175
Faletto, Enzo, 9
Farsoun, Samih, 160, 208
Feinberg, R. E., 109, 215
Fergany, Nader, 216–217
Field, Michael, 158, 188, 189, 204, 211
Financial Times, 175
Foreign attachments, 226, 232, 240–242
Fornos, Werner, 62
Frank, André Gunder, 9
French colonial rule, 8, 18, 19
French, Wendell L., 61, 90

Gellner, Ernest, 24
Gerth, H. H., 4
el-Ghanoushi, Rashid, 10, 165, 170
Goodsell, Charles T., 108
Gross, Jonathan L., 10
Gulf Cooperation Council, 64, 65, 192, 204, 240
Gulf region, 18, 28, 181, 186
Gulf states, 49, 50, 60, 61, 99, 105, 116, 119, 121, 122, 175, 187, 189, 232
Gulf War, 49, 66, 111, 116, 121, 122, 159, 186, 189, 198, 205, 220, 240

Hadar, Leon T., 232, 241
Haim, Sylvia, 26
Halliday, Fred, 197
Halpern, Manfred, 35, 156, 160, 169, 170
Hamilton, Alexander, 71
Harik, Iliya, 208
Hawatmeh, George, 132
Haykal, M. H., 56, 149
Heady, Ferrel, 6, 8, 12, 13, 17, 23, 36, 59
Hepburn, D., 183
Herman, Barry, 13
Hinnebusch, Raymond A., 61
Hisham, Ahmed, 224
Hofstede, Geert, 10
Horan, Hume, 167
Hourani, Albert, 19, 26, 31, 62
Hourani, Hani, 117
Hudson, Michael C., 52, 230, 231
Human development, 13, 20, 50, 55, 87
Huntington, Samuel P., 8, 11, 17

Ibrahim, Saad Eddin, 42n, 205, 230
Institute for Peace, 168
Institutional capacity, 6, 41, 47, 56, 71, 136, 165, 203, 211, 235–239

Inter-Arab relations, 116, 119, 158, 181, 205, 218–220, 226, 233
International Monetary Fund, 15, 98, 100, 115, 116, 206, 207
Iran, 23, 170, 171, 187
Iraq, 19, 31, 36, 37, 47, 49, 50, 54, 64, 159, 187, 190, 224, 240, 242; administrative development, 77–78
Islam, 155, 156
Islamic Action Front in Jordan, 115, 117
Islamic banking, 175–176; economics, 172–175; management, 176–177; political movements, 155, 157
Islamist ideology, 10, 23, 157, 166
Islamists, 10, 23, 38, 64, 96, 115, 155, 223, 233
Israel, 19, 34, 116, 120, 121, 122, 132, 160, 224, 240

Jabbra, Joseph G., 60, 61
Janowitz, Morris, 6
Japan, 8, 183, 210
Jordan, 20, 50, 54–55, 59, 60, 64–66, 71, 137–146, 150, 166, 204, 211, 220; administrative reform, 73, 76–77, 86, 123, 143; civil service, 77, 114, 123, 124, 125, 127, 128, 130; corruption and mismanagement, 114, 126, 141; *Jordan Times,* 116, 152n; parliamentary election, 113, 116–118; public budgeting, 47–48, 119, 121, 129
Jreisat, Jamil E., 13, 57, 67, 111, 113, 121, 132, 207, 225, 231, 234

Kattan, Iyad, 131, 132, 145, 146
Kazziha, Walid W., 35
al-Kawakibi, Abdul-Rahman, 26
Kedouri, Elie, 37, 231
Kennedy, Paul, 8
Keynes, John Maynard, 14
el-Khadra, Basheer, 177
Khalidi, Rashid, 26, 41
Khomeini, Ayatollah, 171–174
Khouri, Rami G., 116, 143, 157, 166n
Kitchen, Richard, 109, 215
Klaren, Peter F., 7, 8
Kohl, Atul, 151
Korany, Bahgat, 230
Kuttner, Robert, 207, 210, 242
Kuwait, 46, 49, 54, 61, 64, 159, 166, 204, 242

Lapham, Lewis, 114
Laqueur, Walter Z., 26, 29
Latin America, 3, 9, 50, 204, 208, 217, 220, 244
Lawson, Fred H., 189, 192
Lazreg, Marnia, 217
Leadership succession, 227
League of Arab States, 49, 71, 99, 219
Lebanon, 19, 50, 135, 157, 190, 204, 205, 224, 226
Leca, Jean, 103, 106, 113, 165
Legal-rational system, 11
Leila, Ali, 57, 61, 71, 75, 98, 106, 109
Lenczowski, George, 28
Lerner, D., 11
Lewis, W. Arthur, 12
Libya, 31, 50, 119
Lowrie, Arthur, 155, 156, 166
Luciani, Giacomo, 186, 230
Luke, Timothy W., 7, 8

Mahasneh, Abdelkarim M., 219
Mahfouz, Naguib, 93
Maksoud, Clovis, 244n
Mandela, Nelson, 102
Mansfield, Peter, 37, 42n
Marxism, 9, 23, 31, 68, 160, 171, 205
Mascarenhas, R. C., 215
Mauritania, 46
McLachlan, Keith, 187
Mendez, Ruben P., 15
Meyer, John W., 20
Migdal, Joel S., 20
Milani, Mohsen M., 171–173
Military, 66, 158–159, 164, 214, 227
Mills, C. Wright, 4
Modernization, 5, 6, 7, 10, 12, 40
Morocco, 50, 54, 55, 61, 67, 119, 190
Moushabeck, Michel, 242
Mukhabarat, 36, 114
Murphy, Caryle, 100, 103, 105
Muslim Brothers, 30, 96, 101, 144, 162
Muslims, 27, 34, 156
Myrdal, Gunnar, 6, 12, 151

Nahdha, 25
Nakbeh, 30
Nasrallah, Elia, 140
Nasser, Gamal Abdul-, 24, 34, 37, 94, 98
Nasserism, 32, 34
Nation building, 5, 6, 12

National planning, 13, 47, 120, 122, 209
Nationalism, 24–32, 37–41, 156
Nelson, Joan M., 8, 16
New Republic, 37
Newsweek, 228
New York Times, 38, 206, 224
Nixon, Frederick, 12, 15
Noble, Paul, 230
Nyrop, Richard, 113

Oil companies, 46, 184, 185, 186, 188
Oil production, 182, 189
Oil reserves in Arab world, 45, 184, 185
Oil revenues, 54, 55, 64, 81, 181, 185, 232
Olson, Mancur, 229
Oman, 46, 50, 54, 64, 67
Organization of Arab Petroleum Exporting
　Countries, 49, 191, 203
Organization of Petroleum Exporting
　Countries, 183
Osman, Osama A., 59
Ottoman rule, 26, 27
Owen, Roger, 4, 5, 94, 102, 230

Palestine, 30, 117, 122, 159, 190, 231
Palestine Liberation Organization, 121, 159
Palestinian children, 54; workers, 116, 123
Palmer, Monte, 13, 57, 59, 61, 71, 75, 98,
　106, 107
Parsons, Sir Anthony, 28
Parsons, Talcott, 11
Perry, William J., 181, 182
Pfeffer, Jeffrey, 228
Pipes, Daniel, 167
Political boundaries, 46
Population growth in Arab world, 48, 62,
　203
Privatization, 206, 207–213; conditions for,
　210, 211
The Progressive, 168
Public debt, 48, 49, 62, 66, 67
Public policy, 4, 212, 213, 220
Pye, Lucian W., 6, 11

Qatar, 46, 64, 74, 190; civil service reform,
　84
Quah, Jon S. T., 109, 215
Quandt, William B., 223, 243
Quataert, Donald, 240

Rayner, Steve, 10

Rich, Bruce, 7, 206, 207, 209
Richards, Alan, 45, 97, 105, 212
Riggs, Fred W., 21n, 57
Robbins, Stephen P., 90
Robins, Philip, 114
Rose el-Yousef, 102, 105n
Rostow, W. W., 11, 14
Rouleau, Eric, 49
Rowan, Brian, 20
Roy, Olivier, 169, 170, 174
Russia, 8

Sadowski, Yahya, 53
Said, Edward W., 8, 9, 26, 155, 158, 159,
　164, 167
Salame, Ghassan, 41, 230
Salem, Paul, 23, 30, 34, 169
Sarayrah, Yasin K., 57, 130
Satloff, Robert, 121
Saudi Arabia, 47, 49, 50, 53, 54, 59, 61, 64,
　73, 119, 165, 172; administrative reform,
　19, 80–81, 86; Basic Industries
　Corporation (SABIC), 211; oil
　production, 184, 185, 188, 189; political
　opposition, 223; public debt, 91n
Sayigh, Yusif A., 6, 8, 9, 12, 191
Schultz, T. W., 216
Scripps, E. W., 135
Sen, Amartya, 15n
Serageldine, Ismail, 220, 237
Sharabi, Hisham, 26, 68, 160
el-Sherbini, Abdel Aziz, 103, 105, 107,
　110
Sherwood, Frank P., 109, 215
Smith, Tony, 9
Sonn, Tamara, 161
Soviet Union, 13, 19, 23, 31, 98, 160
Springborg, Robert, 35, 36
Sudan, 31, 47, 54, 55, 59, 67, 119, 190;
　administrative reform, 83–84
Suez Canal, 55, 99, 100, 105, 240
Sullivan, Denis J., 207
Syria, 31, 34, 36, 37, 50, 54, 61, 67, 119,
　190, 220; administrative development, 73,
　78–80, 86

Tanzer, Michael, 240, 241
Tessler, Mark, 162
Third World, 7, 8, 9, 16, 205
Thomas, Jim, 10
Thompson, Fred, 110

Thompson, Victor, 108
Tibi, Bassam, 25, 26
Time, 86
Todaro, Michael P., 14
Traditional system, 11, 14
Tunisia, 48, 50, 64, 67, 165, 220;
administrative reform, 74, 81–83, 86

Unified Arab Economic Report, 49, 230
United Arab Emirates, 19, 46, 47, 50, 74,
190; objectives of administrative reform,
84–85, 86
United Nations, 46; Development Program,
13, 50, 54, 63, 77, 126, 216, 240;
Committee for Development Planning,
13; Human Development Index, 13, 51,
54, 55, 119, 174
United States, 8, 46, 49, 60, 66, 99,
123, 158–160, 166, 232, 240; Agency
for International Development, 7,
207, 208; objectives in the region,
181, 183; relations with Saudi Arabia,
188, 197, 198, 232; social science,
7
Urbanization, 62–63
al-Ummah, 38, 162, 171

Viorst, Milton, 52
Vitalis, Robert, 7

Wahhabi sect, 194, 195
Washington Post, 163
Waterbury, John, 45, 97, 205, 216, 230
Weber, Max, 4, 11, 106, 109, 235
Weiner, Myron, 8, 12, 16
West Bank and Gaza, 54, 121, 170
Western Europe and Arab oil, 183, 186
Western imperialism, 8, 30, 37, 241, 242
Western press, 37, 39, 204, 228
Wiarda, Howard J., 8
Wilson, Mary C., 115
Wilson, Rodney, 120
Wilson, Woodrow, 4
Wirth, Tim, 50
Wilbern, York, 239
Women and development, 50
World Bank, 7, 15, 18, 46, 63, 66, 101, 120,
174, 203, 204, 206–209, 220

Yapp, Malcolm, 187
Yassin, El Sayed, 57, 61, 71, 75, 98, 106,
109
Yemen, 19, 31, 36, 50, 54, 55, 64, 67, 119,
166; comprehensive reform program, 74,
85–86
Yergin, Daniel, 181, 182, 183, 187

Zakat, 157
Zurayk, Qustantin, 35

About the Book

A candid critique of the institutional systems and practices that define, and in many cases limit, the administrative state in the Arab world, this study centers on the factors contributing to the failure of development efforts.

Almost all Arab leaders, points out Jreisat, have promised bureaucratic reforms, but their political-administrative structures have not succeeded in building the institutions necessary to meet societal needs. Neither have they cultivated a professional managerial class with skills, commitment, and ethics compatible with development objectives.

Addressing a cycle that seems to sustain and even reinforce institutional ineffectiveness in Arab governance, Jreisat offers a subtle understanding of the way context and culture affect state capacity. He calls for reform strategies that recognize the importance of leadership and institutional development in setting objectives and in implementing them, in all sectors and according to concrete targets and codes of conduct.

Jamil Jreisat is professor of public administration and political science at the University of South Florida. His numerous publications include *Managing Public Organizations: A Developmental Approach to Administrative Theory and Process, Public Financial Management and Budgeting;* and *Administration and Development in the Arab World: Annotated Bibliography.*